THE 'DEATH OF THE EXPLAINED

James Heartfield

CONTENTS

| Preface | Who is the Subject? | P5 |

PART ONE

Introduction	Degrading the Subject in Theory	15
Chapter One	The Beginning and the End of the Subject	22
Chapter Two	The Socially Constructed Subject	37

Althusser, Communitarianism, Feminism.

| Chapter Three | Decentring the Subject: The Other *Hegel* | 57 |
| Chapter Four | Process without a Subject | 68 |

Foucault (power); Habermas (intersubjectivity); sociobiology

| Chapter Five | The Ersatz Subject | 87 |

Identity + individualism (Popper + Hayek) — methodological

| Conclusion | More than a Theory | 99 | *individualism* |

PART TWO

Introduction	The Common Ruin of the Contending Classes	102
Chapter Six	Algeria and the Defeat of French Humanism	111
Chapter Seven	Althusser and the Death of the Subject	129

PART TWO continued

Chapter Eight	The Agency Debate	139
Chapter Nine	'There Is No Alternative'	154
Chapter Ten	The Third Way	174
Conclusion	Apathy Becomes a Material Force	202

PART THREE

Chapter Eleven	The Retreat of the Elite	207
Chapter Twelve	Symptoms of Degraded Subjectivity	224
Conclusion	The Subjective Factor	237

Preface

WHO IS THE SUBJECT?

The freely willing human Subject is the cornerstone of contemporary society. Every aspect of our civilisation takes the free Subject as its basic assumption.

In Britain in April 1999 27 million men and women had entered into a contract with an employer; in 1997 just over half of the adult population had entered into a contract of marriage; 16 million homes were privately owned, the rest of the 20 million homes rented. In 1998 goods and services to the value of £843.7 billion were sold; in 1998 nearly 20 million cars were privately owned and in 1997 private motorised road transport accounted for 616 billion kilometres travelled, while a further 85 billion kilometres were covered in buses, coaches and by rail; in May 1997 30.5 million people voted in a general election followed by 26.8 million in June 2001.[1]

In each and every single one of these billions of relationships, the principle is that these millions of people are constituted as freely willing Subjects. To undertake a job of work for pay, to marry, to buy and sell, to drive on the roads and to vote in the election each person is cast as a Subject. As a Subject, one assumes responsibilities and expects rewards. But most pointedly as a Subject, one expects to decide for one's self exactly what one is – or is not – prepared to do. Voluntarism is the guiding principle. Coercion – whether in slavery, forced marriage, economic monopoly, arbitrary policing or the suspension of democratic representation – is reviled as an evil. Of course nobody believes that freedom means that whatever you think ought to happen will happen. Recognising ourselves as free Subjects we recognise others as free Subjects, with their own goals.[2] Meeting the resistance of others does not mean that freedom is nullified. It only means that one must engage the agreement of others to advance one's own ends.[3]

Even those coercive powers that are acceptable, on the grounds that they defend our liberties – the state's powers of taxation, requisition, detention and imprisonment – are heavily qualified with safeguards. Where these are breached, as in the infamous 'miscarriage of justice' cases in Britain in the 1980s, the reverberations are profound. The coercive power of the state derives in principle from a higher voluntarism. Only the higher aggregation of the collective will derived ultimately from parliament may override the rights of individual property as in taxation or compulsory purchase.[4] So, too, do the exceptional powers of the police derive their authority from elected government. Where individuals are denied their freedom, the argument goes, they are held to an implied contract with society to uphold the laws of the land.

The freely willing Subject is the presupposition that makes all of these relationships possible. Without engaging the voluntary actions of the vast majority of its citizens, society would collapse. If just a fraction of the billions of freely willed obligations taken on by these millions of Subjects were not honoured, the effects would be disastrous. Jobs would be left undone, products unsold, shops empty or looted, children abandoned, cars crashed, government exposed as a sham. Since all turns on the axle of the autonomous Subject, if that axle was to break then the finely balanced wheels of all these social relations would break free, clashing and grating against each other like the gears of a broken engine. Both actively and negatively, society needs to engage the passions and ambitions of its members in their own, freely willed activity. Those political regimes that have sought to crush freedom and supplant the democratic will have been marked not just by violent repression, but, perhaps more appallingly, by a slow degeneration, as the population withdraws consent, turns inward, refuses to engage and ceases to produce.[5] Subjectivity is not an optional extra. It is the basis upon which contemporary society reproduces itself. No regime, no matter how efficient, could hope to substitute its own planning for the myriad decisions and choices – individual and collective – of its citizens.

The integrity, sustenance and growth of contemporary society depend upon subjectivity as their foundation and principle. The principles of a free society, of democracy and the rule of law are universally embraced by all serious commentators. There are precious few who will actively and vocally embrace a programme of repression and dictatorship. Even those marginal organisations of the far right must pay lip-service to the principles of freedom, however perversely, in the guise of 'Rights for whites'.[6]

This Subject then is the foundation of society and, say Hobbes, Locke and Rousseau, he has been around as long as Man has. For the great humanist thinkers of the seventeenth and eighteenth centuries society was the creation of individual Subjects. For them, we are all naturally individuals, with appetites and fancies, and a natural liberty. If we trade our natural liberty for civil rights, it is because we can, being already free Subjects. The Subject is a man of action. He challenges, he contests, he defeats. Resistance is an obstacle to be overcome by him, and failure a disgrace, still more so acquiescence which threatens to destroy him altogether. The Subject is also thoughtful and reflective. 'Our Glassy Essence', the inner life of thought and conscience, is divided from the outer world in the Subject. The Subject withdraws from the world into his own thoughts, to consider and plan what he ought to do. The Subject works. Work is not a shame to him, but a source of pride. Hard work endured is like a hero's quest to him, or a battle; he comes home exhausted, but glad. Making things is the best (though he might hesitate to call it anything so expressive as creativity). The Subject's relationship to nature is double-edged. He is a natural man, but he aims to master nature. He is fascinated by nature, and tortures her to make her surrender her secrets.[7] He masters nature to make her yield up her fruits. Nature is his domain. The Subject is perhaps most importantly the bearer of rights. Liberty is his watchword. Against the Church and the King he asserted his own right to determine his future. The individual's freedom of conscience,[8] speech,[9] association,[10] from arbitrary arrest[11] and of private property[12] were all asserted by the Subject. With such freedoms the Subject built our own civilisation.

The Subject is political, understandably seeing himself reflected in those ancient political animals of Athens. But this also implies that the Subject may be a collective, as well as an individual. A people is the collective Subject of a national epic, as well as party to a contract, as in the opening line of the Constitution of the United States of America: 'We, the people of the United States....' Other collective Subjects include, notably, corporations, which, whilst having a bad press lately, are recognised as legal Subjects, with rights and obligations, and, though less in evidence than before, trades unions, whose demand for 'free collective bargaining' was attacked in the 1980s. There are still others, such as juries, (whose decisions are not to be disarticulated into separate opinions by investigation), or families.

In the second half of the twentieth century, the political opposition of left and right generally found each side pressing one version of

Subjective freedom. For the right individual rights took precedence over democracy, while for the left, collective decisions carried more weight than any one man's selfish interests. These political oppositions were theorised by 'Cold War liberals' like Isaiah Berlin on the one hand,[3] and 'collectivists' like CB Macpherson on the other.[4] But the separation and counter position of the individual and collective Subjects is a modern trend. In treating the two as only relatively opposed, but essentially similar, I follow the earlier orthodoxy established by Rousseau in his *Social Contract*, or Hegel in his *Philosophy of Right* (where an undifferentiated 'Will' is the basic building block out of which all right is made). Of course, the general will can and does contradict the individual, as with taxation or imprisonment. Similarly, the individual will can (and must) dissent from the collective. But these are relative oppositions. In truth, both are mutually dependent principles. A collective that was not made up of freely willing individuals would be incapable of deliberative decision making. An individual who was outside of all society would, as Rousseau understood, have a natural liberty but no civil rights.

Contemporary critics of the Enlightenment are not so impressed by the claims of the Subject. They doubt that society depends upon him and reckon he has only been around as long as Hobbes, Locke and Rousseau. The great error of the Enlightenment was to take its own eighteenth-century bourgeois citizen as the model for all people in all time, as though the Iroquois lived only to open a shop. Today, there is a powerful question mark over the Subject, that central character of the free society. The doubts over the possibilities of free subjectivity are the subject-matter of this book. The doubt is that everyone, and not just the far right, is paying lip-service to the idea of a free Subject. Imagine that the principles of freedom, of civil and political rights, of contracts and promises were being observed, not honestly or with conviction. Instead, consider the possibility that these are observed rather in the manner of routine etiquette or ritual – a ritual that has lost its meaning, but persists out of force of habit and the lack of an obvious alternative. The words 'freedom', 'liberty' and 'rights' spring readily to the lips. But they are worn thin. Politicians and salesmen are too willing to turn these ringing words into advertising slogans and soundbites. In 1994 opponents of the British government's proposed Criminal Justice Act took to the streets to protest its repressive agenda. But at the moment when their cause had the nobility of the People's Charter or Women's Suffrage, the campaigners were gripped by an ironic self-deflation, shown by the adoption of the slogan 'Fight for the right to party'. It is as if it was just too gauche to stand up for civil liberties without a knowing wink to the audience.

Martin Amis' hapless author Richard Tull proposes a History of Increasing Humiliation: 'it would be a book accounting for the decline in the status and virtue of literary protagonists. First gods, then demi-gods, then kings and great warriors, great lovers, then burghers and merchants and vicars and doctors and lawyers. Then social realism: you. Then irony: me. Then maniacs and murderers, tramps, mobs, rabble, flotsam, vermin.'[5] Amis is describing the way that the human Subject has travelled from the periphery to the centre, only then to be de-centred. If the emergence of the nineteenth-century novel's hero corresponds to the emergence of a human Subject, then the modern age is one in which the Subject is losing its centrality. Increasingly, it seems, the literary protagonist is other people, people who are alien to us, 'maniacs and murderers, tramps, mobs, rabble, flotsam, vermin'.[5]

What if the free subjectivity at the core of our social order is all used up? In the past repressive regimes sent tanks to put down a rebellious people. The complex paraphernalia of intimidating policing – rounding up the ringleaders, spies and informants, making an example of troublemakers, censorship and dirty-tricks – is all designed to deal with people who are determined to be free. Their own struggle informs the specific character of their repression.

The late Jean Baudrillard proposes a witty reversal of the model of repression and resistance in his little book *In the Shadow of the*

Silent Majorities. There he imagines that the indifference of the masses, rather than any rebelliousness, is their most potent force. 'One begins to foresee...that withdrawing into the private could well be a direct defiance of the political, a form of actively resisting political manipulation.'[16] This mass, is, according to Baudrillard, 'an opaque nebula whose growing density absorbs all the surrounding energy and light rays to collapse finally under its own weight. A black hole which engulfs the social'. The increasingly feverish attempts to articulate the masses' ambitions and desires, whether politically or in marketing slogans, meets only with a powerfully subversive indifference.

Baudrillard's fantasy is not accurate. It is itself a fatally doomed and ironical attempt to articulate the outlook of the Silent Majority, as if it were a strategy, which of course it never could be. But it does indicate something of what a society which had lost its conviction in free subjectivity would look like. Such a society would be in danger of collapse having had its cornerstone chiselled away. As long as there was no movement, the structure would stand, but attempts at repair would only expose the fault and accelerate the collapse. The whole edifice of our society is built upon this cornerstone of the freely willing Subject. The families, homes, working lives, transportation, orderliness, lawful behaviour, political representation takes as its starting point that elusive character, the Subject.

Perhaps the real danger to liberty today comes not from the expected quarter of the forces of direct repression, but from within. If the rights-bearing Subject is but a shadow of his former self, then who will be the bearer of rights? A recent collection of essays asked the question, 'What comes after the Subject?'.[17] Overwhelmingly the contributors replied, not with an alternative, but with a deconstruction of the question itself. Why should there be a 'what' they said, intuiting that the form of the question implies another Subject.

As we shall see, the Subject is under attack. In words and deeds, the role of subjectivity is being questioned. The sovereign individual is being knocked from his perch. Maybe he deserves it: selfish, strutting, bantam cock that he is. And maybe the society that has been built around him deserves to be shaken to the ground. Perhaps, as is argued, the free Subject is a myth that serves to disguise a real world of repression and exclusion. If that is so, our society needs to be reappraised from top to bottom. This book is an attempt to start that reappraisal, and to ask whether we ought to dump the Subject or resurrect him.

Slovenian philosopher Slavoj Zizek opens his book *The Ticklish Subject* with this pastiche of *The Communist Manifesto*: 'A spectre is haunting Western academia...the spectre of the Cartesian subject. All academic powers have entered into an unholy alliance to exorcise this spectre.'[8] Slavoj Zizek names feminists, New Age obscurantists, postmodern deconstructionists and deep ecologists as differing intellectual trends which now coalesce in their hostility to what he calls the Cartesian subject.

In Part One I explore what Zizek calls the unholy alliance against the Subject in theory. The first three chapters deal with the direct critique of the Subject. The idea that the Subject is historically contingent and redundant is dealt with in Chapter One, which also considers attempts to rescue the Subject from the effects of relativism. Chapter Two examines the social construction of the Subject, investigating in particular the similarities between poststructuralist and communitarian accounts of subject formation, and contemporary feminist critiques of the discriminatory exclusivity of subjectivity. Chapter Three is an account of the origins of 'the Other' in the elimination of the Subject from Hegel's Master-Slave dialectic.

Chapter Four outlines three attempts to theorise society without the Subject: Foucault's theory of power, Habermas's concept of intersubjectivity, and sociobiology. Finally Chapter Five looks at the limitations of two modern versions of individualism, the theories of identity that arose along with poststructuralism, and the methodological individualism of Popper and Hayek which were the major theoretical influence on the free market conservatism of the late twentieth century.

Part Two changes the pace of the investigation to look at the real world conflicts through which the Subject has been called into question. In particular I am concerned to isolate those factors which helped to take anti-humanism from the margins of the French left in 1968 to its place as one of the key assumptions of mainstream Western politics by the end of the twentieth century. These trends are introduced by two chapters on the formative political experiences of the French intelligentsia, who were the most influential critics of subjectivity. Chapter Six looks in detail at the pivotal role of France's war against Algeria in the development of anti-humanist ideas. The double failure of French republicanism and the French communist left to back the cause of national liberation cast Enlightenment humanism as the agent of repression and the Algerian masses as its irreconcilable Other. In Chapter Seven the key events in the life of Louis Althusser graphically illustrate the political dynamics of the denial of subjectivity.

Chapter Eight analyses the crisis of the left which developed after the events of 1968. It is particularly concerned with the combined impact of the historical defeat of organised labour in Europe and the New Left's contemporaneous search for new agents of social change. The failure of the New Right in Britain and America to revitalise a triumphant individualism despite the defeat of the left is the subject of Chapter Nine. Chapter Ten analyses the character of politics after the end of left and right with particular reference to the 'Third Way' administrations of Bill Clinton and Tony Blair. The focus is on the development of politics as 'a process without a subject', one which contrasts sharply with classical political theory.

Part Three turns from politics to society, and sketches the social contours of a world without the Subject. It looks both at the retreat of the elite from leadership in society, and at the involution of social relations based on degraded subjectivity.

I am indebted to Peter Ramsay, Eve Kay, Michael Savage, James Panton, Alex Cameron, Kelly Al-Saleh, Sharon Kinsella and

Graham Barnfield for their good advice and assistance in the preparation of this book. I dedicate it to Patrick Hughes, who drew the cover illustration.

Part One

DEGRADING THE SUBJECT IN THEORY

In the 1960s and 1970s a number of different thinkers started to question the validity of the human Subject. Their ideas were ahead of their time. A variety of different theories arose out of the philosophy called 'phenomenology' and the sociological outlook influenced by the linguistic theory 'structuralism'. Together, these ideas coalesced into an outlook popularised as postmodernism. The origin of these ideas is mostly French, but postmodernism caught a mood amongst academics, and more broadly amongst opinion-formers and the culturati, to gain quickly a currency in intellectual life in the 1980s and 1990s. By the end of the Millennium the new papal encyclical found John Paul II embracing postmodern despair rather than giving a message of hope. Noting that postmodern 'nihilism has been justified in a sense by the terrible experience of evil which has marked our age', the Pope asserts that 'such a dramatic experience has ensured the collapse of rationalist optimism, which viewed history as the triumphant progress of reason, the source of all happiness and freedom'.[19] His Holiness warns against 'a certain positivist cast of mind' which 'continues to nurture the illusion that, thanks to scientific and technical progress, Man and woman may live as a demiurge, single-handedly and completely taking charge of their destiny'.

The Pope is echoing the judgement of the postmodernists. It was Jean-François Lyotard who best summed up the assessment of the modern age and its overriding ideologies. 'I will use the term modern to designate any science that legitimates itself with reference to a metadiscourse...making an explicit appeal to some grand narrative, such as the dialectics of Spirit, the hermeneutics of meaning, the emancipation of the rational or working Subject, or the creation of wealth.'[20] Rejecting these defining narrative structures of modernity, Lyotard announced the post-modern age in the following way: 'I define postmodernism as incredulity towards metanarratives.'[21] As is now well-known, postmodernism was defined as a time when we could do away with the ideologies upon which we had relied. They were just so many tall tales, designed to make the listener happy and satisfied, but with no greater significance. Socialism, the free market, Christianity, the nuclear family, scientific progress were 'exposed' as so many bedtime stories told to lull us children into sleep.

It was not immediately clear that the implications of the theory called first 'post-structuralism' and later postmodernism were hostile to subjectivity. Indeed the opposite appeared to be the case. The postmodernists were first and foremost charged with an excessive subjectivity that jeopardised objectivity. To scientists and conservatives the hallmark of these new ideas was their scepticism towards a singular objective truth. The charge of relativism was made against postmodernists.[22] In a celebrated assault on the postmodernists, scientists Alan Sokal and Jean Bricmont wrote: 'A second target of our book is epistemic relativism, that modern science is nothing more than a "myth", a "narration" or a "social construction".' To postmodernism's critics it seemed as if subjective predilection had been elevated over objective fact in this new outlook. Moral philosopher Alain Finkielkraut parodies the postmodern reprobate as saying 'Let me do what I want myself!'. Finkielkraut continues: 'No transcendent or traditional authority, and not even a plain majoritarian one, can shape the preferences of your postmodern Man or regulate his behaviour.'[23] The shortcoming of the postmodernists, then, was that they resisted all authority, in a riot of subjective preference. The critics pointed to the promiscuous way that the postmodernists deconstructed each and every scientific and moral certainty as if these were no more than big stories, meta or grand narratives. But according to the postmodernists, such metanarratives tended to eradicate differences, imposing a lifeless uniformity. Where metanarratives reduced complexity to self-sameness, the method of deconstruction restored the fundamental difference of things.[24] To the natural scientists and conservatives, such a singular elevation of difference suggested a thoroughgoing subjectivism, in which objectivity was sacrificed to personal subjective responses.

But the deconstruction was not only directed outward towards the objective world, as the critics feared. The very promiscuity of the postmodern deconstruction of all grand narratives meant that the grandest of all narratives, that of the Subject itself, would not remain untouched. Jacques Derrida, for example, insists that difference is so primordial that it cannot be kept outside of the Subject, but must call into question the Subject itself:

> 'What differs? Who differs? What is différance?....if we accepted this form of the question, in its meaning and its syntax ("What is?" "Who is?" "What is that?"), we would have to conclude that différance has been derived, has happened, is to be mastered and governed on the basis of the point of a present being as a Subject a who.'[25]

Derrida's style is wilfully demanding. (In *Of Grammatology* he insists that his intention is 'to make enigmatic ... the very words with which we designate what is closest to us'.[26]) But allowing for his specialised vocabulary, the meaning is clear enough. It is not that there are differences between Subjects, he is saying. That much would simply be a pluralistic outlook: 'different strokes for different folks'. But that does not go far enough for Derrida. If we were just talking about differences between people, then we would have already assumed the existence of these unitary Subjects prior to difference. And then difference would only be a predicate of these previously existing Subjects. But for Derrida, difference, or différance, comes before the Subject. To ask what or who differs assumes the prior existence of Subjects who differ. Derrida is insisting on the priority of difference over the Subject. The implication is that the Subject, too, cannot be assumed to be a unitary whole without difference, but rather, must in turn, itself be deconstructed.

In *Of Grammatology*, Derrida makes it clear that his deconstruction of the claims of objectivity go hand in hand with the deconstruction of subjectivity.[27] Just as claims to objective truth are a narrative that must be dispelled, so too is subjectivity a myth. In his book *Of Spirit*, he goes one step further in rejecting subjectivity. The book is a discussion of the philosopher and Nazi Martin Heidegger. In it Derrida indicates that Heidegger's appeal to the Spirit of the West is a perverse outcome of the rational Subject of Enlightenment thinking. Derrida goes on to criticise 'opposition to racism, totalitarianism, to Nazism, to fascism' that is undertaken 'in the name of the spirit, and even of the freedom of (the) spirit, in the name of an axiomatic – for example, that of democracy or "human rights" – which directly or not comes back to this metaphysics of Subjectivity'.[28] Here, the narratives of freedom and democracy are being criticised because they imply the emancipation of a Subject (in this case a people). In Derrida's eyes, that appeal to the 'metaphysics of Subjectivity' puts them on a par with fascism, because fascism, as represented here by Martin Heidegger, also appeals to a Subject, the Spirit of the West.

The turn of Derrida's argument is surprising. How readily he associates democracy and fascism! And that the common strand should be their shared commitment to subjectivity! It is tempting to think that Derrida is simply making an unduly formal abstraction, while carried away with a complex argument. Perhaps on some plane one could say that fascism and democracy are the same since both are political forms of organisation. In such a case it would simply be a rather forced parallel, like the insight that Hitler, Stalin and Saddam Hussein all have moustaches. But Derrida means more than this. The common bond between fascism and democracy is not incidental, but a fatal flaw; and the specific bond that Derrida alights upon is subjectivity. Phillipe Lacoue-Labarthe, another philosopher, influenced by Derrida, makes the point more forcefully, when he writes that 'Fascism is a humanism':

'in that it rests on a determination of humanitas, which is, in its eyes, more powerful, ie, more effective, that any other. The Subject of absolute self-creation, even if it transcends all the determinations of the modern Subject in an immediately natural position (the particularity of race), brings together and concretises these same determinations and sets itself up as the Subject, absolutely speaking.'[29]

Lacoue-Labarthe makes explicit the meaning of the deconstruction of the metaphysics of the Subject. Self-creation, once a virtue, is here seen as fascistic. Humanism is a fascism, it is argued, because humanism puts Man at the centre, makes Man's activity the substance of history. The initial reaction against the poststructuralist thinkers was to protest at their extreme subjectivism and consequent dismissal of 'objective truth'. But what that criticism missed was that the Subject was also the target of deconstruction, perhaps especially so. Implicit in this double movement is the possibility that Subject and object are not opposed, but mutually supporting terms. If the singular objective ground is called into question, then so too is the singular and unified Subject. And, perhaps more importantly, the degradation of the Subject destroys the basis of a sustained investigation of the objective. In prosaic terms, if we cannot be sure of the investigator, there can be no investigation.

It was the poststructuralist thinkers who turned most pointedly upon the Subject. But this trend was not restricted to those French researchers around Jacques Derrida, Michel Foucault, Louis Althusser and Jacques Lacan. If they enunciated the critique most directly, others too lent their own distinctive quality to the critique of the Subject. Historians and social commentators were more often struck by the limitations of subjectivity. It seemed to them that the Subject was exclusively male, propertied, white, heterosexual, adult. In these criticisms a fine line was being drawn – ought free subjectivity to be broadened to include those social groups excluded? Or, conversely, was the Subject in any event so narrowly defined as to be a poor model for the excluded to imitate? It did not follow that the norm established by the White European Male was the right one for those who were already set apart by that very norm. That is to say, the problem might not be the denial of subjectivity, but on the contrary, subjectivity itself could be intrinsically domineering and exclusive. If that were the case, then the criticism of exclusivity becomes directly a criticism of subjectivity. The claim of the universality of subjectivity was challenged, and exposed as its opposite, partiality. The universal outlook of Man, was revealed to be biased in terms of gender, property, race, sexual orientation and age. The centrality of Man was challenged, precisely for its one-sidedness. Humanism was shown to be Eurocentric, ethnocentric, and ultimately anthropocentric. Having fought to de-throne gods and kings to take his rightful place at centre stage, the Subject was now de-centred in turn. In his place stood the excluded Other.

In all respects the claims of human agency were put to the test. The central character of the human story had been taken for granted until

For the 1st time human agency was tested.

this point. But now, he was to be taken apart, or deconstructed, knocked off his pedestal, or de-centred. A great involution in thinking was taking place. There had always been disagreements before about how to live, about morality, about social and political organisation, about how to interpret historical events. But as a rule it was accepted that human freedom was a venerable goal, whatever disagreements there might be about achieving it. Now for the first time – outside of the extremes of conservative thinking – a misanthropic strain emerged that questioned whether Man was indeed the central figure of the human story, and whether he deserved to be.

Chapter One

THE BEGINNING AND THE END OF THE SUBJECT

'As the archaeology of our thought easily shows, Man is an invention of a recent date. And one perhaps nearing to its end....one can certainly wager that Man would be erased, like a face drawn in the sand at the edge of the sea.'[30]

Michel Foucault's conclusion to The Order of Things is startling. In the argument which precedes this conclusion, Foucault demonstrates that the centrality of Man is not a universal human condition, but a modern preoccupation that has been with us only since the seventeenth and eighteenth centuries.

Conventional thinking has it that people throughout time have been essentially similar, only their circumstances changing. Naturally enough, when trying to imagine the lives of people in other ages you draw upon your own self-image to fill in the gaps. School history projects invite pupils to imagine what a child's life would have been like in Roman Britain. Often they start by imagining what life would be like without television. But it is more difficult to understand that childhood itself is an invention of a later age, and that the definitions between infancy, adolescence and adulthood that structure our lives would have been alien to most people in most ages. Yet more difficult to understand is the idea that the centrality of Man, as the autonomous Subject of history and society, is far from being a universal condition of the human species. But in *The Order of Things* Foucault takes the relatively late development of the human sciences, economics, psychology and philology, as an indicator of the appearance of their subject matter, the human Subject. He writes:

> 'The eighteenth century did not hand down to them [the human sciences], in the name of Man or human nature a space, circumscribed on the outside but still empty which it was then their role to cover or analyse. The epistemological field traversed by the human sciences was not laid down in advance: no philosophy, no political or moral option, no empirical science of any kind, no observation of the human body, no analysis of sensation, imagination or the passions, had ever encountered in the seventeenth or eighteenth century, anything like Man; for Man did not exist.'[31]

Foucault's point is that the human sciences did not discover Man, as an empirical fact, waiting to be investigated. Rather, he argues, these very scientific discourses themselves brought Man into being: 'They appeared when Man constituted himself in Western culture as both that which must be conceived of and that which is to be known.'[32] Here it is Western culture, including the human sciences, which constitutes the Subject. More conventional thinking would have said that it was Man who created Western culture, including the human sciences. In this respect, conventional thought follows the basic outline established in the seventeenth and eighteenth centuries by Hobbes, Shaftesbury, Locke and Rousseau: Man exists naturally as a free Subject first, only afterwards entering into civil society. Foucault reverses the order of things, by making civil society the author of the free individual.

However provocative Foucault's mode of expression is, he was pushing at an open door. The evidence for the historically limited nature of the human Subject is well established. A greater sensitivity to historical change amongst nineteenth and twentieth-century theorists led to a criticism of the natural right theories of the eighteenth century. The German philosopher GWF Hegel was amongst the first to question the 'fiction of the state of nature' suggesting that in such theories 'the desired outcome is presupposed' as if it were a natural condition.³³ The nineteenth-century socialist Karl Marx criticised Ludwig Feuerbach's humanism precisely because it uncritically adopted 'the standpoint of civil' which is to say, capitalist, 'society'.³⁴ Following Marx, the Canadian political scientist CB Macpherson faults John Locke for 'having read back into the nature of men and society, certain preconceptions about the nature of seventeenth-century man and society which he generalises quite unhistorically'.³⁵ What Hegel, Marx and Macpherson are all doing is qualifying the claims of the eighteenth-century individual to a natural existence. Instead, they are suggesting, this character has a history. In certain historical circumstances the possibilities of the free individual come into being. By implication, these circumstances can be expected to pass into the historical past. The absolute claim of the natural individual has been qualified historically.³⁶

However, for poststructuralists like Foucault, the Hegelian and Marxist analyses of the historical limitations of the bourgeois subject do not go far enough. The poststructuralists understood that these historical qualifications upon the bourgeois Subject did not imply a rejection of the historical Subject as such. Rather, as the poststructuralists saw it, these analyses tended to criticise the specific form of the bourgeois Subject, only as a feint, through which an idealised human Subject could be promoted. With Hegel, the specific historical instances of subjectivity were seen to be manifestations of a transhistorical Subject, the Idea.[37] Following Hegel, Marx also rejected the specifically truncated form of the individual bourgeois Subject to champion the working class subject: 'The proletariat alone is a really revolutionary class', he writes. 'The proletarian movement is the self-conscious, independent movement of the immense majority, in the interests of the immense majority.'[38] The Marxist Georg Lukacs, deploying the language of German philosophy, argues that for Marx, the revolutionary proletariat is the identical Subject-Object of the history of society' – meaning that the working class is both the active Subject of history, as well as an objective force.[39] As we shall see, the poststructuralists could never be satisfied with this trumpeting of the proletarian Subject of history, which seemed to fall short of their critical insight into the historical contingency of the Subject. They did not want to restore the Subject in a more plausible version. To them it seemed that Marx in particular had simply back-tracked on the critique of the Subject, criticising the Subject in the name of the Subject and smuggling the old reprobate back in, disguised with clogs and a cloth cap.

Jean Baudrillard explained:

'Historical materialism, dialectics, modes of production, labour-power – through these concepts Marxist theory has sought to shatter the abstract universality of the concepts of bourgeois thought (Nature and Progress, Man and Reason, formal Logic, Work, Exchange, etc). Yet Marxism in turn universalises them with a "critical" imperialism as ferocious as the other's.'[40]

'Marxism' Baudrillard disparages 'is the vision of a future "freedom" based on a conscious domination of nature' and therefore 'it is not radical' but 'led despite itself to reproduce the roots of the system of political economy', ie, capitalism.[41] Here Baudrillard anticipates one of the central motifs of the degradation of the Subject, the charge of anthropocentrism. Most pointedly, though, it is the charge that Marxism is contiguous with the social system it sought to challenge, in promoting the idea of a real freedom. For Marx of course, that was precisely the point of the criticism of the alienation of human powers in capital: to institute a real subjectivity, in place of the empty husk of the bourgeois subject. Amongst poststructuralist thinkers it was only Althusser who kept faith with the name of Marx. For the rest, they sought a more radical historicisation than Marx or Hegel could offer.

Foucault found his radical historicism in the nineteenth-century German anti-philosopher Friedrich Nietzsche. Nietzsche's *Genealogy of Morals* in particular was a model. Nietzsche drew upon the increasing historical and philological evidence regarding the moral systems of other times and cultures, in particular of the ancient Greeks and the early Christians. Morality had been seen as fixed: what was right was right for all time. Nietzsche shows that right and wrong are historically specific categories, arising largely from the slave-mentality of the early Christians. Moral claims that had been assumed to be set in stone were broken apart by Nietzche's caustic criticism. This was for Foucault a model for dislodging the eternal claims of the natural individual. Indeed, Nietzsche anticipates the dislodging of the subject with this aside: 'science still...has not disposed of that little changeling the "Subject".'[42] It was a challenge that Foucault took up on science's behalf. Foucault was adopting Nietzsche's 'genealogical' method in uncovering the transitory and fleeting character of Man.

Derrida, by contrast, drew upon Martin Heidegger's philosophy as the basis of his own approach, which he called 'deconstruction'. Heidegger felt that philosophy, especially his own chosen field of philosophy, the 'philosophy of being' or ontology, was unduly dominated by a preoccupation with the Subject, due to the influence of the seventeenth-century thinker Rene Descartes. It was Descartes, who enthroned the thinking Subject as the arbiter of certain knowledge, when he famously declared, *'ego cogito ergo sum'* or 'I think, therefore I am'. Heidegger bemoaned the fact that such concepts as 'the *ego cogito* of Descartes, the subject, the "I", reason, spirit, person' 'have served as the primary guides' but 'remain uninterrogated'.[4] Under the heading 'The Destruction of Ontology',[44] Heidegger says this: 'if the question of Being is to have its own history made transparent, then this hardened tradition', he means the domination of Descartes' thinking Subject over philosophy, 'must be loosened up...dissolved'. 'We are to destroy the traditional content of...ontology'. It was Heidegger's chosen task to strip away the superficial overlay of modern Cartesian subjectivity that Derrida adopts. As we saw in the discussion of Heidegger's Nazism, where Derrida faults Heidegger it is for the lingering trace of such Subjectivity that he suspects still lurks in the master's work. It is Heidegger's 'Destruction of Ontology' that suggests Derrida's deconstructionist approach. Like Heidegger, Derrida sets about excising the merely recent excrescence of Subjectivity.

One should not necessarily make too much of the theoretical sources that the poststructuralists drew upon to found their historical relativisation of the Subject. The poststructuralists were thinkers who were responding to quite distinctive problems and times. What is important is that the sense of Man's transience was usefully articulated by reference back to Heidegger and Nietzsche rather than to Hegel and Marx, who were 'compromised' by their optimism towards the possibilities of the Subject, however modified. It was Heidegger and Nietzsche who formulated the demand for the destruction of the Subject altogether. Their approach was to substitute the temporal contingency of the Subject for an argument. Merely to specify the Subject historically, to situate its emergence in time already seems to call it into question. Why the thing being criticised ought to be rejected does not need to be stated. It is the kind of criticism popularly expressed in the phrase 'that's so old'.

Rescuing the Subject

Some philosophers and political scientists have tried to separate the question of the historical emergence of the Subject from its implied transience. In a cunning feint the American pragmatist Richard Rorty happily acknowledges that 'we are free to see the self centreless, as a historical contingency all the way through'.⁴⁵ But, he argues, 'a sense of human subjectivity as a centreless bundle of contingencies...is compatible with any sort of politics, including liberal politics'.⁴⁶ Rorty is saying that the knowledge of the historical relativity of the Subject does not make a politics based on the free Subject, liberalism, impossible. It is a daring manoeuvre. He is jettisoning the longstanding claim of the eighteenth-century founders of liberal politics that the individual is in a state of nature, born free. Instead Rorty occupies his opponents' ground, acknowledging the historical facts that the Subject is a thing of recent invention, and says, 'a jolly good one, too'. In this way the question of the end of the Subject is sidestepped altogether. The onus is back on the critics to make the case against the Subject.

Rorty explains the revision of natural right theory: 'Even if nothing else survives from the age of the democratic revolutions, perhaps our descendants will remember that social institutions can be viewed as experiments in cooperation rather than as attempts to embody a universal and ahistorical order.'⁴⁷ Rorty is saying that we do not need to believe that liberty is a natural faculty of Man to believe that it is a good thing. We can just adopt it as the last, best hope of humanity. German political scientist Karl-Otto Apel makes a similar objection to Rorty when he rightly asks whether Enlightenment values really have 'proved to be culture-dependent not only by their genesis but with regard to their validity?'.⁴⁸ He is saying that because historically individual rights happened to arise in the Western corner of Europe that might mean that their genesis 'proved to be culture dependent'. But it does not follow that they are valid only for Europeans. Rather, he is suggesting, they are valid for all peoples, whatever their culture.

Rorty sums up his political philosophy with the witty self-description 'postmodernist bourgeois liberalism'. He explains that 'I call it "bourgeois" to emphasise that most of the people I am talking about would have no quarrel with the Marxist claim that a lot of those institutions and practices are possible and justifiable only in certain historical, and especially economic, conditions'. Adding, 'I use "postmodernist" in a sense given this term by Jean François Lyotard, who says that the postmodern attitude is the "distrust of metanarratives"'.[49] So the sense of the historical contingency of the liberal Subject, for example, does not necessarily clash with the postmodern 'distrust of metanarratives'. Rorty is tweaking the poststructuralists' tails when he tells them that their historical contingency is owed as much to Marx as to Nietzsche or Heidegger. But he suspects that they would not be satisfied that Marx's historical relativisation was sufficient when he admits that his postmodern bourgeois liberalism 'sounds oxymoronic'.[50]

Like Rorty, the legal theorist John Rawls seeks to save the rights-bearing Subject while conceding the unlikelihood of his emerging ready-made from the state of nature. Rawls wants to save his Subject from being the mere effect of his cultural context. He wants to sustain the notion of an 'unencumbered Self', that is a Self that can stand apart from any vested interests it may have, despite finding the natural individual implausible. What Rawls is trying to do is to rid the liberal order, in which free individual Subjects hold sway, of the charge of partiality, of bias towards the wealthy, those who have succeeded in the 'rat race'. Rawls has recourse to the following thought experiment: imagine the social order that you would choose, if you were wholly ignorant of where you were likely to end up on the pecking order. Rawls suggests that, from 'behind the veil of ignorance' you could be expected to choose a social system that favoured liberty and the possibilities of self-advancement – because very few people would write off their own chances to gain by their efforts. At the same time, he says that since most of us fear that poverty would be a fall from which we would not recover, most too would prefer to see a safety net of welfare in place, since 'behind the veil of ignorance' one cannot know where one will end up. The thought experiment of the veil of ignorance usefully leads to the expected result: that a liberal society with a welfare state, Rawls' own, is the one that most would choose if the choosing were 'fair', which is to say, not undertaken from one's actual social standing, but from a disinterested vantage point. 'The veil of ignorance' is a theoretical device that substitutes for 'the state of nature' of natural right theories, a secular, non-natural basis for individual rights. As we shall see, Rawls' 'unencumbered Self' is open to more objections that Rorty's centreless self.

The late Cornelius Castoriadis, social activist and iconoclastic thinker, takes the historical emergence of the Subject as axiomatic, but at the same time sees the Subject, like Rorty, as worthy nonetheless. 'Of [human subjectivity] one ought to say that, as a relatively recent historical creation, it is virtual in every human being, but it is certainly not a fated process.' At which point he is in full agreement with the poststructuralists – perhaps not surprisingly, since many of them, like Lyotard, studied with Castoriadis in his radical group Socialism or Barbarism in France in the 1950s and 1960s. But unlike Derrida, Castoriadis associates the authoritarian regimes of the mid-twentieth century with the extinguishing of subjectivity, rather than with its reign. 'Recent and present history offers massive and horrifying examples in which the last traces of reflectiveness and of a will of one's own, which human beings can possess are reduced to nothing by the social (political) institution.'[51]

Indicative of a wholly distinctive political engagement to that of the poststructuralists who came after him, Castoriadis sees fascism and Stalinism as the negation of subjectivity, where they would see them as the culmination of subjectivity. Castoriadis directly answers the charge that any defence of the individual implies a naturalistic theory of individualism. The individual should be seen not as a natural given, but an historical achievement. 'Is there a unity to the singular human being beyond its corporeal identity and the chronological container of its "history?"', he asks. 'There is a unity that is aimed at or that we ought to aim at: the unity of reflective self-representation and of the deliberate activities one undertakes.' And to rebut the specific charge of ahistoricism, he adds, '"Unity" here does not mean, of course, invariability through time'.⁵¹ But even in that last qualification, one can sense a certain defensiveness in Castoriadis' tone.

With Rorty and Castoriadis, the Canadian Hegel-scholar of the old New Left, Charles Taylor seeks to subvert the postmodern historicisation of the Subject with his book *The Sources of the Self*. The book is a great compendium of the differing historical contributions to modern subjectivity, or the Self, showing the distinctive sources, from the Attic legacy through the Renaissance and Enlightenment to the Romantic modifications of subjectivity. The effect is to lay claim to a deep understanding of the way that the Self has been historically constituted in an implicit challenge to some of the more glib statements about the 'recent invention' of the Subject. But at the same time, Taylor is demonstrating the nobility of this historical achievement. His approach to historical development is Hegelian and positivistic, embracing the real in all of its development, rather than Nietzschean and negative. But as we shall see later, Taylor's Subject is bounded in other ways than historically.

For all of the attempts to sidestep the historical relativisation of the Subject, it is difficult not to think that these are posed defensively. The belief that the human Subject is transient is more of an intuitive response than a rational one. It is not necessarily susceptible to a rational argument. The claims of liberal societies that Rorty and Rawls are defending are precisely what are called into question in the presentiment of the transcendence of the human. Conceding the transience of the Subject but defending liberal norms is not likely to satisfy the critics of subjectivity. The sense that the Subject is intrinsically limited is well expressed in Lyotard's introduction to his book *The Inhuman*. There he argues that 'the socioeconomic decision-maker' uses the discourse of free subjectivity 'to legitimate his or her options: competitiveness, better distribution of costs, democracy in society, enterprise, school and family. Even the rights of Man can be appealed to in reinforcement of the authority of the system'.[53] With this degree of distrust and alienation from family, democracy and school and even the idea of rights, the modest defence of liberal democracies made by Rorty and Rawls is simply missing the point.

The posthuman

In an essay on the fall of the Berlin Wall and the subsequent war in the Gulf, Lyotard expresses his distance from the competing 'systems' in these conflicts with the observation that 'the hero' in 'this fable' 'is no longer Man'.[54] Instead, Lyotard sketches a fable narrated by 'the system', in which energy dispersed in particles in 'the vastness of the cosmos' undergoes 'internal differentiation' before 'Entropy' leads to 'random distribution'. On the surface of the Earth '"living" systems' reverse entropy and develop 'sexed reproduction' giving rise to 'the chance of mutations ("misreadings")'. 'After some time, the system called Man was selected' and 'after some [more] time, it happened that systems called liberal democracies came to be recognised as the most appropriate for the task of controlling events in whatever field they occur'. 'In liberal democratic systems, everybody could believe what they liked...provided that they contributed to the system as energetically as they could.'

> 'Given the increased self-control of the open system, it was likely that it would be the winner in the competition among the systems all over the Earth....Nothing seemed able to stop the development of this system except the Sun and the unavoidable collapse of the whole star system.'[55]

Thus far the meaning of Lyotard's fable is to re-tell human history without the human subject – except as the illusion of freedom in liberal democratic societies. By making human history a mere episode within the infinitely greater history of the cosmos, Lyotard succeeds in belittling Man and his achievements. But at this point, Lyotard's fable takes an interesting turn:

> 'In order to meet this predictable challenge, the system was already in the process of developing the prosthesis that would enable it to survive after the solar sources of energy, which had contributed to the genesis of the living systems, were wiped out....research was devoted to the problem of adjusting or replacing living bodies so that human brains would still be able to work with the only forms of energy left available in the cosmos – thus preparing for the first exodus of the negentropic system far from the Earth.'

> 'What Man and "its" brain or, better, the Brain and its man would look like in the days of the final terrestrial challenge, the story did not say.'

Lyotard's speculations are misanthropic, and bear the imprint of a sense of helplessness and futility towards the historic events unfolding in front of him. His bleached-out natural history of Man combines the dumb essence of sociobiology with the dehumanised systems theory influenced by cybernetics. This, perhaps, is the culmination of the radically historicised theory of Man. Set in a cosmic context so vast that all his subjectivity is diminished to an illusion fostered by a self-reproducing system, of which he is merely the organ. But it is the conclusion that is compelling. 'The end of the world is nigh', the old lunatic with the sandwich board used to warn us. But a more bizarre fate now unfolds. Even extinction offers no release from the self-reproducing system, as humanity is transcended. Though he does not name it here, it is the figure of the posthuman that has arrived.

'You are posthuman and hardwired', sing the American Goth band Marilyn Manson, briefly notorious after being scapegoated for having 'inspired' the 1999 Columbine High School massacre.[16] The image of an evolutionary transcendence of the merely human has been with us since Nietzsche's *Man and Superman*, and a mainstay of adolescent culture from the American comic book characters the X-Men to the seventies British TV series *The Tomorrow People*. It is perhaps a normal enough fantasy to imagine oneself the mutant originator of a wholly new species, the next stage of evolution after homo sapiens. Those earlier biological mutations generally aspired to 'special powers', telepathy and the like. But today's 'posthumans' draw their inspiration from the internet rather than genetics.

Max More, founder of the Extropian Institute suggests that humanity's time is almost up: 'Not because we will destroy ourselves, but because we will transcend our humanity. We are becoming transhuman persons in transition to a posthuman era in which human limits will have been overcome.' The Transhumanist FAQ prepared by Nick Bostrom *et al* explains that 'A posthuman is a human descendant who has been augmented to such a degree as to be no longer a human'. Lyotard's vision of 'research...devoted to the problem of adjusting or replacing living bodies so that human brains would still be able to work' is embellished in the Transhumanist FAQ. The most potent image is that of 'Uploading (sometimes called "mind uploading" or "brain reconstruction")...the hypothetical process of transferring a mind from a biological brain to a computer'. One can copy an electronic file of data onto your computer from another through the telephone wires, which is called downloading a file from 'the Net'. The network of possible telephone connections between computers, personal and institutional, sustains the illusion of a realm known as the internet, or more poetically, cyberspace.[17] Uploading reverses the image, to imagine that one's 'brain waves' or 'synaptic patterns' (the images are drawn from different eras of science fiction) could be copied in the opposite direction, onto 'the Net'. Once projected into the cybernetic ether, the personality has transcended its corporeal form, to become part of the traffic of information that passes through the internet.

Donna Haraway's *Cyborg Manifesto* was an early inspiration to the current generation of posthumans. Haraway has speculated about the way that technology could break down the traditional Subject. Specifically, she looks forward to a new race of beings, part man and part machine, cyborgs. In principle, she is saying, the future is already here. Pacemakers, prosthetic limbs and modern warfare all indicate the growing interface between human biology and technology. She is conscious of the irony that a positive embrace of technology's possibilities is more usually associated with nineteenth-century ideologies: 'The main trouble with cyborgs, of course, is that they are the illegitimate off-spring of militarism and patriarchal capitalism, not to mention state socialism. But illegitimate offspring are often exceedingly unfaithful to their origins....From one perspective, a cyborg world is about the final imposition of a grid of control on the planet, about the final abstraction embodied in a Star Wars apocalypse waged in the name of defence, about the final appropriation of women's bodies in a masculinist orgy of war. From another perspective, a cyborg world might be about lived bodily and social realities in which people are not afraid of their kinship with animals and machines, not afraid of permanently partial identities and contradictory standpoints.'[58] Technology, as Haraway sees it can break with the patriarchal and domineering to dissipate the Subject into fractured identities and contradictory standpoints. Pointedly the posthuman cyborg sloughs off the accoutrements of the merely human subject:

> 'The cyborg is a creature in a post-gender world; it has no truck with bisexuality, pre-Oedipal symbiosis, unalienated labour, or other seductions to organic wholeness through a final appropriation of all the powers of the parts into a higher unity. In a sense the cyborg has no origin story in the 'Western' humanist sense....The cyborg is resolutely committed to partiality, irony, intimacy and perversity....The cyborg would not recognise the Garden of Eden; it is not made of mud and cannot dream of returning to dust.'[59]

Haraway's posthuman cyborg seems irreligious here. But the desire to transcend the merely human form has marked echoes of religious sentiment. The sense of the historicality of the human subject began as an insight into the way that men, rather than God, shaped their own circumstances and remade themselves.[60] But increasingly that insight has been turned into its opposite. The sense of Man's transience in the world reverses the humanist dethronement of God in favour of Man. Where the humanists made Man the central character in his own story, the tendency of the historical relativisation of Man has, perversely, led to a diminishing of Man's standing. Now we are to be cowed in the face of Eternity, our own brief appearance on that vast continuum a mere happenstance.

In the final movement of the transcendence of Man in the posthuman we can see the degradation of the human Subject assume a familiar form. The 'Higher Source' religious cult believed that the Hale-Bopp comet contained a space ship that would deliver them to a 'higher evolutionary level' after they shed their bodies. In March 1997, 39 of them poisoned themselves along with cult leader Marshall Applewhite.[61] The posthuman is a playful speculation, but one that expresses a sense of alienation from humanity and a fantasy desire for transcendence. In its most extreme form, it leaves piles of poisoned bodies and reduces the human essence to a video message left for those of us who still cling doggedly to the human form.

Chapter Two

THE SOCIALLY CONSTRUCTED SUBJECT

'Ideology interpellates individuals as Subjects', Louis Althusser [62]

Althusser₁ structuralism.

Louis Althusser was a theoretician of the French Communist Party in the sixties and seventies as well as a lecturer at the elite Ecole Normale Supérieure with Foucault and Derrida. Like them he was concerned to dislodge the Subject from its exalted status. In the essay 'Ideological state apparatuses' of 1970 Althusser argues that 'ideology has the function of "constituting" concrete individuals as subjects'.[63] He means that the Subject is an effect of the ideology, not the other way around. Ordinary thinking would have it that persons – Subjects – have ideas, or perhaps more cynically that an ideology is crafted to deceive these Subjects about their true conditions. But Althusser goes further than that. He is saying that ideology does not only deceive you into thinking things like 'this war is a just war', or 'wealthy people worked hard to get where they are'. Althusser argues that even the idea of oneself as a Subject, author of your own destiny, is an illusion fostered by ideology.

Althusser's argument exemplifies the thinking that sees the Subject as socially bounded. In other words the Subject does not exist before society. Society is not a contract between fully formed Subjects. Rather the Subject owes its existence entirely to the social order. Furthermore, once the Subject is seen as the contingent effect of society, then subjectivity is revealed as partial rather than universal. Those that society deigns to ennoble as 'Subjects' turn out to be a narrow and particular caste of individuals, exclusive of other sections, such as the lower classes, women, non-Europeans, and others. Like the insight that the Subject is historically bounded, the view that the Subject is socially limited is unquestionably true. What is at issue is the conclusions to be drawn from that insight. Does it follow that since the Subject is a product of society that it is merely illusory, or that the Subject ought to be subordinate to society? Does it follow from the exclusion of some sections from the rights and status of subjectivity, that those grapes are sour, and that subjectivity itself should be abolished?

Althusser recalls, 'in Marxism and Marxist theory I discovered a system of thought which acknowledged the primacy of the bodily activity and labour'. 'I at last discovered the primacy of the body and the hand as the agent of the transformation of all matter.'[64] 'I later took from it my description of history as *a process without a subject.*'[65] For Althusser, then, Marx suggested a more or less biological process, of bodily activity. This would indeed be a process without a subject. But to make Marx the cloak of the historical process with no subject, Marx had to be tailored to fit. Unfortunately, Marx's writing is imbued with a sense of the historical Subject, albeit one that is in the process of formation. Moreover, the fashion in Marxist circles at the time, heavily influenced by the official Marxist policy of the 'Communist' Soviet Union in the East, was to emphasise the 'humanist' Marx.

Althusser rightly intuited that the stress upon Marx's humanism from official Soviet ideologues was shaped by the political imperatives of the Russian state. In particular the Soviet policy of 'peaceful coexistence' sought to win time for Russia to build up its economy, and make friends amongst the Western intelligentsia, as a buffer to criticism. As a member of a party with fraternal links to the Soviet Union, Althusser had to frame his criticisms cautiously and in the judicious language of philosophical disagreement. With a note of sarcasm he wrote, 'I wonder even whether socialist humanism is not such a reassuring and attractive theme that it will allow a dialogue between Communists and Social-Democrats, or even a wider exchange with those "men of good will" who are opposed to war and poverty. Today', he continued ironically, 'even the high road of Humanism seems to lead to socialism'.[66]

And then, as a reprimand to the humanists, Althusser adds, 'In fact the objective of the revolutionary struggle has always been the end of exploitation and hence the liberation of man, but, as Marx foresaw, in its historical phase, this struggle had to take the form of a struggle between classes'.[67] Althusser is arguing that for Marx, a humanism that embraces all humanity is a myth that only succeeds in papering over the urgent differences between classes, exploiters and exploited:

> 'He [Marx] drove the philosophical categories of the Subject...etc from all the domains in which they had reigned supreme. Not only from political economy (rejection of the myth of *homo economicus*, that is of the individual with definite faculties and needs as the Subject of the classical economy); not just from history (rejection of social atomism and ethico-political idealism); not just from ethics (rejection of the Kantian ethical idea); but also from philosophy itself: for Marx's materialism excludes the empiricism of the Subject (and its inverse: the transcendental Subject).'[68]

Althusser finds in Marx a rejection of the 'bourgeois' Subject of economics, and liberal ethics. He rightly understands that it was Marx who explained that a humanism that pretended that Moneybags and Rent-roll were on the same plane as the wage-slave was a lie designed to cover up those differences. But Althusser puts more on Marx than he ought to bear. Marx criticised the bourgeois Subject for its limitations. He did not aim to abolish the historical Subject altogether. In particular Althusser's characterisation 'Marx's theoretical anti-humanism'[69] is misplaced. As Althusser sees it Marx 'replaced the old couple individuals/human essence in the theory of history by new', and suitably impersonal, 'concepts (forces of production, relations of production, etc.)'.[70] However Marx's theoretical terminology was not intended to blot out the human agency, but to highlight the barriers to its full realisation. But then Althusser's knowledge of Marxism, despite his reputation, was to say the least, sketchy, as he acknowledged in his memoirs.[71] In fact Althusser's underlying inspiration in the battle against the Subject was drawn from his contemporaries, in spite, not because of, the Marxist idiom he adopted.[72]

Althusser's account of ideological Subject formation is far from common sense. He is saying that the creation of the Subject is one of repression, not liberation. The example he gives in 'Ideological state apparatuses' is of a policeman hailing 'Hey You', and so creating a 'You', to which the passer-by answers, accepting the ascribed status. Identification here becomes a repressive act, rather than the recognition of a free Subject. Perversely, the very terms of Subjective recognition in Althusser's account are an imposition from outside, that impose a given identity rather than liberating the Subject of the policeman's address. The account of Subject formation as repression has been widely taken up. Michel Foucault gives an alarming historical telling of the formation of modern Subjects in his books *The Birth of the Clinic* and *Discipline and Punish*. There modern institutions from the prison, through the schools and the hospitals are all involved in the disciplining of bodies through techniques of surveillance and interview. The all-pervasive gaze of these new authorities transfixes the individual, making him a Subject with guilt and conscience.

In her book *The Psychic Life of Power: Theories in Subjection*, Judith Butler develops the 'paradoxical' account of 'subjection'. 'If, following Foucault, we understand power as forming the subject', she writes, 'power imposes itself on us, and weakened by its force, we come to internalise or accept its terms'. 'Power, that first appears as external, pressed upon the subject, pressing the subject into subordination, assumes a psychic form that constitutes the subject's self-identity.' It is the internalisation of the 'discourse' of power that creates the Subject. 'Subjection consists precisely in this fundamental dependency on a discourse',[73] leading Foucault to talk of the 'discursive production of the subject'.[74] In Butler's telling the terrible burden of subjectivity seems more or less established until she checks herself to ask 'how can it be that the subject, taken to be the condition for and instrument of agency, is at the same time the effect of subordination, understood as the deprivation of agency?'.[75] How indeed?

The first answer is that the theory depends upon a play on words. The word 'subject' has two, related, meanings. It can mean the active party, the subject in the sentence, 'He threw the ball', which is related to the wider meaning of the rights-bearing Subject, who is a free agent. Otherwise, subject can be a verb meaning to impose, as in 'I subject him to torture'. Or subject can be the noun for those under the King's rule.[76] All these different meanings are connected. The word comes from the latin *jacere*, to throw or cast, and its meaning was widened to mean 'exercise power over'.[77] The shifting meaning of Subject in Butler's play on words, though, has its origin in social changes.[78] Where few people exercised power, that power was for most, the experience of subjugation – hence the Crown's subjects, ie, recipients of the exercise of power. The historical subjection of the sovereign power to democratic control gives us the more contemporary meaning of Subject as master of his own destiny. The modern meaning carries the older meaning within it, in the sense that the word still means something like subjugate, but now with the implication of a mastery over circumstances rather than people.[79]

But this lingering trace of the older meaning is a foothold for Butler. The reversal of meanings whereby Subject formation becomes enslavement rather than liberation begins with the critique not of *subjectification*, but of *objectification*. Specifically, it was feminist thinkers who first showed how ideological representations of women could serve to render them as 'objects of the male gaze'.[80] In 'slasher' films, for example, camera shots made the audience 'both voyeur and aggressor'.[81] For Susanne Kappeler pornography 'shows one and only one constant element of representational content: the woman-object.[82] But there is another constant factor: the male-subject, producer and consumer of representation...the viewer plays the imaginary hero in relation to the woman-"object"'. Here the objectification of woman divides the pornographic worldview into male subjects and female objects. The question arises, is objectification a necessary consequence of subjectification? Kappeler writes, 'The woman objectified implies a subject, a hero of her degradation.'[83] Is the opposite also implied, that a Subject, a hero, implies objectification and degradation? If that were true then the entire project of subjective freedom is called into question. All subjectivity would be compromised as complicit in the degradation of others. Conversely, the critique of objectification would seem to imply that women demand to be treated as Subjects in their own right, though not all have seen it that way.

Maeve Cooke writes, for example, that 'feminists have rejected the ideal of autonomy' that defines the Subject.[84] Judith Butler takes a similar view. 'Do the exclusionary practices that ground feminist theory in a notion of "women" as subject paradoxically undercut feminist goals...?', she asks.[85] In this reading, women's liberation is an 'exclusionary practice' because it implies a Subject, women, of liberation, excluding the possibility of a non-subjectively grounded feminism. 'What sense does it make to extend representation to Subjects who are constructed through the exclusion of those who fail to conform to unspoken normative requirements of the Subject?... The identity of the feminist subject ought not to be the foundation of feminist politics.'[86] Butler means that a movement that sees women as Subjects reproduces the basic structure of the society that it is challenging. Feminism for Butler advances a critique of the Subject *per se*, not simply a reformist demand for the extension of the 'normative requirements of the Subject' to encompass women. The implication is clear: it is not the male monopoly over the rights of the Subject that is at fault, but the very 'ideal of autonomy' itself. Women in adapting the mantle of Subject, conform to these unspoken, normative requirements. At this point one has to wonder whether Butler is carried away with her own dialectical skills. What began as a criticism of the monopoly over freedom exercised by men has turned, paradoxically, into a criticism of freedom as such.

Seeing the individual as an effect of social forces, and an illusory one at that, Althusser completed the account of history as a process without a Subject. Althusser's prioritisation of society over the Subject has its own particularities, but it also has antecedents in much sociology. The view that the individual is socialised into given roles was already part of the canon of Western sociology.[87] Indeed it is an idea that goes back to the anti-Enlightenment reaction that sought to emphasise the priority of the social whole over individual rights. 'Man', wrote the arch-reactionary Joseph De Maistre, nearly two centuries before Althusser, 'is sociable in his essence'. Conservatives, more than radicals, are associated with the argument of the priority of the social over the individual. So the Hegelian political philosopher TH Green would write dismissively of 'the delusion of natural right' in which 'the Individual, it is thought, [has] a right, not derived from society'.[88] 'It is on the relation to a society – to other men recognising a common good – that the individual's rights depend', wrote this English Victorian. 'A right against society', he continued, 'is a contradiction in terms'.[89]

Community conformity

Today the surprising accompaniment to Althusser's demotion of the individual before the social structure is to be found in the American social philosophy of communitarianism. The origin of communitarianism is Michael Sandel's polemic against John Rawls' *Theory of Justice*, published as *Liberalism and the Limits of Justice*.⁹⁰ Sandel was dismayed by the narrowly founded conception of justice, and of society, that he found in Rawls' book. Characterising Rawls' approach 'contractarian', because it had no firmer foundation than the contract between individuals, Sandel called his own argument, communitarian. In doing so, he coined a term that caught the imagination of a great many philosophers, from social catholic Alasdair MacIntyre to small-town America enthusiast Amitai Etzioni, as well as politicians from US Republican William Bennett to Democratic President Bill Clinton and British prime minister Tony Blair.

Sandel takes issue with Rawls' attempt to found society on a contract between 'unencumbered selves' – unencumbered that is, by the knowledge of their own social standing, because choosing their society from 'behind the veil of ignorance'. Sandel objects that 'to assert the priority of the self whose sovereign agency is assured, it was necessary to identify an "essentially unencumbered" self'.⁹¹ That is necessary in Rawls' argument because if the choosing self is already situated socially, then his choices will be biased. But as Sandel explains, the 'unencumbered self' is a tortuous construction that has the capacity 'to dissolve into a radically situated subject'.⁹² What Sandel is saying is that we cannot so easily forget who we are, in its particulars. Pretending that our choices are made from a studiously impartial standpoint 'behind the veil of ignorance' only strips us of what makes us worthwhile. Worse still, the show of impartiality can serve as a disguise for the partisan interests of the well-heeled 'radically situated subject'.

Sandel's alternative to Rawls is to give community priority over the individual. When Sandel's ideas began to attract attention, many radicals took issue with what they saw as a straightforward expression of moral conservatism. But whatever his politics, Sandel's social philosophy was surprisingly similar to Althusser's structuralism in its

interpellation — an interruption / interjection

account of the interpellation of the individual. 'Community describes not just what they have as fellow citizens but also what they are, not a relationship they choose but an attachment they discover, not merely an attribute but a constituent of their identity.'[93] Community here constitutes identity, not the other way around. Like Althusser, Sandel charges his opponents, by reference to Rawls' 'antecedently individuated subject', with assuming individuation rather than explaining it.[94]

The preoccupation of the communitarians is with the corrosive effect of individualism upon social cohesion. Amitai Etzioni calls the 1980s 'a decade in which "I" was writ large, in which the celebration of the self became a virtue'. Instead, he says it is time to 'put a new emphasis on "we", on values we share'.[95] Alasdair MacIntyre deplores the way that 'the social order of modern individualism' 'replace[s] earlier shared forms of belief with the pluralism of indefinite and growing disagreement'.[96] Sandel suggests that 'given the increasing scarcity of energy and other basic resources facing modern advanced societies, combined with the breakdown of consensus and loss of common purpose',[97] morality is threatened. And 'the breakdown of certain political and civic attachments may represent a moral loss that even a full measure of justice cannot redeem'.[98] As Charles Taylor puts it 'there is an important set of conditions for the continuing health of self-governing societies...these include a strong sense of identification of the citizens with their public institutions and political way of life'.[99]

A reaction to celebration of "I".

The revealing side of the communitarian argument is the constant counterpoise between 'rights' and 'responsibilities'. 'Claiming rights without assuming responsibilities is unethical and illogical', says Amitai Etzioni.[100] So stated, Etzioni's point is compelling, but not necessarily for the reasons that he puts forward. For Etzioni, rights and responsibilities are different animals. We get rights; we owe responsibilities — to the community. In fact, what he means by responsibilities is something more like duties, obligations that we owe. As he tells it, there is a kind of trade-off. We should be glad we have rights, and therefore be willing to do our chores. The tenor of his approach is that too many rights have been granted and too few duties observed, therefore the balance must be redressed. Rights must be curtailed, responsibilities enhanced. And there he reveals his essentially conservative view of what rights are. In Etzioni's telling rights are more like privileges granted by society to individuals.

A natural right approach would be quite different. The bare statement 'claiming rights without assuming responsibilities is unethical and illogical' would certainly gain the agreement of a natural right theorist. Indeed the defender of natural rights would mean it more logically than the communitarian. For the natural right theorist, rights are responsibilities. Self-government means that you assume responsibility for yourself. As a rights-bearing individual your word is your bond. The duty owed arises out of the right. The responsibility owed is ultimately a responsibility to one's own conscience. The rights-bearing individual expects, demands even, to be held to account for what he does. Lawful behaviour is binding because the rights-bearing individual lives in a civil society in an implied social contract. 'America, love it or leave it' are just the plain words for that obligation. All of the rights-bearing individual's responsibilities arise directly out of his rights and are their necessary corollary. He enjoys the liberty to enlarge his property and he obeys the law of the land that honours such a right.

Etzioni appeals to this correspondence between right and duty, but smuggles quite different obligations in under the rubric of responsibilities, like careful driving, looking after the environment for future generations and so on. Such obligations in fact arise out of our concern for the welfare of our fellow man, and have no direct relationship to rights. 'Welfare', Kant reminds us, 'has no principle'. Etzioni ought to understand that greater liberty would correspond to greater responsibility, not contradict it. Annealing the welfare of the community to the need to limit our rights, Etzioni reveals the substantial interest he has in the community and in responsibility. They are really just slogans under which rights can be restrained. The community he believes in is just the negative of those he sees as greedy selfish egotists. The responsibility he embraces is just the negation of rights. Their value is as a limit upon individual subjectivity.

With a very different pedigree from the poststructuralists, the communitarians have come to one strikingly similar conclusion: the demotion of the individual Subject. Like Althusser, Charles Taylor belittles the individual Subject. 'Modern identity', he complains, 'remains too narrow [because] it is still entirely anthropocentric, and treats all goods which are not anchored in human powers or fulfillments as illusions from a bygone age'.[101] Michael Sandel suggests the contrast of the 'ideal family situation' to individualistic societies. In the family, he says 'the questions of what I get and what I am due do not loom large in the overall context of life'.[102] Harking back to old-fashioned illusions and the self-sacrifice of family life are not modes of expression designed to curry favour with deconstructionists and feminists. But for all that Sandel and Taylor are surprisingly contemporary in their attitude to the contingency of the self, and the need to circumscribe the egotistical Subject. Juliet Kristeva, the feminist critic of psychoanalysis, is equally critical of the choosing Subject, finding him to be trivial and incapable of the goal of liberation. 'Who can revolt if the human being is increasingly reduced to a conglomerate of functions, ie, he is not a "Subject" but rather a "patrimonial individual"...who is free only to "zap" and choose his "channel"?'[103] Kristeva's hopes for 'revolt' seem to be at odds with Taylor, Sandel and MacIntyre's healthy society. But for all the difference in the way that the overarching goal is framed – as revolution on the one hand, order on the other – the judgement on the egotistical Subject is surprisingly similar.

The exclusive Subject

Juliet Kristeva does add a special contribution to the critique of the Subject socially constituted. That is the charge that his is not a universal outlook, but rather a vested interest, trying to pass itself off as a universal outlook. This is the argument that the Subject socially constituted is far from being synonymous with all human animals. This criticism is made most pointedly by the feminist critic Carole Pateman (though of course it is a criticism that can and has been extended to embrace several other kinds of exclusion).

> 'The fraternal social contract story shows that the categories and practices of civil society cannot simply be universalised to women. The social contract is a modern patriarchal pact that establishes men's sex right over women, and the civil individual has been constructed in opposition to women and all that our bodies symbolise, so how can we become full members of civil society or parties to the fraternal contract?' [104]

Carole Pateman's argument is that membership of civil society excludes women. The fictional contract between freely willing Subjects is the mythical origin of society as told by the natural-right thinkers of the eighteenth century. According to the story, men, born free, made a compact amongst each other to recognise the laws of the land as a binding contract. In that way they undergird the security of each individual, so that he can protect his possessions, only giving up what is his freely in trade. The social contract has always been understood as a fiction to describe the way that modern societies derive their authority from the consent of the ruled. However, as Pateman points out, in the essay 'The fraternal contract', and in greater depth in *The Sexual Contract*,[105] the history shows that women, as well as servants and children,[106] were not part of the original contract.

Drawing on CB Macpherson's account of *The Theory of Possessive Individualism: From Hobbes to Locke*, Pateman can show that women were not originally seen as rights-bearing Subjects. Even the most radical elements of the English Revolution, the Levellers, who were crushed by Cromwell, opposed stretching the suffrage to women, and to servants, rights that were refused right up until the twentieth century.[107] Historically then, the social contract was, in Pateman's words a 'fraternal contract'. It signalled the end of paternal rule by the King, but brought it back in the changed shape of a patriarchal right in the home that was an Englishman's castle.

'The social contract is the point of origin, or birth, of civil society, and simultaneously its separation from the private sphere of real birth and disorder of women', writes Pateman.[108] She derives the oppression of women from the public-private divide. 'The civil body politic is fashioned after the image of the male "individual" who is constituted through the separation of civil society from women', she writes.[109] Her point is that enslavement in the home exists before we even get to civil society, as its pseudo-natural basis. 'Women are oppressed socially', writes feminist lawyer Catharine Mackinnon, 'prior to law, without express state acts, often in intimate contexts'.[110] Women in this form of social organisation are defined by their domestic slavery, which not only runs alongside of civil freedom, but is its basis. The 'civil body politic is fashioned after the image of the male "individual"' because the individual attains his individuality only as a householder, which is to say, on the backs of his wife and servants.

Catharine Mackinnon spells out the conclusion that the extension of civil rights to women cannot resolve the prior problem of oppression in the home. 'If one group' – men – 'is socially granted the positive freedom to do whatever it wants to another group' – women – 'to determine that the second group will be and do this rather than that, no amount of negative freedom legally guaranteed to the second group will make it the equal of the first', she writes. In other words, equal rights in wider society will always be undercut by oppression in the realm of the home. 'For women, this has meant that civil society...has been placed beyond reach of legal guarantees.'[111]

The authority of the feminist critique of the Subject in social contract theory is compelling. Historically it is undeniable that 'natural rights' theorists took it as natural that women were not free but propertied men were. In its original conception, then, the rights-bearing Subject is exclusively the property-owning male. The argument runs that the principle of free Subjectivity is poisoned at its source, built upon the denial of freedom to women and other subordinate classes. But this argument is open to the answer that maybe it was so, but is no longer. Indeed, women have the vote. Was the campaign for women's suffrage 'simply the universalisation' of the 'patriarchal pact that establishes men's sex right'? That would seem to be a perverse judgement.

The example that Pateman cites of the restricted franchise proposed by all wings of the English Revolution of 1649 poses a fascinating problem. The reason given by the Levellers for their restricted franchise was that they did not want to give political rights to people who in social terms lacked independence. Household servants, it was felt, would not be at liberty to cast their votes freely. On the contrary, it was assumed that being dependent upon a master, their votes would simply create additional votes for that master.[11] Pateman and Mackinnon both alight on the same condition that the original Levellers cited to restrict the franchise – the persistence of a state of dependence for given sections of society. The English Revolution enfranchised not the abstract Subject of political theory, but the actual, empirical men of independent means. These alone could be recognised as rights-bearing Subjects.

The insight that human beings are not necessarily Subjects is wholly correct. All societies exclude some human beings from the rights owed to Subjects. Infants are denied a say in the running of all societies, and understandably so. Catatonic patients are not consulted about their healthcare. If some instances of the restriction of rights appear to be inevitable, others arise out of the balance of forces in a society, between different social castes and groups. The extension of the realm of rights-bearing Subjects has been gradual and much fought over. The introduction of the rights of association and the franchise to the labouring classes was a begrudging concession to agitation and protest. Women, too, forcibly insisted upon their right to be treated equally to men, as Subjects, with the right to dispose of their own property, to divorce, to vote.

But according to Pateman's criticism, all of these reforms are compromised by the intrinsically male character of such rights. Civil rights presuppose the cleavage between public and private as their necessary basis. The existence of a private sphere is an essential part of liberal societies. If all are permanently engaged in public life, then the possibility of withdrawing to reflect on one's own ambitions and desires is impossible. Freedom of conscience, the original claim of the non-conformist sects that made the English Revolution, implies a withdrawal from the public realm into a private world. Without mastery of one's own home, the Subject lacks the independence to be a Subject. It would appear that Pateman's argument is unassailable, civil liberty implies domestic domination of women. However, one cannot help but feel that the argument is being stretched when women are the majority of the workforce, the nuclear family is severely strained and marriage for life a minority pursuit.

In very different circumstances the German political theorist Franz Neumann argued that the limitations upon equality were not a reason to dispense with it. He criticised those 'who seize upon the obvious inadequacy of mere legal equality and constitutional equality, and charge that formal equality tends only to conceal socio-economic privilege and exploitation'.[13] Neumann's answer though was not to deny the charge, on the contrary, he said, wryly, since they were criticisms he was more than willing to make 'we must concede some justice to their accusations'. But Neumann's objection is that 'they make no attempt to transform the socio-economic structure so as to make the formal equality real. Instead, they use a legitimate critique to abolish even legal equality'.[14] Neumann's point has legs. He is saying that just because equal rights do not necessarily lead to social equality, it does not follow that you should junk equal rights. It is hypocritical to denounce legal inequality as inadequate, when there is no desire to make social equality adequate to it. And hypocrisy is ever that vice that pays homage to virtue. The very reason that the criticism of the disparity between equal rights and social inequality has force is that inequality is abhorrent. If you point up the inequality that lies beneath the superficially equal appearance, the discovery is doubly sickening. Not only is there inequality, but there is a pretence of equality. But the very reason that these criticisms bite is that inequality is repellent. If the criticism does not aim to extend the realm of free Subjects to embrace the excluded, then the call on our sense of outrage is just a show.

Are Pateman and Mackinnon sincere in their criticisms of inequality? We will never know for certain, but we can judge by their comments. Firstly we note that their rhetoric, so forceful in the denunciation of social inequality, is strangely woolly when it comes to saying what they are for. Mackinnon talks of a 'new model' a 'society in which equality is a fact, not merely a word', whilst warning that even her own intermediate campaign against pornography is 'almost impossible'.[115] 'In this new model, principle will be defined in terms of specific experiences, the particularity of history, substantively rather than abstractly.' But of course, as Mackinnon reminds us, equality is an abstraction. It follows that Mackinnon's ideal society in which principle will be defined substantively rather than abstractly is one without equality and in which there will be no expectation of equal treatment before the law. Perhaps circumstances will be such that we will not need to cling jealously to our rights, but what these circumstances might be, Mackinnon barely hints at. 'When this day comes silence will be...a context of repose into which thought can expand, an invitation that gives speech its shape, an opening to a new conversation.'[116] Poesy steps in to fill the vacuum where Mackinnon's ill-formulated commitment to social equality ought to be. Nor is Carole Pateman's version much better. 'The most profound and complex problem for political theory and practice is how the two bodies of humankind and feminine and masculine individuality can be fully incorporated into political life',[117] she says taking refuge in a conundrum. 'How can the present of patriarchal domination, opposition and duality be transformed into a future of autonomous, democratic differentiation?' Notwithstanding the 'How?', you could be forgiven for asking 'What?' when offered a future of 'autonomous, democratic differentiation'.

The vague nature of these hints at a positive alternative to the present state suggests that these are not sincere attempts to overcome inequality. In fact that much is already indicated in the theory. Extending equality to all adult persons as equal subjects would, in the view of Pateman and Mackinnon, be to force women into the straitjacket of a male model of the free Subject. There have been a great many criticisms of the limited extent of those natural rights claimed by eighteenth-century freeholders. The original meaning of the Social Democracy of the nineteenth century was the extension of rights to embrace not just the civil but also the social realm. After the Chartists in the nineteenth century, Suffragettes fought for women's rights in the twentieth, followed by the struggle for colonial freedom and for civil rights in America and Northern Ireland. What all of these campaigns had in common though, was that their explicit intention was to extend the realm of free Subjectivity, to have themselves reckoned as Subjects with rights comparable to their former masters. Now, arguably, these movements were in a state of false consciousness. It could be said, that they were revolts against the very principle of subjectivity – because it is necessarily implicated in oppression. But to follow that argument means transforming the great democratic struggle of the modern era into a revolt against the Subject, rather than for its propagation. One can annex these past movements into the contemporary attitude of disdain for the Subject, but to do so is to do violence to their own stated intentions and real practices. It would be more accurate to say that this history has been reinterpreted in the light of a more recent history. In much the same way, Butler's critique of subjectification is a novel emergence within feminism.

The Subject of society

Like the historical critique of the subject, the social critique has a real basis. It is not refutable. The Subject is a social product, in the same way that it is a historical product. Human beings become individual Subjects in and through society, as Althusser, Sandel and Taylor say. Furthermore, not all human beings are recognised as Subjects, that is, not all have had the rights that mark the person as a free Subject extended to them, as Pateman and Mackinnon indicate. All of these things are true. And these insights make the modern critic erudite and insightful, where the eighteenth-century natural rights theorist is, by contrast, a naïf. The modern critic understands that the individual apart from society will never attain the independence that the socially situated Subject will. The naive theorist of natural rights persists in the foolish belief that men, fully formed, with an innate sense of their abilities and interests, set about building a society by common consent. The modern critic is sensible to the way that society set limits upon the extent of who was and who was not recognised as a Subject. The natural rights theorist turns a blind eye to the many exclusions from a supposedly natural equality.

For all that, the arch sophistication of the modern critic has some drawbacks, and even the naive natural rights theorist has some advantages. As analysis, the modern critic's take seems profound. But as statement of intent it is feeble. Indifference if not downright hostility to free subjectivity lies beneath the modern critic's sophistication. The greater sense of the Subject's historical contingency and social delimitation arises not just from a greater understanding. It also follows from an underlying rejection of the rights and responsibilities that come with a real love of freedom. How very profound it is to point out that Jefferson kept slaves, Ireton beat his wife and Saint Just had servants. The camp sensibility adores the details of human foibles, but is curiously indifferent to the broad canvass on which these – yes, flawed! – heroes painted a new society in which ultimately slaves were freed, women emancipated and servility abolished.

The insight that the Subject comes to be through society is analytically correct, but there is a blurring of lines between what is the case and what ought to be the case. Do any obligations ensue from the *anthropocentric — human centered.*

observed fact that individuals arise in society, and if so, what are they, and to whom? For the communitarians the analytical point supports a moral proposition: that the individual is subordinate to the social order. But like Althusser, communitarians have a curiously dehumanised view of society. Is society something other than the massed ranks of humanity? The selfish egotism of an Aleister Crowley ('do as you will shall be the whole of the law') or Max Stirner (*The Ego and His Own*) is an easy target, but hardly anybody fits the caricature. Rather, most understand that individual needs and desires must be mediated with others. In whose name is the individual to submit? Community sketched out as a bare abstraction means very little. Tradition, duty, responsibility are words that, if not specified, rapidly reduce to mere slogans, or worse ciphers with which any authoritarian proposition may be justified. Charles Taylor expresses the communitarians' alienation from humanity when he complains that 'Modern identity remains too narrow [because] it is still entirely anthropocentric, and treats all goods which are not anchored in human powers or fulfilments as illusions from a bygone age'. It is strange to find anthropocentrism offered as an example of what is wrong. Who should be at the centre, if not humanity? Taylor seems to be saying that modern identity, being too narrow, ought to be broadened to include the non-human. Presuming that this is not an apology for bestiality we must assume that it is a religious appeal. There is a kind of tragedy in *Sources of the Self* that Taylor manages to describe the full majesty of man's liberation from servitude to alien powers, only to end with this plea for a return to the subordination of man before the non-human. The communitarian argument appears to be humane, asking only that the balance between individual and society be redressed, so that the selfish lout will pay more attention to his community. But on closer inspection, 'the community' is a lifeless abstraction, invoked only as the restraining limitation upon the individual Subject.

NB — No, an appeal to politics.

The view that the individual Subject is constituted through society, whether in its communitarian or structuralist version, is evidence of the growing alienation from Subjectivity. It weakly suggests an alternative of the collective Subject, the social, that will overpower the individual Subject, but this collective Subject turns out to be no Subject at all. In Althusser's case, history is a 'process without a subject'. In Taylor's the quest is on for 'goods not anchored in human powers'.

Intriguingly, the sociological account of Subject formation has its blind-spot precisely when it comes to society. The 'society' that is invoked is superior to the individual. But at the same time, both communitarians and poststructuralists are reluctant to give credence to a collective subjectivity. Their society is an abstract category that simply swamps the individual, absorbing any independent initiative that the individual might undertake. That society, too, is made up of acting Subjects they find impossible to conceive. Society is a closed book to Althusser, as it is for Taylor. The aggregation of humanity does not bring a new social standpoint because the social remains the blind carrier of impersonal forces. Ironically this apparently sociological account more accurately describes the narrow standpoint of the isolated individual. Why? Because for him society is always 'out there', what comes before and shapes, an impersonal force of domination or tradition. To individuals who are isolated, society ceases to be an extension of themselves, and becomes instead a vast impersonal force. The more isolated and helpless the individual feels, the more adamantine in its indifference is society. By contrast, confident and gregarious individuals will tend to sense the possibilities of social action, in the informal networks and more structured organisations that present themselves. To such an individual, the apparently seamless structure of society begins to look more manageable, or even a means to achieving his ends rather than an absolute barrier. The sociological analysis is one that is deeply alienated from society. Like the historicisation of the Subject, the meaning of the theory of the socialised Subject is an expression of the degradation of subjectivity in theory.

Chapter Three

DECENTRING THE SUBJECT: THE OTHER

'The Orient is not only adjacent to Europe; it is also the place of its civilisations and languages, its cultural constant, and one of its deepest and most recurring images of the Other. In addition, the Orient has helped Europe (or the West) as its contrasting image, idea, personality, experience.' Edward Said

Said's book Orientalism first published in 1978 was a remarkable counter-blast to an age of Western triumphalism in the Middle East.[18] Said showed how Western perceptions of the Orient, in literature and anthropology, consistently overlaid the real geographical and social area described with images drawn substantially from the West's needs. At a time when not only hostile images, but also patronising stereotypes of the Orient stood in the way of a proper understanding between East and West, Said's book turned the tables on the Western intelligentsia and held them to account for their statements.

But beyond its influence as engaged criticism, Said's book also popularised the philosophical notion of 'the Other'. This capitalised adjective-turned-noun carries a surprising wealth of meaning. In the above from Orientalism, Said shows how the Orient, as Other to the West, defines the West. He means something like, 'all the negative features that the West see in the Orient are really just projections of its own fears'. Those things that we value we see as specifically Western, and, to make the point more forcefully, we find their opposite in the East. The negative images of the East serve to delineate what the West values in itself.

There is a fascinating example in *Orientalism* of how a change in Western self-perception demands an alteration in the description of the East, to fulfil its function as Other to the West. In much of the material that Said accumulates, drawn from the eighteenth and nineteenth centuries, there is a stereotype of the East as licentious.'[9] As Said notes, 'for nineteenth-century Europe...there was no such thing as "free" sex'. Prurient Europeans projected what they feared (and desired) in their own society onto the Orient. Today, of course, the imaginary opposition of Eastern licentiousness and Western rectitude has been more or less inverted. Not in fact because of any change in the sexual mores of the East, but rather because the West has in the latter half of the twentieth century become sexually more liberal, the East appears, by contrast, to be sexually repressive. The imaginative transformation of the licentious East into the sexually repressive East is entirely independent of what actually happens there. Rather it is the expression of changing sexual manners in the West.

The explanatory power of the concept of the Other has led to its broad adoption in cultural and social criticism. So, for example, we have analyses of childhood as the Other of adulthood, nature as the Other of humanity, and, the most illustrious line, analyses of woman as the Other of man. Like all concepts, 'the Other' can illuminate, but it can also obscure meaning. Routine application of a received idea can become a barrier to thinking. Specifically, in the case of the concept of the Other, as a consequence perhaps of its promiscuous reproduction in the social sciences, the unspoken presuppositions in the theory are rarely made explicit.

The development of the concept of the Other is a theoretical assault on the Subject. The Other describes the negation of subjectivity. Said acknowledges this when he says, with an attractive candour, 'because of Orientalism the Orient was not (and is not) a free subject of thought or action'.[120] Descriptively, that is a harsh but broadly accurate judgement. For the greater part of modern history, the Orient has been dominated by the West, and has not been a free Subject of thought or action. However, Said puts the cart before the horse when he says that the reason is Orientalism. It would be more true to say that the intellectual outlook of Orientalism has taken hold because the Orient has been denied the status of a free Subject of thought or action. But the flaw in the theory of the Other, is that it tends to absolutise the opposition between the Self and its Other. Said's analysis of Orient as Other to the West, is telling because of the real subjugation of the East by the West. Even there, though, Said's approach tends to treat the relationship as one that is set in stone, as if the East could only occupy the position of Other to the West. Consequently, the account becomes repetitive, as if there were no modulations in the relationship. In particular, the universalising moment in Enlightenment thinking, its optimism for a singular human family, is ignored or worse, assimilated into the romantic emphasis on the Otherness of the East.

The concept of the Other has been so woven into contemporary social and philosophical thought that it appears to be unremarkable, an ordinary part of the language. But this is a concept with an origin, and its origin is in Hegel's dialectic of Master and Slave as it was revised by French philosophers after the Second World War. It was from Hegel's account of the clash between Master and Slave that

Simone de Beauvoir and Jean-Paul Sartre took the categorical opposition of Self and Other and made it into an absolute. To understand the significance of this absolute opposition it will be helpful to trace the intellectual development of the theory of the Other – with the proviso that intellectual histories do not explain the contemporary appeal of the idea.

Hegel's dialectic of Master and Slave is a philosophical account of the emergence of the Subject. Hegel's predecessor Kant, tended to assume the existence of the Subject and the potential for harmonious relations amongst Subjects, as in the formula 'be a person and respect others as persons'.[121] Hegel, by contrast, showed the emergence of the Subject as the outcome of a struggle that he idealised in the 'Master-Slave dialectic'.[122] There are a great many subtleties to these passages in Hegel's *Phenomenology of Spirit*, but for present purposes, and at the risk of vulgarising, the relevant stages in the argument can be summarised in the following way.

Men meet on the battlefield in a struggle to the death. The victor in such an encounter, suggests Hegel, is the one who risks death – 'He who dares wins', as the British Special Air Service motto runs. In risking physical death, the victor has made an important step. For him honour is more valuable than mere animal subsistence. His selfhood is emerging as something higher, an ideal, realised in his new status as Master. The vanquished has preferred survival to honour and pays by being reduced to a slave, little more than a beast of burden.

Thus far, the clash has only produced Slave and Master in opposition. But Hegel intends to show how this relationship transforms its two terms. In the first instance the slave is the Other to the master, the Self. The slave makes himself the corporeal body of the master's will – 'your wish is my command'. However, the relationship is unsatisfactory for the master. He has domination over the slave. What he wanted, though, was honour, or recognition of his mastery. The love owed him by his slaves will never satisfy him, because it is not freely given. Furthermore, the master, having made himself

Hegel's dialectic.

master through action becomes lazy. Superficially it appears that he calls the shots. He snaps his fingers and the slaves come running to wait upon him. But already the slaves are, without realising it, the active parties. Their labour creates all the possibilities available to the court. If they would but realise the fact that they make everything happen, they would shake off the mantle of slave. Then they would cease merely to be the Other, and attain the character of Selves.

Hegel describes the stages of consciousness that the slave goes through as he approaches knowledge of himself as a Self. First the slave decides to embrace his servitude manfully, in the attitude of a Stoic, taking pleasure in his labour. Second the slave shrugs off the external world of servitude, in the attitude of the Cynic, for whom mere existence is an illusion. Then the slave creates a spiritual realm of freedom, in the attitude of the Christian, who renders unto Caesar that which is Caesar's, and to God that which is God's. Through this process the slave gradually withdraws his complicity in his own servitude making the transition from obsequiousness through dumb insolence to establish freedom of conscience. This last is the preparatory stage to the demand for mutual recognition, or emancipation and civil rights. The fascinating aspect of the dialectic of the master and the slave is the way that Hegel gives the slave's consciousness the active role of developing full subjectivity and selfhood. Consequently, Self and Other, in Hegel's Master-Slave dialectic are relative terms, not absolutes. The Other passes into selfhood. This is what marks out Hegel's original working up of the terms from the later interpretation that became current in France just before the Second World War.

Hegel achieves the relativisation of the Self-Other opposition by making both into expressions of the development of the Idea, or Spirit. In other words the different social positions that people occupy are not intrinsic to them. They are just vessels for the underlying spiritual development. By manifesting itself in these successive shapes – Master, Slave (Stoic, Cynic, Christian), mutually recognising selves – the Spirit develops and comes into consciousness of itself.

This transformation of human history into the development of the Spirit is unconvincing to modern sensibilities, and certainly was in pre-war Paris. But Hegel, not yet published in French, had a useful interpreter in the Russian *émigré* Alexandre Kojève. The trend to secularise Hegel begins with Kojève's celebrated lecture series on Hegel's *Phenomenology of Spirit*.

The most influential part of Kojève's telling of the Master-Slave dialectic was its secular, humanistic reinterpretation of Hegel's religious spirituality. Kojève 'read' Hegel to be describing the development of human institutions 'in the guise' of describing a spiritual progression. Where Hegel's book is a 'phenomenology of Spirit', Kojève's lectures describe an anthropogenesis.[123] In Kojève's version the subject is Man ('Man is self-consciousness'[124]), in Hegel's the subject is Spirit. We merely have to shed the arcane language of 'spirit' to understand Hegel's real humanistic message, Kojève is saying.

The difference between Kojève's anthropogenesis and Hegel's phenomenology of Spirit is this: Hegel relativises the independence of the self-consciousnesses as so many subordinate terms in the movement of Spirit. Hegel writes: 'What still lies ahead for consciousness is the experience of what Spirit is – this absolute substance which is the unity of the different independent self-consciousnesses which, in their opposition enjoy perfect freedom and independence.'[125] It is because the substance of the independent self-consciousnesses is Spirit that the different structures of consciousness, of Master and of Slave, can be superseded as merely intermediate manifestations of Spirit.

For Kojève, however, Spirit has been banished in favour of Man. What, then, allows 'the "dialectical overcoming" of both' Master and Slave? The corresponding concept to Hegel's Spirit (as substance of forms of consciousness) in Kojève is society: 'the human reality can come into being only as social reality', though 'society is human – at least in origin – only on the basis of its implying an element of Mastery and an element of Slavery'.[126] The nearest thing then to the over-arching concept of Spirit that could allow a movement beyond the entrenched positions of Mastery and Slavery in Kojève is society. But this universal is underdeveloped, appearing to be little more than the reiteration of the clash of Master and Slave.

Kojève stripped out the Spirit to put Man in its place. His was a secular humanism which shared something of Hegel's optimism. Later Hegel scholars shared Kojève's resistance to the Spirit, but were cautious, too of his humanism, thinking it shared something of the religiosity of Spirit. In principle though, whatever the subsequent differences, this one underlying project to strip spirituality out of Hegel is the enduring theme of Hegel scholarship in the period after the Second World War.

A dispirited Hegel, secularised and rendered more prosaic seems to fit our times. But there is a difficulty in re-reading Hegel in this way. The passage of the Spirit is fundamental to Hegel's phenomenology – it is the substance of which the forms of consciousness are the phenomena. Most importantly, Spirit is the concept to which all other forms are subordinate. Hegel's method of relativising specific positions and stances depends upon their being partial, one-sided expressions of the over-arching totality of Spirit. The historical overcoming of these specific forms of consciousness and of being is only possible by virtue of these forms being made the subordinate clauses of the central proposition. Historical transition, the transcendence of each and every specific manifestation of Spirit is possible because they are only partial expressions.

Spirit as a concept might be out of keeping with our contemporary sensibilities. But without it, Hegel's historical movement stands in danger of being jettisoned. Unless a more prosaic substitute can fulfil the same goals of relativising contingent positions, then these must necessarily solidify into absolute polar opposites, without the possibility of being transcended. The forms of consciousness that in Hegel are merely staging posts on the way will ossify into insurmountable barriers. The antagonisms of Master and Slave will simply fall asunder into mutually exclusive oppositions without any possibility of their supercession. Alienation ceases to contain the possibility of its own overcoming, but is arrested at the point of mutual incomprehension and hostility. Roughly speaking, this is what has happened with the secularisation of Hegel's thought.

Once secularised in this way, Hegel made his most important bequest to twentieth-century philosophy, the mutually defined concepts of Self and Other which are categories of the Master-Slave dialectic. The opening line of Hegel's account is 'Self-consciousness exists in and for itself when, and by the fact that, it so exists for another'.[127] In the subjugation of Slave by Master 'there is posited a pure self-consciousness, and a consciousness which is not purely for itself, but for another....The former is lord, the other is bondsman'.[128] After Kojève the categories of Self and Other took on a life of their own, first in the works of Jean-Paul Sartre and Simone de Beauvoir, and extending outwards to become the commonplace terminology of a large body of social and philosophical writing. What is the meaning of this transformation of the Hegelian categories in the hands of these postwar French philosophers? We can say that the Master-Slave dialectic has been removed from its pseudo-historical context and made mundane. In the place of the historically specific relations of Master to Slave, we now have universal relations of Self and Other. The relations that in Hegel are projected back into a notional historical era prior to the emergence of civil society are dragged forward into the present. Conflicts that in Hegel are elaborated in a fictional pre-modern era, are seen as resonating in the present. While the historical shell of lordship and servitude falls away, its inner content, the problematic and unsatisfactory relations of Self and Other, persists.

It was Simone de Beauvoir who first transformed Hegel's categories of Self and Other into the modern concept of the Other. For her groundbreaking book *The Second Sex*, de Beauvoir is much praised as the first person to insist that one is not born a woman, one becomes a woman. 'The biological and social sciences no longer admit the existence of unchangeably fixed entities that determine given characteristics, such as those ascribed to woman, the Jew, or the Negro', she writes.[129] With such a non-biological approach one would think that the eternal status of woman is to be dislodged. But having downgraded the biological differentiation, De Beauvoir rehabilitates the opposition in as trenchantly enduring terms. 'The category of the Other is as primordial as consciousness itself. In the most primitive societies, in the most ancient mythologies, one finds the expression of a duality – that of the Self and the Other.'[130] 'Thus it is that no group ever sets itself up as the One without at once setting up the Other over against itself....Jews are "different" for the anti-Semite, Negroes are "inferior" for American racists, aborigines are "natives" for colonists, proletarians are the "lower class" for the privileged.'[131] The biological differences between men and women are inserted into this eternalised psychological form: 'Here is to be found the basic trait of woman: she is the Other in a totality of which the two components are necessary to one another.'

Jean-Paul Sartre followed de Beauvoir in elevating the Self-Other distinction into an absolute. He rejected Hegel's resolution, accusing Hegel of an 'ontological optimism',[132] which he explained as follows: 'Thus when Hegelian monism [ie, the monism of Spirit] considers the relation of consciousness, it does not put itself in any particular consciousness. Although the Whole is to be realised, it is already there as the truth of all which is true.'[133] Sartre is saying that in making Spirit the substance of the particular figures of consciousness from the outset, Hegel is smuggling the conclusion of the problem in at the beginning. Sartre answers Hegel: 'we should not..."surpass" the Other toward any inter-monad totality. So long as consciousnesses exist, the separation and conflict of consciousnesses will remain.'[134] In Sartre's *Being and Nothingness*, Hegel's phenomenology of Spirit must founder on the 'Reef of Solipsism', along with everyone else. Separation and conflict are an ever-present condition of the existence of consciousnesses. As Self and Other, Master and Slave are trapped in their conflict, and their mutual incomprehension for all time.

Sartre's unbridgeable opposition between Self and Other appeared to be radical in the face of the apologetic social pacifism of the post-war day. While government spokesmen and ideologues promoted an unproblematic harmony, Sartre's insistent problematisation of human relations pointed up the shortcomings. The embrace of the case for the Other took on a radical significance. So, for example, Franz Fanon, the intellectual of the Algerian revolution, adapted Sartre's refusal of commonality to the conflict between Europe and Africa: 'The two zones are opposed, but not in the service of a higher unity. Obedient to the rules of pure Aristotelian logic, they both follow the principle of reciprocal exclusivity.'[135]

But while the Self-Other opposition was radical in its rejection of amelioriative reforms, it does not readily lead to radical solutions either. Rather the whole point is that the Reef of Solipsism cannot be crossed. Self and Other are radically incommensurable. The tension is relocated from a specific and historically transient form of social organisation to the human condition itself. It cannot be overcome.

What the secularisation of Hegel's Master-Slave dialectic achieves, then, is not finally a humanisation of Self and Other, even though it appeared to be that way. Rather it is the removal of the Subject from the Master-Slave dialectic. This is the case because Hegel's idealised Subject is the Spirit. And it is this Subject which overcomes the condition of Otherness. The elevation of the Other into the dominant principle is an effect of the demotion of the Subject. The theory of the Other is a degradation of the Subject. This much can be seen in the growing number of religious theories of the Other. These begin with the Hasidic theologian Martin Buber's radical opposition of Self and Other as 'I and Thou', an opposition that leads quickly 'toward the fringe of the eternal Thou; in each we are aware of the breath from the eternal Thou; in each Thou we address the eternal Thou'.[136] Paradoxically the excision of Hegel's religiously expressed subjectivity allows God to rush into the vacuum between Subjects, to become the eternal Other. In Buber's follower Emmanuel Levinas, we can again see the way that the elevation of the Other is in fact a demotion of the Subject. In his book *Outside the Subject*, Levinas' essay 'The rights of Man and the rights of the Other' deploys the concept of the Other to circumscribe the 'egotism of a being persevering in its being'. Levinas elevates the notion of the absolutely Other, which is '"more other", so to speak, than are the individuals with respect to one another within the "same species" from which the I has freed itself'.[17] By this introduction of big Other, the merely individual other is overshadowed, by God, in fact.

Like the concept of the posthuman, the elevation of the Other corresponds to a degradation of the Subject. The desire to relinquish the Self, leave the species, stop persevering in one's being are all essentially the same death-wish.

Chapter Four

PROCESS WITHOUT A SUBJECT

Beyond the theoretical degradation of the Subject stand attempts to theorise life without the Subject. Amongst these are the attempts to theorise society in terms of power, or as a conversation – the theory of intersubjectivity – and the sociobiological accounts of genes as destiny, as well their sociological reinterpretation, memes.

Powering down

The theory of power has come to the fore in social analysis in recent times, popularised by Michel Foucault in his books *The History of Sexuality*, *Discipline and Punish* and *The Birth of the Clinic*. Power recommends itself to Foucault as a critical concept precisely because it excludes the priority of the Subject.

'Power relations are both intentional and nonsubjective', writes Foucault. 'There is no power that is exercised without a series of aims and objectives. But this does not mean that it results from the choice or decision of an individual subject.'[38] There is intelligence, then, in the structures of power, but not as a consequence of any design. The category 'power' here has the effect of making social organisation non-specific, because no hand can be discovered on the levers of power. Like Althusser's depersonalised categories of forces and relations of production, the category power seems to make things more vague rather than clearer.

'The analysis made in terms of power, must not assume that the sovereignty of the state, the form of the law, or the over-all unity of a domination are given at the outset; rather, these are only the terminal forms power takes', according to Foucault. This is his famous argument against the repressive hypothesis. He objects to the version of history, the 'repressive hypothesis', in which a Subject, 'the people' struggles to free itself from the domination of the repressive state. Foucault is interested in the forms of social control and regulation that preoccupy libertarian visions of the state. But he resists the binary opposition of a people struggling against a singular state apparatus. The reason is that such libertarian schemas contain as their presupposition a Subject of liberation when Foucault has already rejected the Subject in all its manifestations. Instead, he says, Subjects are formed through the regulatory instruments of power, as we have seen.

Foucault's rejection of the schema of a Subject-of-liberation forces him to revise the accepted model of state power. Instead of a singular state power, he insists, 'power must be understood in the first instance as the multiplicity of force relations immanent in the sphere in which they operate and which constitute their own organisation'.[39]

'Where there is power, there is resistance and yet, or rather consequently, this resistance is never in a position of exteriority in relation to power. [With] the strictly relational character of power relationships...existence depends upon a multiplicity of points or resistance...

present everywhere in the power network. Hence there is no locus of great Refusal, no soul of revolt, source of all rebellions, or pure law of the revolutionary. Instead there is a plurality of resistances.'[40] Foucault has theoretically dismantled the repressive state apparatus into 'the multiplicity of force relations'. And this allows him in turn to dismantle the Subject of liberation, otherwise known as 'great Refusal', 'soul of revolt' and so on. Foucault means to rubbish the liberationist dreams of his fellow rebels of 1968. His revolution-within-the-revolution rejects the Subject as the model of resistance most thoroughly implicated in the existing order. As Butler writes: 'Such subjection is a form of power that not only unilaterally acts on a given individual as a form of domination, but also activates or forms the subject.'[41]

This much we already know, but the intriguing aspect of the 'power theory' is the way that it works to make the operations of 'power' unspecific. Where the hallmark of power is its dispersal into localised discourses of power, 'seizing power' becomes a quixotic task.

More than a century ago, Friedrich Engels had occasion to complain about the philistinism of what was then called 'The Force Theory of History', or would today be called the theory of power. Engels was replying to the socialist Eugen von Dühring.[42] For Engels the major problem with the force theory was that it was tautological, leaving everything essentially unexplained: 'The question at issue is how we are to explain the origin of classes and relations based on domination, and if Herr Dühring's only answer is the one word "force," this leaves us exactly where we were at the start.' Engels' complaint is that 'force' (or 'power' just as much) is too loose a category to explain anything. Like an enormous spanner that fits every single nut but grips none of them, the 'force theory' remains at too great a level of generality. 'The mere fact that the ruled and exploited class has at all times been far more numerous than the rulers and exploiters, and that therefore it is the former who have had the real force in their hands, is enough to demonstrate the absurdity of the whole force theory', Engels continued. 'The relationships based on domination and subjection have therefore still to be explained.' Similarly Engels complained that Dühring's phrase "Property founded on force" 'proves here also to be nothing but the phrase of a braggart intended to cover up his lack of understanding of the real course of things'. As with Dühring we do find in Foucault a combination of a very general category, power, with very specific empirical material, leaving us with the feeling that the two are not really meeting. Foucault's celebrated mobilisation of telling and evocative historical evidence illustrates the 'power' theory superficially, but without really being integrated into it. One feels that the broad sweep of his historical knowledge, for all his insistence upon historical specificity lacks just that.

One of Foucault's more pointed claims in *Discipline and Punish* is that the judicial regulation of subjects had priority over the later economic emergence of the factory system. Foucault argues in effect that the very success of the prison and workhouse in disciplining subjects made them the model for the historically later form of the factory system of regulation. In *The History of Sexuality*, he rejects the accepted socialist view that repression is coincident with capitalism: 'By placing the advent of the age of repression in the seventeenth century, after hundreds of years of open space and free expression [taking this last to be ironic], one adjusts it to coincide with the development of capitalism.'[43] Foucault argues, by contrast, that the repressive formation of the Subject precedes capitalism, indeed the very success of the prison system means that factories have to be built, on the same model, to finance the growing burden of this new repressive apparatus.

Frederick Engels parodied this selfsame argument when it was made by Eugen von Dühring:

'when Robinson Crusoe made Friday his slave...that was an act of force, hence a political act. And inasmuch as this enslavement was the starting-point and the basic fact underlying all past history and inoculated it with the original sin of injustice, so much so that in the later periods it was only softened down and "transformed into the more indirect forms of economic independence"; and inasmuch as "property founded on force" which has been maintained right through up to the present day, is likewise based on this original act of enslavement—for these reasons it is clear that all economic phenomena must be explained by political causes, that is, by force.'

But, argues Engels, only 'Herr Dühring could regard this view as so very "original," which it is not in the least. The idea that outstanding political acts and state actions are the decisive facts in history is as old as written history itself, and is the main reason why so little material has been preserved in regard to the really progressive evolution of the peoples which has taken place quietly in the background behind these noisy scenes on the stage.' Of course, for Foucault's purposes, the 'really progressive evolution of the peoples' is a version of the myth of the Subject-of-liberation. But Engels has a point in suggesting that the priority given to political and administrative history implies a blind-spot towards the underlying social development.[144]

Not only is the force theory unoriginal, lacking explanatory power and apologetic, it is also conservative, argues Engels, because it elides the difference between the violence of the oppressed and the violence of the oppressor. This is a counsel against resistance, says Engels, anticipating the later trajectory of the theory of power.

'For Herr Dühring force is the absolute evil; the first act of force is for him the original sin; his whole exposition is a jeremiad on the contamination, which this brought about, of all subsequent history by this original sin....That force, however, plays another role in history, a revolutionary role...of this there is not a word in Herr Dühring. It is only with sighs and groans that he admits the possibility that force will perhaps be necessary for the overthrow of the economic system of exploitation—unfortunately, because all use of force, forsooth, demoralises the person who uses it.'

For Foucault too, the deployment of power by the repressed is problematic – and not just because we cannot talk about the repressed. Implicit in his vision of power dispersed is an account of the way that the 'seizure of power' means that power seizes us, and makes us into obedient Subjects. Foucault promotes an idea of the intellectual as someone 'who destroys evidence and generalities, the one who, in the inertias and constraints of the present time, locates and marks the weak points, the openings, the lines of force, who is incessantly on the move, doesn't know where he is heading nor what he will think tomorrow for he is too attentive to the present'.[45] The sense of caution and indecision are painfully obvious, as is the adopted mien of the hunted refugee clambering through the power structure. But what possible purpose it could serve to locate and mark the weak points and openings is anybody's guess. Openings for whom, if not for the Subject of liberation, and weak points for what assault but that of the soul of revolt?

Foucault would probably not have said that the utilisation of power 'demoralises the person who uses it' as Engels has Dühring say. But the difference in idiom should not blind us to the similarity in the shape of the argument. Power is complicit in the formation of the Subject. Rhetorically, Foucault challenges, 'Did the critical discourse that addresses itself to repression come to act as a roadblock to a power mechanism that had existed unchallenged up to that point ['No', cries the audience] or is it not in fact part of the same historical network as the thing it denounces by calling it repression?' ['Aaahhh, so that's it', goes up the cry]. 'Was there really a historical rupture between the age of repression', Foucault continues, 'and the critical analysis of repression?'. Or in other words, 'doesn't the use of force demoralise the user?'. As Castoriadis puts it, 'Foucault presents all society as caught up entirely in the nets of power, thereby erasing the struggles and the internal contestation that put power in check half the time'. Foucault, according to Castoriadis, 'has discovered the "plebs" – who, however, are "reduced to nothing" as soon as they "become fixed in a strategy of resistance"'. Castoriadis parodies:

'Resist if it amuses you – but without strategy, for then you are no longer the plebs but power.'⁴⁶

The theory of power is such a tempting short-cut to real analysis that it has been invented and re-invented again and again, generally in periods when critical movements are in abeyance. Take this from Bertrand Russell's *Power*.⁴⁷ 'It is only by realising that love of power is the cause of activities that are important in social affairs that history, whether ancient or modern, can be rightly interpreted', promises Russell, happily subordinating all historical periods under the one law. 'The fundamental concept in social science is power, in the same sense as energy is the fundamental concept in physics.' But in case you think that this is too general Russell qualifies, pointlessly: 'Like energy, power has many forms, such as wealth, armaments, civil authority, influence on opinion. No one of these can be regarded as subordinate to any other, and there is no one form from which all the others are derivative.' Which does away with any need to order these different categories.

'The love of power is the chief motive producing the changes which social science has to study', says Russell anticipating Foucault by 40 years. Power explains everything, which is to say it explains nothing. Power explains all of history, which is to say that all history is collapsed into that one 'night in which all cows are grey'. Needless to say the theory that unlocks the key to all human history was never heard of again from that compulsive writer, Russell, despite its spectacular explanatory powers.

The sheer banality of the theory of power is so compelling that the banal reproduce it in all its unintelligent abstraction over and over. So for Talcott Parsons we should 'treat power as a specific mechanism operating to bring about changes in the action of other units, individual or collective, in the processes of social interaction'.⁴⁸ Parsons' curiously antiseptic and non-committal language speaks volumes – not persons, or peoples talking and struggling, but 'units, individual or collective, in the processes of social interaction'. The power theory blanches all the specificity out of human relations. Seen as mere nodal points on the field and lines of force, human Subjects become impersonal units. Indeed, the resurgence of the Dühring/Russell 'social analysis of power' could only happen where the vacuum left by the ejected Subject demands to be filled. As Castoriadis wrote, 'Foucault places omniscience and omnipotence not in individuals but in this mysterious entity called "power" – or "powers," or "networks of power". Therefore, for Foucault, in history there is an impersonal instance of absolute rationality. Hegel transcended? Give us a break!'. 'Now, this myth is obviously what power would like the enslaved to believe.'[49]

The Intersubjective

In Germany, largely due to the work of Jurgen Habermas, a social theory that puts a premium upon the intersubjective is prominent. Habermas' emphasis upon the intersubjective would appear to be distinct from the explicit denunciations of the Subject to be found in French philosophy, and he has publicly attacked the poststructuralists as 'a counterpart to neoconservatism'.[50] But curiously the ideal of 'intersubjectivity' in Habermas work becomes reified to the extent that it actually displaces the subjectivity that one would imagine it was derivative of. Like sociological theories of the Subject, the Subject is demoted before a formal category, only this time, read 'intersubjectivity' for society.

For Habermas, modern philosophy took a wrong turn at its birth in the Enlightenment in adopting a 'Subject-centered' rationality. This problem is aggravated by Hegel and Marx who are described as having modelled their concepts of reason (in the former) and the emancipation of labour (in the latter) on the self-conscious Subject. The model of a process of self-education on the part of this Subject, or collective Subject, is flawed because of its circularity.[51]

'Marx' according to Habermas promoted a 'utopia of self-activity – emancipation from heteronomous labour' which 'suffered, I believe from two mistakes'. In keeping with his mentor, Theodor Adorno, Habermas suggests that 'the first was the productivist bias'. By that he means that Marx's emphasis upon the capacity of increased productivity to increase the realm of human freedom was mistaken. Rather, he thought, like Adorno that greater rational control over nature would only lead to an enslavement of man. Already this was a negative assessment of human subjectivity, since it saw 'instrumental reason' as fundamentally flawed, precisely because it was deliberately willed activity bent towards a given end. His preference is for the non-finality of reflective debate. And it was this failure of Marx to see that it was the process of social interaction itself that was worthwhile that Habermas sees as 'the second' and more important 'error...not to realise that the only utopian perspectives in social theory which we can straightforwardly maintain are of a procedural nature'.[52]

Habermas explains:

> 'By "interaction", on the other hand, I understand communicative action, symbolic interaction. It is governed by binding consensual norms, which define reciprocal expectations about behaviour which must be understood and recognised by at least two acting subjects. Social norms are enforced through sanctions. Their meaning is objectified in ordinary language communication. While acceptance of technical rules and strategies depends on the validity of empirically true or analytically correct statements, the validity of social norms is grounded only in the intersubjectivity of mutual understanding of intentions and secured by the general recognition of obligations.'[53]

The procedural utopia that Habermas outlines is sometimes called the 'ideal speech situation', where, as he describes above, 'binding consensual norms' are 'enforced through sanctions' because they are based upon 'mutual understanding' and the 'general recognition of obligations'. All of these restraints are implied, according to

Habermas in intersubjectivity, and it becomes apparent that 'intersubjectivity' is a restraint upon the Subject. But it is clear in Habermas' work that the collective Subject troubles him just as much as the individual Subject, and the 'ideal speech situation' restrains collective actors just as much as it does individual ones.

According to Habermas's follower Axel Honneth, 'Habermas... dropped the notion of a unified subject of history', such as the Marxist 'self-emancipation of labour'.[54] In this Habermas was drawing upon the ideas of Martin Heidegger as much as of the Frankfurt School. In a veiled attack on his Marxist rival Georg Lukacs, Heidegger had written in 1926 that mass man 'is not something like a "universal subject" which a plurality of subjects have hovering above them'.[55] Heidegger was rejecting the socialist version of the collective Subject that Lukacs championed: the collective power of the working class. Heidegger thought that mass man would never be a collective Subject, and Habermas agrees. Habermas developed his own theory of intersubjectivity studying Heidegger and Lukacs, though he decided that in the end, Lukacs's collective subject 'wouldn't work'[56] and that his *History and Class Consciousness* was merely 'a historical document', of no interest today.[57]

Habermas argues that 'since the collective subject of a meaningfully constituted lifeworld borrowed from transcendental philosophy, has been shown, at least in sociology, to be a misleading fiction, the concept of system is proposed'. Like many sociological arguments, system here describes a dehumanised order, from which subjectivity has been squeezed out. 'Social systems are unities that can solve objectively posed problems through supra-subjective learning processes',[58] he writes. The collective Subject as a historical actor is ruled to be 'misleading'. But this does not mean, in the manner of neoconservative criticisms of collectivism, that the individual subject is to be set free. On the contrary, Habermas looks around for a transcendent principle to replace the collective Subject and finds a 'supra-subjective' in the 'system'.

As Honneth explains 'with the concept of "communicative action" Habermas places the process of intersubjective understanding in the central position that had been occupied by social labour in social theory reaching back to Marx'.[59] In other words, the intersubjective displaces Marx's collective Subject, 'social labour'. In fact Habermas' critique of subjectivity works by making Marx's collective Subject the equivalent of the narrowly egotistical Subject of free market theory. A plague on both your houses, Habermas is saying.

Consequently, Habermas looks forward to the day when we can do away with 'subject-centred reason and future-oriented consciousness'. 'To the extent that we become aware of the intersubjective constitution of freedom, the possessive-individualist illusion of autonomy as self-ownership disintegrates', Habermas promises ominously. And in a telling comment, he ridicules the Subject for his indifference to tradition: 'the self-assertive Subject that wants to have everything at its disposal lacks an adequate relation to any tradition.'[60] The socialist revolutionary James Connolly joked that 'Our goals most modest are, we only want the Earth', while City high-flier and mother Nicola Horlick insisted on 'Having it all'. For both, Habermas has a simple message: 'Don't get above your station in life' – or 'don't get above your ideal speech situation'.

Not subjectivity, but intersubjectivity is the basis of freedom, he says, where intersubjectivity means the negotiation between subjects, rather than the will of subjects. It is a distinction that can appear to be a bit pedantic, but in the development of his ideas it makes more sense. Habermas is saying that the thing we should value is not our free will, but the way that the clash of many wills prevents any one will from taking precedence. He means that the rules we all observe to get along are more important than what any one of us wants. This is a theory that puts a premium not on subjectivity, but on the constraint of subjectivity, meaning more laws to govern our behaviour.

Habermas's theory of intersubjectivity is the basis of an important strand of social theory that demotes the Subject in favour of norm-governed behaviour. In the 1980s a resurgence of 'civil society' theories drew upon Habermas' social theory. In Andrew Arato and Jean Cohen's *Civil Society and Political Theory*,[161] a Habermasian typology was deployed to analyse the emerging citizens movements in Eastern Europe and elsewhere. Confusingly some social movements were characterised positively, like the East German 'citizens list', while others were 'totalitarian', like the Peronist movements in Argentina, though the reasons were unclear. The Polish Solidarity movement, for example, was positive when out of office, but once in office became totalitarian. The reason was that Arato and Cohen were drawing on Habermas' conception of the priority of the intersubjective over the Subject. Movements that aimed simply to open up dialogue, like the civic groups of Eastern Europe were good, but those that aimed to exercise power, like the Peronists were bad. Lech Walesa's doughty shipyard workers were worthy of Cohen and Arato's patronage when they were breaking up the old order, only to see it withdrawn when they dared to try to rule themselves. Their error was to formulate themselves as a collective Subject, whereas before they had been part of an emerging intersubjectivity.

Other theorists who put a premium upon the conversational aspect of social interaction include Theodor Zeldin whose *Intimate History of Humanity*, moves away from the grand version of human history as great movements and leaders, to look at the small-scale interactions between people.[162] Zeldin's anthropological style is elegantly engaging, and he neatly side steps the apparently passé world of politics and social institutions. Others have drawn on the Russian formalist Mikhail Bakhtin's 'dialogism' – a theory of the dynamics of language that makes dialogue take priority over formal codes of language.[163] This picture of society as 'cafe society' in which the art of conversation is more important than the outcome is a flattering self-portrait of the educated classes. It has the effect, though, of removing the decisive, urgent side of human behaviour and emphasising instead the chit-chat of people who are essentially filling in time.

More recently Habermas's theory of intersubjectivity has provided the basis of the sociology of 'reflexive modernisation', proposed by Ulrich Beck, Scott Lash and Anthony Giddens. Like Habermas, Beck proposes that 'instrumental reason' is limiting and limited. But he emphasises this point by showing the increasing effect of the unintended consequences of human action upon modern societies. In particular, he has in mind pollution and other man-made disasters. Rather than seeing these as random events, says Beck, we should understand that modernisation is impacting upon itself in an increasing chain of unintended consequences. Modernisation is now reflecting back upon itself, hence 'reflexive modernity'. Whereas classical modernity was characterised by intelligible decisions with discrete impacts, reflexive modernity means that new technologies also create 'manufactured uncertainty'. The consequence is the emergence of a 'risk society'.[164]

Though Beck drew upon the sociology of industrial pollution, he does not consider reflexive modernity to be restricted to industry. On the contrary, society as a whole is dominated by reflexive modernity. The consequence is that individual autonomy is necessarily problematic, since actions are connected in unforeseen ways. 'Even if the image of individual autonomy flutters around in people's minds, such ways of living can be practised only by participating in and being dependent upon a variety of institutions.'[165] Following Habermas, Beck sees individual subjectivity as illusory. The collective Subject, too is rendered impossible by Beck's reflexive modernity. That is because of the domination of unintended consequences over intended ones in reflexive modernity. As he says, 'the side-effect, not instrumental rationality (as in the theory of simple modernisation) becomes the motor of social history'.[166] Beck draws out the consequences of rejecting purposive action, or what is now known pejoratively as 'instrumental rationality'. If intentions are divorced from their effects, frustrated by the manufactured uncertainty of the risk society, then there can be no subjective decision-making. All decisions will be subverted so as to make deliberation meaningless. More than that, Beck sees systemic social change by-passing any kind of collective will. 'Reflexive modernisation, therefore, asserts exactly what is considered out of the question...by...Marxists...namely that there will be no revolution but there will be a new society.' Boasting that he is 'breaking a taboo', Beck continues, 'the idea that the transition from one social epoch to another could take place unintended and apolitically, bypassing all the forums for political decisions, the lines of conflict and the partisan controversies, contradicts the democratic self-understanding of this society'.[167] Beck is drawn to paradoxical and precocious formulations, and in saying the unsayable here, he is only drawing out the consequences of the rejection of a collective Subject. Democracy in the sense that Lukacs described it, as 'societal self-determination',[168] is rendered impossible by 'manufactured uncertainty'.

In place of a Lukacsian subjectivity, Beck proposes a sub-politics motivated principally by fear. 'Basically one is no longer concerned with attaining something "good" but rather with preventing the worst; self-limitation is the goal that emerges....the commonality of anxiety takes the place of the commonality of need. The type of the risk society marks in this sense a social epoch in which solidarity from anxiety arises and becomes a political force.'[169] Except, of course, that as Habermas argued, 'future-oriented consciousness' is illusory, so political action can only be about 'self-restraint' not about planning outcomes. As Anthony Giddens puts it 'individually and as collective humanity, we can seek to remoralise our lives in the context of a positive acceptance of manufactured uncertainty'.[170]

In Beck and Giddens' hands, risk becomes a morbid version of Habermas' intersubjectivity. Like intersubjectivity, risk is in the nature of complex societies. It represents the subordination of the Subject before a social process that is out of his control. Freedom, such as it exists, is the freedom to modify one's behaviour to the overriding imperative, whether intersubjectivity, or reflexive modernity.

Sociobiology and memes

In 1994 the publication of *The Bell Curve: Intelligence and Class Structure in American Life* sparked a major intellectual controversy. Its authors claimed that cognitive ability, as measured in Intelligence Quotient (IQ) tests, is an inherited trait which substantially accounts for inequalities in wealth, income and education. Controversially, they estimate that, on average, white Americans are a full 15 points more intelligent than blacks. The claim that some races are naturally superior to others has been taboo ever since Nazi racial policies led to the Holocaust. When Murray and Herrnstein broke that taboo, critics in liberal newspapers like the *New York Times* and Britain's *Guardian* reacted with outrage, and even right-wing commentators like William Safire and the leader writer of the British *Spectator* balked at *The Bell Curve*.

Herrnstein had already courted notoriety with previous work on intelligence. His co-author, Charles Murray, is no stranger to controversy either. His previous book *Losing Ground: American Social Policy 1950-80*, along with countless articles and lectures, warned of a dangerous underclass of demoralised and welfare-dependent poor developing in America's inner cities. At the heart of the controversy over *The Bell Curve* is a correlation between tested IQ, income and race. According to Murray and Herrnstein, 'wages earned by people in high-IQ occupations have pulled away from the wages in low-IQ occupations, and differences in education cannot explain most of this change'.[71]

The debate over *The Bell Curve* ended with a pointed rejection of sociobiological arguments to do with race amongst most commentators. The overwhelmingly hostile reaction to *The Bell Curve* seems to suggest that sociobiological arguments about race differences have had their day.[72] Certainly following the debate over *The Bell Curve* proponents of so-called 'scientific racism' like Chris Brand at Edinburgh University and Richard Lynn at Coleraine University received much rougher treatment than was ever given Charles Murray.

Brand was forced out of his job after protests by students and Lynn, heavily cited in Murray and Herrnstein's book, found that his own book was refused shelf-space by all the major bookshops in Britain.[73] But the apparent rejection of sociobiology is deceptive. Whilst those old-fashioned sociobiologists who echo the Social Darwinists of the early twentieth century with talk of racial superiority are reviled, sociobiology still is making a considerable impact.

The book that really shifted the terrain was not *The Bell Curve*, but the much earlier *The Selfish Gene*, by scientist Richard Dawkins. Dawkins' account of genetic inheritance was well argued. The organism, as Dawkins put it, reversing our expectations, was the gene's way of reproducing itself. Imputing a 'reason' to the gene, of self-replication, Dawkins gave the Darwinist account of evolution a contemporary feel. Where the *The Selfish Gene* connected with the spirit of the age was in its apparent explanation of human behaviour as biological destiny. The gene's 'selfishness', its 'desire' for self-reproduction seemed to provide a warrant for selfishness amongst persons. 'Nice guys finish last', wrote Dawkins, connecting with a mood of resurgent free market individualism in the seventies. Dawkins, unlike Murray and Herrnstein, or Lynn and Brand, is a scientist first and a commentator on human relations second. He is at pains to distance himself from any racism. But he has still caught a mood in his explanation of human behaviour in terms of the mute operation of a natural genus.

Much ink has been spilled since in the so-called nature-nurture debate. Critics of Dawkins and other sociobiologists have challenged his account of human behaviour, intelligence and other characteristics as being the product of biology. Educationalists, sociologists and many natural scientists have resisted the sociobiological argument. Their objection that sociobiology tends to explain everything, either one way or the other is appropriate: sociobiological arguments have been deployed to support the idea that humans are innately individualistic (*The Selfish Gene*) or innately sociable (*The Moral Animal*, Matt Ridley);

genetics has been cited to explain *Why Sex is Fun* (Jared Diamond) and also homosexuality (*The Sexual Brain*, Simon LeVay). Critics suspect that the biological arguments are not predictive but merely take up whatever empirical content is available. If the norm is that men are breadwinners, then this will be traced back to the cavemen, when 'men went out to hunt'. On the other hand, when the status of women improves, other sociobiological arguments will be mobilised to show that women are naturally more co-operative and better adjusted than men. In sociologist Anthony Giddens' choice phrase, there is 'a pronounced tendency to naturalise social problems'.[74]

As pointed as the sociological criticisms of sociobiology are, it is sometimes difficult to see what the difference turns on. As it is understood, the nature-nurture debate is about what proportion of our characteristics are inherited genetically and which are socially determined. Most agree that physical characteristics are generally inherited (though even here one must be careful, given the increase in the average height of the Japanese in the postwar years, illustrating that a presumed racial characteristic turned out to be a nutritional one). The differences arise over moral and intellectual characteristics. But while most sociologists attribute these to social influence and sociobiologists attribute them to natural inheritance, the underlying similarity in outlooks is rarely commented upon. In both instances the overwhelming ambition is to explain away human behaviour as causally determined. The result is a Dutch auction in which both sides are fighting as to who can provide more causal explanations for more facets of humanity. As so often in a stale argument, neither side is listening closely enough to the other to notice that they are fundamentally in agreement that humanity has very little control over its own destiny. In this unspoken assumption both sides agree and in fact reinforce each other's prejudices.

Richard Dawkins, perhaps anticipating a certain blind spot in the argument that human civilisation is due to genes, contributed another, fascinating theory to the debate in *The Selfish Gene*, that has come into its own since: the theory of memes. Dawkins proposed in *The Selfish Gene* that genes were not the only self-reproducing sequence. Alongside the gene was the meme. The meme is wholly without any natural existence, but instead is a unit of cultural inheritance. Mimetic reproduction, unlike genetic reproduction, passed through human civilisations by imitation. Examples of memes include compulsive tunes that once hummed cannot be forgotten, and can pass from one listener to the other, infecting them in turn with the compelling repetitive clause. More seriously, Dawkins has suggested that world religions are an example of mimetic reproduction, as might be ideologies or political movements. Other authors such as Daniel Dennett and Susan Blackmore have taken up Dawkins' memes.[75]

The weakness of the meme theory is that it describes the reproduction of unconscious, routine behaviour rather than more deliberate, higher functions. Much human behaviour is routine: humming tunes, saying the rosary, canvassing votes in an election. The meme well describes routine behaviour that is not particularly considered. But higher intellectual functions cannot be got by multiplying the lower. Composing the tune, a crisis of faith, or planning an election campaign are less routine and more demanding. Of course one can look at what other people have done in your circumstances, but decision-making is at the fore. Daniel Dennett has it the wrong way around when he writes that 'human minds are themselves to a very great degree the creation of memes'.[76] It would be truer to say that memes are the product of the human mind. They are routines laid down to avoid reinventing the wheel each time. Of course, to the extent that subjectivity is evacuated, then the mind will reduce to the level of a collection of memes.

What is fascinating about the meme theory is just how close it is to contemporary sociology. For all the differences between the sociologists and the biologists in the explanation of human behaviour, Dawkins' meme theory has reproduced all the major aspects of much of modern social thinking, whilst doing it on the model of genetic reproduction. If Dawkins had called his memes 'structures', or 'fields of power' instead he could surely have become a professor of the social sciences. Mimetic reproduction, like Althusser's 'interpellation of the Subject' wholly demotes autonomous subjectivity. And surely Foucault would have understood Dawkins's meditation that 'perhaps the subjective "I", the person that I feel myself to be, is the same kind of semi-illusion. The mind is a collection of fundamentally independent, even warring agents'.[77]

Chapter Five

THE ERSATZ SUBJECT

The theoretical degradation of the autonomous Subject has been accompanied by a recuperation of an ersatz subject, pallid and more compromised than the original he displaces. Something must occupy the space left by the evacuation of the Subject. In the following we examine two versions of the truncated subject. First we look at identity theory, in which the Subject is displaced in favour of an 'identity'. Then we look at the methodological individualism adopted defensively by rights theorists to shore up the individual Subject, only to find his subjectivity is exhausted in the process.

The identity parade

Perhaps the most cogent assertion of the self to be found in contemporary conditions is in terms of identity. The right to have one's identity recognised for its validity is among the most contentious issues today. According to Chris Gilligan's estimates of the occurrence of the word in the titles of academic journal articles, identity has soared in importance, rating a stable 200 or so mentions between 1981 and 1989, before embarking on a steady climb to more than 700 in 1998.[78] Despite its contentious nature, identity, sadly, is a peculiarly truncated substitute for subjective autonomy.

Identity theory began as a component of psychology, to describe child development. The process of identity formation was seen as an important stage that individuals pass through. In 1950 the Freudian analyst Erik Erikson wrote about the difficulties young people had establishing stable identities in his book *Childhood and Society*.[79] Elsewhere, the 'behaviourist' psychologist Erving Goffmann was developing the theory of 'social roles' and 'role-playing' to describe the way that individuals adopted given identities in social interaction.[80] These psychological theories helped develop the terminology of identity theory. These early developments in the theory were conducted in the manner of observations from the outside. Psychologists were preoccupied with the 'problem' of misidentification, such as the American Psychiatric Association's notorious classification of homosexuality as a mental disorder.[81] Conversely, they were concerned with the difficulties of identity formation, as in Erikson's discussion of the youth 'problem'. Characteristically, the normative aspects of identity were assumed (eg, heterosexual), and deviance from the norm categorised and 'treated'.

In the 1960s and 1970s identity theory came increasingly to adopt the standpoint of the fugitive identity. Deviance from the norm was no longer considered pathological. To the contrary, identity theory today takes as its starting point those identities that are formed in opposition to the old norms. In this version, the conditions of exclusion are inverted to become a source of pride and strength. Identifications that carried a negative cachet are reversed to become moments of self-assertion. Sociologists in particular were drawn to the expressions of Black Pride, and later Gay Pride as the creation of identities of resistance and opposition to the dominant culture.[182] The emergence of these apparently oppositional identities suggested new ways in which the priority of the ideal-type of the free Subject could be compromised. Juliet Mitchell pointed out that 'each class has aspects of its own culture, which are relatively autonomous. The fact is illustrated by such phrases as "working class culture", "ghetto culture", "immigrant culture", etc, and by the absent phrase – "middle class culture"'. The fact of the cultures of exclusion limits the perceived universality of 'middle class culture'. 'We don't think of "middle class culture" as something separate – it simply is the overall culture, within which are inserted these isolable other cultures', Mitchell objects.[183] As she suggests, though, the very fact of the excluded culture calls into question the claim of the middle class culture to be the archetypal culture. If the norm is refused, then it is no longer the norm.

Cultural identity is a site of resistance, and hence of action. However, identity is markedly different from subjectivity. Whereas the Subject presents itself as pure, abstract and universal, identity is specific and local. In Heidegger's typology, determinate being ('being-there') takes priority over the abstract Being.[184] Those very features that were portrayed as flaws, or even impurities by Enlightenment thinkers are instead held up as a badge of pride. The particular stance that was rejected before for its partiality is now recognised for its special insight. And that insight is precisely the limit point of the presumed generality of the dominant identity. It appears that the now-embraced identification has a power to disrupt the norm, revealing the one-sidedness of what had purported to be all-sided.

As an ideal of resistance, though, identity is flawed. Unlike the classical model of subjectivity, identity is contextual and situated. It draws its authority from its given nature, rather than its future orientation. With identity theory, survival itself is the virtue. The conditions of exclusion or oppression are seen as a source of inner strength and nobility. It seems as if we are in the presence of a return to the stoical consciousness that endures hardship with equanimity. Where the principle of subjectivity is self-determining, identification takes identity from its context and location. The Subject is intrinsically *undetermined*, in the sense of not having its goals prescribed for it from without. It is not, however, *indeterminate*, because the Subject determines itself (not of course meaning that all obstacles are removed, but in the sense of deciding its own course, while taking such obstacles into account). By contrast, identity remains a response to identification. It is an inner reworking of externally imposed norms, but still remains a response, and more, a cleaving to those conditions of its formation. 'I come from a proud heritage', Identity says to Subject. 'Don't ask me where I'm from, ask me where I'm going', Subject says to Identity.

With the development of the theory identity has come to be seen as paradoxical to many in the field. On face value, identity is disruptive, rebellious, a challenge to the received order. But this meaning of identity is strictly within context. As against the dominant model, the excluded identities are disruptive, but intrinsically they reproduce the very limitations they illuminated. Judith Butler objects to the 'foundationalist reasoning of identity politics'. She says that 'the feminist *we* is always and only a phantasmatic construction, one that has its purposes, but which denies the internal complexity and indeterminacy of the term and constitutes itself only through the exclusion of some part of the constituency that it simultaneously seeks to represent'.[185] She means that once the 'Subject' of the movement is determined as 'women', then the differences between women get covered up. Do straight women have the same goals as lesbian women? Not necessarily. It is pointed that Butler insists on the 'indeterminacy of the term', the term 'feminism' we presume. But surely the point is that, at least minimally, 'feminist' is a determination, that delineates and circumscribes its object – a movement for, and of, women. Butler wants to recover the indeterminacy, or open-endedness that corresponds to the idea of freedom. But identity theory in its nature takes as its starting point a bounded identity: identity that is identical to itself. It is born from a refusal of universality, and must take into itself that character of being limited.

Over and over again we find the paradox of identity theory replayed: it conjures up a feisty spirit of taking on the world, but at the same time it revels in its chains. Identity theorists having based their claims upon determinate being are constantly looking around for the undetermined moment that is contained within identity theory. How can freedom be rediscovered within the slave compound? One response is to multiply identities. Stuart Hall writes, for example, that the postmodern subject is 'composed not of a single, several, sometimes contradictory or unresolved identities'.[86] Furthermore, identity is 'formed and transformed continuously in relation to the ways we are represented or addressed in the cultural systems which surround us'.[87] Hall emphasises continuous formation and transformation to try to resurrect the open-endedness of free subjectivity. Stability and order would hardly appear to be ambitious goals. But in fact this indeterminacy is false. It is not indeterminacy for us. Rather it is the unpredictability of our outlying conditions, of 'the ways we are represented or addressed', which is an indeterminacy that is all the more limiting. As Herakleitos says, 'the more one puts oneself at the mercy of chance, the more chance will involve one in the laws of necessity and inevitability'.[88] Being buffeted from one representation to another is not an indeterminacy that is open to self-determination, but rather the uncertainty that makes freedom impossible. 'Give yourself up, the cultural systems have got you surrounded!', Hall might be saying. Nor indeed is the multiplication of determinations equal to open possibilities. It is just more and more determinations, or more external shaping. The minimal freedom of 'playing off' one imposed identification against another is a peculiarly lacklustre alternative to free subjectivity – corresponding to trading for a marginal advantage. The fact that identity theorists feel obliged to talk vaguely of indeterminacy, the unresolved and so on, is not to be taken at face value. On the contrary, it is closer to the bad conscience that resists facing the determinate resolution that is identification.

Judith Butler in particular has grappled with the moment of closure that is identification, trying to hold on to the sense of subversion of identity. The parodic subversion of identity in drag interests her because of the way that it turns the imposed identification against itself. For Butler adopting a gender identity involves the continuous performance of the many gestures that make up that identity. This identification is, she says 'a process of repetition' that 'enforces its rules'. 'All signification takes place within the orbit of compulsion to repeat; "agency," then, is to be located within the possibilities of a variation on that repetition.' Butler continues, 'it is only within the practices of repetitive signifying that a subversion of identity becomes possible'.[189] As agency goes, this is an agency of a remarkably limited kind – 'variation on repetition'. The subversion of identity seems to have slowed to the pace of natural evolution, and quite at odds with the remarkably swift changes in socially acceptable identities in recent times. One wonders what the barrier to a more fulsome rejection of repetition is. Butler explains:

> 'The critical task for feminism is not to establish a point of view outside of constructed identities; that conceit is the construction of an epistemological model that would disavow its own cultural location and, hence, promote itself as a global Subject, a position that deploys exactly the imperialist strategies that feminism ought to criticise.'[190]

To do more than vary the repetition would be to risk stepping outside of the constructed identity. Such conceit would, 'disavow its own cultural location', which is to say, abandon the identity ascribed to women. Worse still, it seems to suggest that taking decisions for oneself is tantamount to invading small and defenceless countries. With this degree of caution it is no wonder that Butler talks down the goal of freedom, pretending that it is pretty much the same thing as slavery, anyway: 'Feminist discourse', she regrets, 'remains trapped within the unnecessary binarism of free will and determinism'.⁹¹ Drawing out the logic of identity theory's displacement of free subjectivity, she writes that 'there is no self that is prior...there is only a taking up of the tools where they lie, where the "taking up" is enabled by the tool lying there'.⁹²

Methodological Individualism

In a very different quarter from cultural studies you can find another, quite different elevation of individuality. Free market theory, as championed by FA Hayek and Karl Popper, has fallen out of favour in recent times but retains an influence from its high tide in the Reagan/Thatcher years. Hayek and Popper were both highly ideological champions of the free market against socialism. In Hayek's case, the argument was more purely made in terms of a philosophy of economics, whilst Popper, less dogmatic against state intervention broadened out the idealisation of the free economy into an 'open society'. If it seems that Popper and Hayek are marred by their association with the official promotion of their work in the West, many of the more left-wing critics of their work have reluctantly admitted that the individualist critique of socialist planning has been vindicated by the failure of the Soviet bloc.⁹³ Whatever the truth or otherwise of the planning debate, our purpose is served by looking at the assertion of the priority of the individual over the collective in their writings.

It was Popper who most poignantly summed up the prejudice in favour of the Self when he, citing Hayek, called it 'methodological individualism'. Happily asserting that this theory is equally applicable to atomic particles, Popper goes on to insist that 'methodological individualism' is 'the quite unassailable belief that we must try to understand all collective phenomena as due to the actions, interactions, aims, hopes, and thoughts, of individual men, and', he adds, with a pointed qualification, 'as due to traditions created and preserved by individual men'.⁹⁴

[margin note: The collective is simply due to individual action.]

Methodological individualism, a presupposed bias towards the individual over the collective in theory, mirrored an ideological bias towards the free market. But it would be foolish to take the ideological bias towards the free market literally. Hayek and Popper both took the view that freedom was synonymous with a market society, one in which the state played as small a role as it could. Their criticisms of collectivism were made in the name of individual liberty. Hayek's 1944 tract, *The Road to Serfdom* was a warning against welfarism, that likened it to fascism. Popper's *Open Society and its Enemies* was a polemic against Marxism. On the face of things, Popper and Hayek were both arguing the case for individual freedom against the oppressive might of the socialist state.

However, the underlying theme of methodological individualism was a polemic against man's hubris in presuming to take control of society. The implication of 'methodological individualism' was that social knowledge was an absurdity. The complexity of developed societies meant that it was impossible to understand them. The conceit of the social engineer was that he presumed to understand something that could not be understood. All action on the basis of such false understanding, then, would also be deluded. The limited conception of the social engineer would always fall short of the complexity of society. Furthermore, planning decisions themselves, in becoming a part of the picture, would be taken into account in the myriad decisions of individual actors. All government action would be subverted by the way that individuals took that action into account and sought to get around it. In other words, 'you can't buck the market'.

Though the free market rejection of socialism was made in the name of individual freedom, it was substantially an argument against the Subject, namely the collective Subject. Hayek and Popper's methodological individualism started with the assumption that collective action was an impossibility. The more argumentative side of their ideas made it clear that they were trying to attack a real living Subject, the collective Subject of organised labour, in the name of an abstract Subject, the free individual. When Hayek wrote that he had succeeded in winning the intellectual argument against his state-spending rival economist John Maynard Keynes, he warned: 'There will be no more urgent need than to erect new defences against the onslaughts of popular Keynesianism.'[95] Here Hayek reveals the unspoken meaning of the campaign against serfdom. While he feared the servitude of the propertied classes before a socialist state, the working classes were properly serfs, against whom one must 'erect defences'. In his essays 'The confusion of language in political thought' and 'Economic freedom and representative government', Hayek argues against democracy on the grounds that representative government limits individual freedom.[96] The collective Subject of 'the People' was of course an absurdity to Hayek, for whom collectivities are delusions.

It is interesting that even as unashamed a capitalist ideologue as Hayek was unable to sustain a positive attitude towards individual subjectivity. In *The Fatal Conceit: The Errors of Socialism* it is clear that socialism is only the express form of a more destructive conceit, reason itself. 'Mind is not a guide, but a product of cultural evolution and is based more on imitation than on insight or reason', he wrote.[97] Whereas he had as a young man insisted that his philosophy was liberal rather than conservative, the older Hayek was to be found arguing that 'tradition is in some respects superior to, or "wiser" than, human reason'.[98] 'Virtually all our benefits of civilisation, and indeed our very existence, rest, I believe, on our continuing willingness to shoulder the burden of tradition.'[99] From warning against the *Road to Serfdom*, Hayek appears in *The Fatal Conceit* to be arguing for it. This is, though, to be expected. Methodological individualism was never what it appeared to be. Superficially it was the case for individual freedom against collective enslavement. In substance it was the case against the conceit of human reason, with reference to the collective Subject. Since the substantial argument was the argument against the conceit of reason, we could anticipate that even individual reason would fall away in the face of a subservience to tradition more in keeping with the communitarians. Furthermore, a methodological individualism would have to be the opposite of a true individual subjectivity. This individualism is not attained, but presumed at the outset. Individuality is not a self-assertion but something that is taken for granted. That contradicts the very meaning of subjectivity as self-determining.

An example of the limitations of methodological individualism can be seen in the work of PF Strawson and his son Galen, both of whom worked in the analytical philosophical tradition on which Popper and Hayek drew. The elder Strawson's book *Individuals* took individuals as a primary fact of existence. Material bodies 'in our actual conceptual scheme', he says, are 'basic particulars'. Persons are identified by the identification of their bodies first, but also by their states of consciousness. It is 'a necessary condition', he says, 'of ascribing states of consciousness, experiences, to oneself, in the way that one does, that one should be able to ascribe them, or be prepared to ascribe them to others who are not oneself'.[200] The so-called 'problem of other minds' has preoccupied analytical philosophers for many years. A philosophy that takes as its starting point the disaggregation, or analysis, of wholes into their constituent parts, or individuals, has problems understanding the overarching moment of communication. Strawson's response here is to derive community from self-reflection. As I see my own mind, I can assume other minds.

This assumption has not stood the test of time. The American analytic philosopher Richard Rorty reflecting long and hard on the possibility of other minds, came to the conclusion that his own – and everyone else's – was an illusion, 'our Glassy Essence', invented by Descartes. In truth we were 'persons without minds'.[201] Rorty meant that there was no need to presuppose the existence of a homunculus seated somewhere in the brain behind your actions. Analysing away, he dispensed with that hypothesis. Galen Strawson, also had reason to doubt the existence of the mind as an independent motivating force. The younger Galen raises a Basic Argument against free will:

1. It is undeniable that one is the way one is, initially, as a result of heredity and early experience, and it is undeniable that one cannot be held morally responsible for these things

2. One cannot later accede true moral responsibility for the way one is by trying to change the way one already is as a result of heredity and previous experience, because:

3. The way one is moved to try to change oneself and the degree of one's success, are determined by how one already is as a result of heredity and previous experience. Furthermore:

4. Any further changes that one can bring about in – 3. Above – will be determined, via these initial changes, by heredity and previous experience.[202]

The way that the younger Strawson's argument works is by a strict application of the law of entailment. The 'way one is' at birth is wholly given by heredity and experience. Common sense dictates that one who is without responsibility for the way one is cannot be held responsible. Clearly, we all know that a child is not responsible for his own circumstances. This common sense starting point gives rise to the later, counter-intuitive conclusion that adults are not responsible for how they are either. Strawson's argument works because it excludes the possibility of the emergence of one thing out of another, that is the emergence of adult responsibility out of childish irresponsibility. The one cannot entail the other, because they are so different. But one could just as easily put the argument the other way around. Since we know commonsensically that adults are responsible, and we exclude the possibility of the emergence of a distinctive factor out of given conditions, then we must assume that infants are responsible for how they are. If one rebel's against this absurd conclusion, it is no less absurd than the one that denies the responsibility of adults. (Indeed, in other ages and societies, the responsibility of infants and even animals has been taken seriously – but I do not mean to advance that case here). Strawson's conclusion is faulty not because of its premise, but because of its method, which excludes the possibility of the emergence of subjectivity in the process of education and encouragement that is growing up. How, he is asking, can one be taught to think for oneself? It is an absurdity to formal logic, but not to a logic of development.

More interesting, perhaps is what the younger Strawson's rejection of individual autonomy tells us about the fragility of methodological individualism. With this negative assessment, the methodological individualism of Cold War ideology turns into its evil twin, Soviet-style determinism. Strawson's approach is characteristic of the empty contrast between free will and determinism in analytic philosophy. To the analytic philosophers free will and the determined were simply opposed. The philosophical answer was given by Hegel in his *Science of Logic* in which he describes the transformation of Substance into Subject in the Doctrine of the Concept. As popularised by Engels, freedom is the recognition of necessity, but it is also the leap from necessity. Like the diving board beneath your feet, necessity is determinate, but it is also the basis of self-determination, where one gives to oneself the law.

MORE THAN A THEORY

In laying out the many varied theories of human interaction in so far as they touch upon the degradation of the Subject, the tendency is to minimise their differences from each other. The debates between schools of thought are passed over, perhaps to the detriment of their case. It is possible though, because of this common trend to minimise the role of the Subject. Throughout a variety of apparently contradictory outlooks we find an underlying unity in the increasing discomfort with the idea of the Subject. Engaging critically with these ideas, I have argued from the standpoint of the despised Subject, as the 'excluded Other' of these texts, if you will. Thus far, I have presented the demotion of the free Subject as if it were an error, so to speak. But this is not quite how it is.

These different thinkers are not making a simple error. Their thoughts are not in a mismatch with the world. On the contrary, it is their sensitivity to the new conditions that drives them to demote human subjectivity in their thinking. They are sensitive to the way that in truth, the Subject is wanting, or degraded. In the engagement with the received ideas of the past, the intellectual systems handed down from previous generations, these theorists have become increasingly troubled by the widening gap between the theoretical Subject and the reality. Existing social and political thinking is ordered around the Subject. The Subject is the starting point of so many intellectual systems from Adam Smith's *Wealth of Nations* and Hegel's *Philosophy of Right* to Lenin's *What Is to Be Done?* or Sartre's *Being and Nothingness*. Finding this Subject still stumbling about in the realm of ideas, more contemporary thinkers were driven to wonder whether he had any correlate in the world, or if he lived up to the promise he offered. The theoretical Subject had been hollowed out, made ethereal like a ghost. The living Subject approximated less and less to the promise. Heideggerian Jean Greisch poses the question 'what are we to do when that double presupposition – a rational animal whose highest expression of value is freedom – becomes problematical...?'.[20] Greisch is talking about the moral Subject, the autonomous individual who makes moral choices. But that Subject is in question, not just theoretically, but also in fact.

There is a kind of élan to the critique of Subjectivity. It moves tentatively first, like a child testing out some new profanity. But finding that there is little resistance it rushes forward, pushing at an open door. It is as if someone worked up the courage to say 'The Subject has no clothes!' and suddenly his nakedness is revealed. Such sudden shifts encourage the criticism. The assault on the Subject takes on the character of a revolt, like storming the Winter Palace. Those that demur are reactionary old fuddy-duddies. Quite quickly the fugitive outlook of yesterday becomes the establishment viewpoint of today. Postmodernism is now an intrinsic part of the syllabus throughout the humanities. Even the Pope has gone pomo.

There is of course, a price to pay, and a heavy one. The theoretical degradation of the Subject is closer to reality than a naive reassertion of natural rights could be. But it is also an accomplice to the present. Whilst the first stirrings represented some considerable labour, groping towards something that was far from clear, the work today is just too easy. No sooner is a proposition made than it can be deconstructed. The question of whether the project of deconstruction is the right one is more and more difficult to ask. What is the degradation of the Subject in fact, and ought theory to be an accomplice to it? Thinking ought to pay attention to the world, but it does not necessarily have to celebrate the defeats of the human spirit. To take the argument further we will have to look more closely at the actuality of the degradation of the Subject. Not just as it is reworked in thought, but as it is lived.

Part Two

THE COMMON RUIN OF THE CONTENDING CLASSES

The ubiquity of the idea of the death of the Subject leads us to ask why it is so widespread. Intellectual fashions and the history of ideas give some clues. But the question remains why it is that the idea is so extensive, and reproduced, at least in its basic tenets, across distinctive schools of thought and intellectual disciplines. That much cannot be explained by intellectual fashion. The real challenge is to explain why it is that the ideas of the death of the Subject have travelled.

One author who worried about the spread of the ideas that he associated with postmodernism was the British socialist Alex Callinicos. In his book *Against Postmodernism* Callinicos gave the following account: 'The political odyssey of the 1968 generation is, in my view, critical to the widespread acceptance of the idea of a postmodern epoch in the 1980s. This was the decade when those radicalised in the 1960s and early 1970s began to enter middle age. Usually they did so with all hope of socialist revolution gone.'[1] Callinicos' point is persuasive. The ideology of the end of modernity and progress corresponds to a sense of retreat from radical ambition. The point is all the more persuasive when one considers that many of those who popularised the ideas of postmodernism were indeed associated with the left in the years leading up to 1968: Althusser was a prominent member of the French Communist Party, Foucault had been a member in the fifties; Jean François Lyotard and Jean Baudrillard were both influenced by Cornelius Castoriadis' heterodox Trotskyist group, Socialism or Barbarism.

The philosophy of deconstruction begins with the deconstruction of the Marxist model of historical progress, as with Baudrillard's book *Mirror of Production* or Lyotard's *Libidinal Economy*. In both early tracts these leftists are concerned to deconstruct the intellectual tradition they knew best, the Marxist one. At first the pointed criticism was that Marxism was not as different from capitalism as it claimed. According to Baudrillard, Marxism was a 'productivist' ideology, like the official economics of the capitalist elite. In *Libidinal Economy* Lyotard parodies sarcastically 'the proletariat is Christ, and his real suffering is the price of his redemption'.[2] Only later, by analogy, was the deconstruction of Marxism broadened out into a blanket dismissal of all grand narratives, by which time Marxism settles back into the series 'the dialectics of Spirit, the hermeneutics of meaning, the emancipation of the rational or working subject, or the creation of wealth'.[3] The deconstruction of the Subject begins on the left, as a deconstruction of the historical Subject of Marxism, the working class.

Certainly Callinicos' notion of postmodernism as an expression of the way that 'the far left disintegrated throughout Europe at the end of the 1970s seems to fit the biographies of those who first innovated this package of ideas. And when Callinicos continues, 'In France, where hopes had been raised highest, the fall was most precipitous', it seems as if there is a good historical reason for the emergence of postmodernism in France.⁴ Callinicos' draws attention to the profound disappointment, felt by French leftists at the stabilisation of De Gaulle's regime after the heady days of 1968. However, postmodernism may have started in France, but it is by no means restricted to France. Indeed, the reputation of its philosophical stars is generally greater beyond her shores. The furore over a rearguard attempt by some Cambridge Dons to block Derrida's proposed honorary degree in 1992 provoked a wave of popular support for the philosopher in his home country that gave him more coverage than he had ever enjoyed previously.⁵ That year, Derrida attracted an audience of 2000 people to an Amnesty International lecture in Oxford – a larger audience than the film star Warren Beatty had drawn just a month before. Plainly the appeal of the postmodern critique of the Subject has an appeal that stretches beyond France.

Like Alex Callinicos, the British critic Terry Eagleton also sees the origins of postmodernism in the political defeat of the left. In his book *The Illusions of Postmodernism* he invites us to 'imagine a radical movement which had suffered an emphatic defeat',⁶ before asking, 'What would be the likely reaction of the political left to such a defeat?'. Eagleton's proposition and question are rhetorical. The condition of emphatic defeat is the defeat of the left in the 1980s, with the rise of the neo-conservative right of Margaret Thatcher and Ronald Reagan. When he asks what the likely reaction of the left would be, we are to understand that this is not just speculation, but how it happened. Patiently Eagleton builds up his picture with hints and jokes. 'It would not be out of the question to run across people who wished to see the Epoch of Man pass away, and voted Liberal Democrat', he writes.⁷ Elaborating upon his theme, Eagelton writes that in such conditions of defeat, the ideology would be surprisingly close to that which we find in postmodernism. 'One would hymn the praises of the schizoid, dishevelled Subject, whose ability to fasten his own shoelaces, let alone topple the political state would be bound to remain something of a mystery.'⁸ Eagleton's picture is compelling. Both Eagleton and Callinicos are pomo refuseniks. They do not want to go down the road to the end of all grand narratives. They do not want to see the working class Subject of socialist emancipation sidelined. Hence their accounts, though informed, are dissident to the trend, in some sense the accounts of outsiders.

The historical turning point that haunts their two accounts, though, is the one that seems to verify the postmodernists' argument: the evacuation of the working class Subject from history. You do not have to endorse Lyotard's millennial account of the End of Man to see that the role of the working class is no longer the decisive factor in contemporary political life that it was.

In the 1970s the working class across the Western world remained highly combative. Many millions of workers were prepared to go on strike in pursuit of better wages and conditions and, less often, in support of political causes. Some workers, like the British miners in 1974, did not balk at bringing down governments to achieve their demands. By the early 1990s that militancy had all but disappeared, and strikes began to appear to be a thing of the past.⁹

Of course, some defenders of trade union militancy cling to the hope that the decline is merely a cyclical response to economic slump, and will reverse again with the boom.¹⁰ Though it is true that there has been some bounce back after the record lows in militancy in the first half of the 1990s, there is no indication of a return to the turbulent 1970s. The comparison with the seventies reminds us that there is no obvious correspondence between recession and reduced industrial militancy. The way that workers respond to slump is informed by their confidence in their organisations, and political outlook, not the other way around. The underlying state of working class organisation indicates that the changes are far from being a simply cyclical effect, but rather have corroded those organisations.

In all the major Western industrialised countries except Canada union membership fell significantly as a proportion of the workforce in the 1980s and 1990s. In the USA and France fewer that one fifth of workers are unionised. In Britain, with historically high levels of unionisation, the membership halved between 1980 and 1999. As important as the numerical changes is the change in the character of the unions. The increasing reliance upon agreeing unionisation deals with management rather than building up independent organisations was the preamble to the decline. The high unionisation rates in municipal employment are indicative of the way that union organisations have come to depend on their relations with employers rather than with employees.

One sociological response to these figures is to see a 'fit' between unionism and industrial work. The growing proportion of service workers to industrial workers, it is suggested, will naturally lead away from mass unionism." It is true that in general rates of unionisation are lower in the services than industry. However, there is nothing intrinsic about service sector work that means that employees are not organised. Rather it is the coincidence of the growth of this sector with the decline of unionism that has led to the difference. It is true, for example, that France, with its very large service sector has a very low level of union density, but the other two countries that have comparably large service sectors, Italy and Britain, have experienced relatively high levels of union density.

What this sociological explanation of the decline of working class self-organisation fails to take into account is the interaction of political opposition and working class organisation. In Britain and America the 1980s saw crushing defeats for the trade unions in major confrontations such as the British miners strike of 1984-85. Internationally, the political programme of the left, the socialism of state ownership and control, was also defeated electorally by resurgent conservative parties, and eventually abandoned both by Western socialist parties and ultimately by the Communist Party of the Soviet Union. The discrediting of state socialism robbed the organised labour movement of its distinctive contribution to political life.

NB Discrediting w/c (socialism) ≠ subjectivity has to die

Having failed to make decisive gains from the opportunities presented by the instability and militancy of the late 1960s and early 1970s, and with its influence in politics and industry largely extinguished, the labour movement became irrelevant to most workers.

But whatever cause the dramatic decline of working class organisation and militancy is put down to, the fact of that decline is hard to deny, and the idea that the grand narrative of the emancipation of labour was a myth begins to look a lot more plausible. The defeat of the working class, and its allies on the political left, that Eagleton describes begins to look like a reasonable account of the roots of the 'death of the Subject' announced in the theory of postmodernism. Marx and Engels had long ago written: 'Oppressor and oppressed, stood in constant opposition to one another, carried on an uninterrupted, now hidden, now open fight, a fight that each time ended, either in a revolutionary reconstitution of society at large, or in the common ruin of the contending classes.'[12] But the prospect of a revolutionary reconstitution of society seemed more distant than ever, as the class struggle of the eighties was won by the capitalists and their political representatives.

Terry Eagleton's version of a more generalised sense of defeat internalised seems to give a better explanation than Callinicos' of the appeal of the idea of the Death of the Subject going far beyond the French generation of 1968. But even Eagleton's account does not seem to explain the universality of the idea. After all the philosophy of deconstruction may have first grown in French soil in the 1960s, but by the 1980s it was gaining popularity in language departments and cultural studies courses throughout Europe. More impressively though, it was in America that deconstruction became truly successful. 'I would risk', wrote Jacques Derrida, 'with a smile, the following hypothesis: America is deconstruction'.[13] Baudrillard agreed, writing his aphoristic account, *America*, as a kind of deconstructed road movie script. Foucault was the first of the theorists then known as 'poststructuralists' to take up a teaching post at Claremont

Graduate School, California, just outside Los Angeles, in 1974.[14] Lyotard was professor of French at the University of California at Irvine, where Derrida holds a visiting appointment. American academia found it difficult to resist the rise of deconstruction and many academics made an important contribution as interlocuters for the French thinkers, such as Baudrillard's translator Mark Poster at University of California at Irvine or Derrida's, Gayatri Chakravorty Spivak at Columbia. In Britain there was some resistance to the new trend, as in the decision of Cambridge University to revoke the structuralist critic Colin MacCabe's lectureship in the early 1980s, or the opposition to Derrida's honorary degree from Cambridge. Also in America, the debate over the universities was stoked by Allan Bloom's best-seller *The Closing of the American Mind* in 1988, which protested the influence of the deconstructionists. But mostly American academia has opened itself to the French philosophy and sought to integrate it into American thinking.[15]

Given the success of the deconstruction of the historical Subject in American academia and letters, it seems that we have to amend the explanation for its influence from simply being the result of the defeat of the left. America is, after all, not a left-wing country. It has very little by way of a labour tradition to deconstruct. Marxism has never been an influential intellectual strand in American life, and socialist politics have been wholly incidental to mainstream American public life. There is no forward march of American labour to be halted, and barely a narrative, let alone a grand one of the socialist Utopia to draw Lyotard's incredulity. Is it plausible that an intellectual framework could be established that refers entirely to events played out elsewhere? No. The only plausible explanation is that in some sense the philosophy of deconstruction also tells Americans about their own society, finding a resonance in conditions that are distinct from those in which the theory first emerged. But how could the theorisation of socialist defeat make any sense to a nation that has no socialist tradition to speak of, and was, after all, the victor at the end of the Cold War?

The prospects seem unpromising. But in some sense the experience of the French militant's disillusion, summarised in the theory of postmodernism, must be emblematic for the superficially opposite experience of the victorious American Cold Warriors.

To understand how this could be, we need to look more closely at the experience of the end of the Cold War in the USA, and amongst the right. Paradoxically we find that the events of 1989 did not lead to a triumphalist ideology, though many tried to give it that spin. Right-wing ideologue Francis Fukuyama echoed the postmodernists first in declaring the End of History, and then, the era of the Last Men. It seemed that the crisis of working class political leadership had developed into a wider crisis of humanity. The exhaustion of the left alternative only exposed the inner weaknesses of the right, long obscured by the anti-Communist rhetoric of the 1980s. The collapse of the political right in the 1990s shook the Western establishment. Ruling parties of the right were caught in a crisis of legitimacy. Political purpose gave way to indecision in Washington, London, Paris and Rome. All the major institutions of the ruling elite were gripped by doubt. It seemed possible that the outcome of decades of class conflict would not be victory for either class, but 'the common ruin of the contending classes' that Marx had warned of. With the Cold War ideologies of individualism, family and patriotism now coming under fire, the philosophy of the Death of the Subject, the philosophy of the defeated French left, found its own fertile American soil.

The claim of the political right to re-establish individual freedom is the subject-matter of Chapter Nine. But first we look in more detail at the beginnings of the anti-humanist idea in the experience of the left. The French left's failure to support freedom for Algeria is the subject of Chapter Six. In Chapter Seven Louis Althusser's own tragic compulsion to live out his theory of the Death of the Subject and its relation to the paralysis of the French Communist Party is examined. In Chapter Eight we look at the long debate on the left about where new agents of change to replace the working class could be found, and ask why it did not succeed. Finally Chapter Ten enquires into the 'Third Way' and what it represents for subjectivity.

Chapter Six

ALGERIA AND THE DEFEAT OF FRENCH HUMANISM

The founding of the modern French state is unique in history. The state is created in the name not just of the French citizen, but of all mankind. The document adopted by the Constituent Assembly in June 1789 is headed Declaration of the Rights of Man and of the Citizen. The declaration is a sincere expression of the sentiments of the revolutionaries who created the state. It was also a beacon to liberals across Europe,[16] and as far afield as Haiti in the West Indies, where the 'black Jacobin' Toussaint L'Ouverture was inspired to lead a slave revolt.[7] The most adamant of the French revolutionaries deplored slavery as they deplored feudal privileges. 'The moment you pronounce the word "slave" you pronounce your own dishonour', said Robespierre, who also defended the civil and voting rights of free blacks in the West Indian colonies.[18] Even after the restoration of a more centralised power under Napoleon Bonaparte's military leadership, France remained a beacon of the universal rights of man to radicals and liberals across Europe. Napoleon's army swept through Europe to be welcomed by some as an army of liberation. The Jewish ghettoes were emancipated. The Code Napoleon is, to this day, the basis of many countries' civil law. Revolutionary France represented the hopes of the Enlightenment, of reason and of humanism for progressive Europe.

The extent of French humanism, though, found its limits. The German middle classes came to resent the French monopoly on universal civilisation, and jealously guarded their own, more grounded *Kultur*. England regarded France's challenge as a threat. In Russia, Napoleon was defeated less by the winter, than by the sheer otherness of Russian society. Russia lacked any comparable enlightened middle class to those who had welcomed Napoleon in Austria and Prague. Napoleon's army did not liberate Russia, but was reduced to a mere army of occupation, without supplies or support, and was defeated.

Revolutionary France's moral mission to realise the 'eternal rights of man' was compromised, but by no means exhausted. French civic republicanism combined with scientific rationalism to exemplify the Enlightenment ideal. There were many setbacks, from the reactionary repressions of 1830, 1848 and 1870 to the anti-Semitism that split French society when Captain Dreyfus was charged with treason. In 1940, the reaction of the French middle classes, resentful of Leon Blum's Popular Front government, to the German Occupation – 'better Hitler than Blum' – cast a dark shadow over France's claim to represent the best in humanity. But the communist-dominated French Resistance kept the honour of French liberty intact. France was occupied, and as long as France resisted could avoid the shame of collaboration with fascism. Much as the postwar French establishment loathed the communists and radicals, they had played a large part in saving France, while much of the upper class had collaborated. French Humanism, as an ideal, lived on in the 'socialist humanism' espoused by the communists, and in Sartre's existential philosophy. 'Existentialism is a humanism', wrote Sartre, although as we have seen (in Chapter Three) Sartre's postwar philosophy would soon distance itself from humanism. If the bourgeois elite had momentarily let go of the banner of humanism, the French left had taken it up.

If French humanism survived the occupation it found its severest test in Algeria's struggle for national liberation. France's empire, its colonies in Indo-China, the Middle East, Africa and the West Indies were always profoundly corrosive of the ideal of the universal rights of man. Colonial rule degraded the indigenous natives of those countries. It also degraded the ideal of a universal humanity. Where real living men and women were denied liberty, in the name of France, then 'French liberty' was reduced to an ideological cover for enslavement. The French Army under Napoleon invaded Egypt in 1798. The Emperor had been at great pains to pose as a liberator come to free the oppressed natives from the Turks. Napoleon also took on the role of defender of the annual caravan to the Holy Places and even expressed a willingness to convert to Islam.[19] However, Bonaparte's pro-Islamic policy was not taken seriously by his officers. A contemporary Egyptian observer recalls: 'They treated books and Quranic volumes as trash, throwing them on the ground and stamping on them with their feet and shoes. Furthermore they soiled the mosque, blowing their spit in it, pissing, and defecating in it.'[20] French rule in Algeria and Egypt remained tied to the demeaning corvée system of forced labour that prevented any substantial extension of civil freedom to the Muslims annexed to the French empire.[21] France's enlightened social scientists were tempted into subdividing the human race into advanced and lesser breeds.[22]

The contradiction between humanism and imperialism reached its apex in Algeria. Algeria was also occupied in 1830 at a tremendous human cost. The population of Algiers was reduced from its eighteenth-century peak of 75,000 to just 30,000. The status of the Algerians and the French settlers was complicated. Under the constitution of 1848

Algeria was officially designated French territory. Algeria was divided into two sections, one civilian, and the other military. The civilian section was largely European, centred on Algiers and the ports. The military section was the countryside and almost wholly native, Arabic and Berber. Divided into three provinces the Algerian natives were ruled through local chiefs recognised by the military governors, rather more liberally than the settlers would have preferred. The rationalist ambitions of Emperor Louis Bonaparte, Napoleon III, for Algeria were to be seen in the Imperial Decree of 1857 for a network of railways, and in the support for the Saint-Simonian socialist Prosper Enfantin's plans to industrialise the region. Enfantin raised funds to extract iron ore in Bone, but French industrialists torpedoed his proposal for a local smelting industry.

The new Emperor disliked the European settlers who had voted against his accession, and listened favourably to native complaints of oppression and land-grabbing. In 1863 Napoleon III wrote to Arabs that: 'Algeria is not strictly speaking a colony, but an Arab kingdom. The natives and the colonists have an equal right to my protection and I am no less the Emperor of the Arabs than the emperor of the French.' Constitutionally that position was unsustainable, but Louis Napoleon kept up his support for native rights as a counter-balance to the fervently republican settlers. The two laws voted by the senate on 22 April 1863 and 14 July 1865, known as the 'Senatus-Consult', defended first the native's land rights and second granted them the right to citizenship. However, in their application, the Senatus-Consult laws ended up discriminating against Arabs and Berbers. In formalising land rights, the courts reduced traditional land-holdings precipitately. Intended to grant citizenship by a 'well-meaning Emperor',[23] the second Senatus-Consult allowed Algerians to apply for French nationality but only if they allowed their Statut Personnel to be French, so subjecting themselves to French courts in such matters as marriage and inheritance.[24] Between 1865 and 1 November 1867 only 56 Muslims and 115 Jews made applications. However, under the terms of the law, all Algerians were subjects of the Empire, and therefore subject to its taxes. Similarly, the Imperial College, open to Algerians, but with the goal of assimilating them into French culture, taught its lessons in the French language, and recruited just 99 Algerian pupils in 1865, 81 in 1866. In 1870 the Algerians under the military zone revolted. French repression redoubled, and the ideal of assimilation was exposed more openly as a lie. The Algerians were not to be treated as equals with equal rights to the French, but inferiors. That same year the Crémieux decree granted French citizenship to Algerian Jews, in a policy of divide and rule, consolidating a loyal intermediary layer of Jews between the natives and the settlers. In fact the French republicans had recreated a system that was, according to Governor General Gueydon 'the serfdom of the natives'.[25] In 1881 the Code Napoleon was supplemented with a special 'native code', which listed 27 imprisonable crimes. These included, most extraordinarily, refusal to carry out corvée labour, an insulting attitude in the presence of French officials and travelling in Algeria without a permit. The flag hanging over the colonial office was the same tricolour that Marianne used to lead the revolutionaries against the King, but the policy imposed under it was closer to the restitution of feudal servitude. According to General Hanoteau, an officer of the Bureaux Arabes: 'What our settlers dream of is a bourgeois feudalism in which they will be the lords and the natives the serfs.'[26] In May 1898, in the heady atmosphere of the anti-Dreyfus campaign, Algeria elected four anti-Semitic deputies to the National Assembly after a week of anti-Jewish rioting that January. Governor Laferrière bent to the colonists' demands for autonomy, granting financial independence and the creation of an elected colonial assembly. Algeria became a 'small French Republic' in which 'the voter's card became the title of nobility in this novel feudal system'.[27]

In truth, though, the Algerian economy was not a throwback to a feudal past. Rather, its limited development was an entirely modern consequence of its subordinate relationship to the French economy.

Algeria exported grain and surplus labour to France. In the early twentieth century the colonists, swelled with poorer Spanish immigrants, made wine, while the most ambitious of Algerian manhood crossed the Mediterranean to find work in Paris. Underemployment was the curse of the growing class of landless labourers, the Fellaheen, who would become the grass roots of the Algerian resistance in the 1950s. Industrialisation was at a minimum, and the director of agriculture wanted it kept that way: 'Is it really in our interest to proletarianise future elements of the population, when social stability presumes an inverse development?',[28] he asked rhetorically.

The political leaders of the Algerians had been committed to reforming the French Republic by winning equal rights for Algerians within it. In 1924 the grandson of the national hero Abdel Kader, emir Khaled, set up L' Étoile Nord Africaine among immigrant workers in Paris, with the assistance of the French Communist Party. In 1926 Messali Hadj became its leader. As Messali organised the migrant labourers, Ferhat Abbas organised middle class Algerians in the Fédération des Élus, founded in 1927 around the demand for equal rights with the settlers.[29] Abbas' moderate demands were based on his own intuition that there was no coherent national sentiment to awaken. 'If I could find the Algerian nation, I would be a nationalist, and I would not blush from it as a crime...I will not die for the Algerian fatherland, because this fatherland does not exist', he told *Entente* on 23 February 1936. Messali disagreed. That year L'Étoile organised mass demonstrations and published a manifesto demanding independence. The French Communist Party (PCF) attacked Messali for playing into the settler's hands by supporting their demands for secession. Without PCF support, L'Étoile was easily suppressed by Leon Blum's popular front government in January 1937.

Algerian nationalists of a new kind led the war of 1954. The rural fellaheen were being made into a surplus population by agricultural improvements. They gravitated towards shantytowns on the outskirts of the major towns. 'The formidable erosion of the peasantry is not balanced by a complementary industrialisation', wrote a young Jean-François Lyotard, then a teacher and Marxist agitator in Constantine. 'The peasants do become industrial workers, but only in France.'[30] Migrant labour was an escape valve for the social pressures building up in Algeria, but in the fifties, an economic downturn shut off the valve. The national struggle erupted and found its social basis in the underemployed landless labourers, men who were called by the National Liberation Front's (FLN) most eloquent spokesman, Frantz Fanon, 'The Wretched of the Earth'.

The Algerian commanders of the Army of National Liberation (ALN) were older veterans of L'Étoile and the struggle of a previous generation. The commandant of the first battalion of the Eastern Base confided to a Western journalist that 'Those under 20 are the most intransigent. For my part, I certainly do not have much sympathy for the enemy I am fighting. But I know another face of France: Voltaire, Montaigne, the Rights of Man, the Commune, Sartre, Camus – in a word, the best there is to know of the enemy'. The commandant might have learned the classical canon of French humanism at one of the few state schools for Arabs, or working amongst communist militants in Paris. But even those narrow avenues for the inculcation of French humanism had been blocked off for the younger generation of Algerians. Only two per cent of the Algerian population was educated in 1950, and whatever influences the French left had on the Algerian national movement were thrown away.

In their reaction to the Algerians' aspiration to freedom and equality, the French establishment rejected the essence of humanism. They denied the common humanity of the Algerians. They denied the Algerians their freedom. They rejected the Algerians' own wishes and substituted what they thought was best. If France had merely torn up the Declaration of the Rights of Man and of the Citizen as a public demonstration that would have been bad enough. But what they did was even more destructive. They denied Algeria its freedom in the name of the Rights of Man. The republican sentiments of the revolution, universal in their aspiration were tied down to the narrow and particular interests of French rule. What was truly human was debased into a narrowly chauvinistic ideology that denied the humanity of the Algerians, even as it pretended to represent all humanity. In Algeria, France debased humanism, and made it into a sham.

Georges Bidault was president of the Council of National Resistance during the German occupation of France and a minister in De Gaulle's first government. 'A choice has to be made: either we believe in the inequality of the races, we consider that democracy, the Rights of Man and parliamentary government are acceptable on one side of the Mediterranean but not on the other – and I would understand if we abandoned the Algerians', he said.[31] Bidault's meaning is so forced that it is not at first clear. He means that a respect for equality, democracy and rights demands that France maintain its occupation of Algeria. Only if one had no respect for such things would it be right to 'abandon [i.e. liberate] the Algerians'. On the other hand, he says, if 'we are humanists, universalists to the end, and we consider that parliamentary democracy, the generalised right of habeas corpus, and the rule of law are preferable for Algerians as well', then we will prefer the assimilation of Algeria into France, as Brittany was assimilated. Another French resistance fighter Jacques Roustelle said, 'we would be arrant swine to abandon to their own destiny people who count on us to liberate them from their own ancestral and religious dependency'.[32] In these justifications of the continued occupation, the meanings of humanism, universalism and liberation are twisted to mean their opposite. People are to be liberated from themselves. The defence of universalism is perverse when substantially Algerians have been denied the rights enjoyed by settlers and by French citizens. But no such contradiction existed in the minds of the supporters of French colonialism. On the contrary, Algeria was occupied in the name of humanism and universalism. The occupation was enlightened, the Algerians backward. Le Corbusier's model for a reconstruction of Algiers, never built, provided an astonishing example of such thinking. The plans attempt to integrate modern apartment buildings with the Arab souk. The meeting of enlightenment rationalism and social exclusion is painfully explicit. The Arab dwellings are medieval and chaotic, a 'warren', as the soldiers hunting FLN fighters would say, running down the hill. At the brow of the hill rise great apartment blocks for settlers to look down on the subject race of Algerians. On stilts a great whiplash motorway hovers over the Arab houses, so that settlers do not have to drive through the souk. It also offers a platform for observation or sniper fire. Corbusier's architectural rationalisation of Algiers could not change, but only make explicit, the racial domination on which it was founded.

Georges Bidault's claim that the occupation was a defence of parliamentary democracy and habeas corpus rings hollow. On 22 October 1956, after negotiations with the French government broke down, the leaders of the FLN were intercepted while flying in a Moroccan plane on the orders of Max Lejeune, Secretary of State for the Armed Forces and imprisoned in France for the duration of the conflict.[33] In January 1957 General Massu led the Tenth Parachute Division into Algiers to smash the FLN in what became known as the Battle of Algiers. They began a systematic policy of detaining and torturing suspected FLN members to identify and break the organisation and its militants. Henri Alleg, an Algerian Jew and communist, was arrested in 1957 by paratroopers. He was subjected to torture by electric shock – *la gégène* – with electrodes attached to all parts of his body. In his account of the torture, Alleg recalls the taunts of the paratroopers: 'You're going to talk! Everybody talks here! We fought the war in Indo-China – that was enough to know your type. This is the Gestapo here! You know the Gestapo?'[34]

Many of the tenth division had fought with the free French. General Massu later protested: 'the left wing in France, intellectuals and communists, all compared my paras to the SS, which was absurd.' And he went on: 'Anyway, I tried *la gégène* on myself; it was not so terrible.' 'To which part of the body did you attach the wires', he was asked by Simon Cortauld. 'I don't remember – it gives you a shock, but I didn't make a tragedy out of it. *La gégène* had been used in other parts of Algeria. I was surprised, but then I was told that it had been in general use since Indo-China. The Battle of Algiers was not something that we enjoyed; but we carried it through with a certain style.' On 1 January 1958 de Gaulle sent Massu a letter sending his best wishes '*à vôtre si belle et brave Division*'.[35]

France's military and political establishment cast themselves in the role of the Gestapo. They suspended such niceties as habeas corpus and parliamentary democracy to use torture and mass detention. Frantz Fanon, the West Indian who joined the FLN editing the underground paper *El Moudjadid*, passed judgement on French humanism. 'Leave this Europe where they are never done talking of Man, yet murder men wherever they find them.'[36] The disaster was that Fanon was not just passing judgement upon France, but upon humanism itself. So pointedly did the European rulers of Algeria claim the authority of liberal humanism, that it seemed evident to Fanon that talk of Man was a sign of practical inhumanity.

But what of the left? In 1940 much of the French elite had been similarly disgraced by their collaboration with the German occupation. Then it was the resistance, and in particular the French left that had saved France's honour. Not this time. According to Fanon, socialist prime minister 'Guy Mollet...explicitly stated...France wants the war'.[37] Then minister of the interior, François Mitterand, who went on to be France's socialist president in 1980, gave a solemn warning that Algeria, centre and heart of the French Republic, guarantee of France's future, would be defended by all possible means[38] – including, it seems torture, detention without trial and summary execution.

Nor was the French Communist Party's record on Algeria any better. From the PCF's original positive involvement in setting up the Algerian immigrant labourers' organisation L'Etoile du Nord Africaine it was all downhill. The PCF described the revolt in Constantine as 'fascist', even after the natives had been bombed into submission. In 1956 it voted special powers to Guy Mollet's socialist government to repress the Algerian revolution.[39] The PCF had opposed Algerian independence since Massali Hadj first proposed it in 1937. In 1955 the PCF complained against charges of disloyalty to the Algerians: 'Have we not already shown that we support a policy of negotiation with the peoples of North Africa for the creation of a true "Union Française"?'[40] – as if the Algerian people were demanding a true Union Française! But with the outbreak of war, the PCF faced some criticism for this uncomradely betrayal of the Algerian people. Rather than take responsibility for the policy outright, they sought to deflect responsibility by shifting the blame onto the working class. In a speech to students, the PCF spokesman Laurent Casanova asked them to take into account 'the spontaneous attitude of the French popular masses on the question'.[41] Writer Francis Jeanson, who undertook clandestine work for the FLN, remembers Casanova speaking more bluntly. 'He used to say, "The working class is racist, colonialist and imperialist".'[42] In fact it was the Communist Party above all that was responsible for spreading chauvinist attitudes towards the Algerian struggle amongst working class people. 'Victims of the myth of French Algeria', wrote Fanon, 'the parties of the Left create Algerian sections of the French political parties on Algerian territory'. The truth was that it was they, before it was the working class, who assumed the right of France to rule over Algeria. In fact, the Communist Party of Algeria (PCA) recruited heavily amongst white settlers in Bab el Oued and Belcourt, according to Michael Farrell, who also charges that many PCA members were later active in the reactionary OAS.[43]

Both left and right had failed to recognise the Algerian claims to independence. And both left and right had sought to justify their stance in the received language of humanism. From Fanon, they received the obvious reply: if that is your humanism, you can keep it. Fanon's book *The Wretched of the Earth* had an electrifying effect on France, as it continues to compel readers throughout the West.

Jean-Paul Sartre, who wrote an introduction, said that it was 'a classic of anti-colonialism in which the Third World finds itself and speaks to itself though his voice'. Clearly the FLN were delighted to have found as pungent a polemicist as Fanon, a valuable editor for *El Moudjhadid* and trusted comrade (named FLN ambassador to Ghana before his death). Fanon was not, though, a part of the 'Wretched of the Earth' by upbringing, but by identification. Born in the French colony of Martinique, and trained in psychiatric medicine in France, Fanon came to Algeria as part of the staff of a French-run hospital – all of which makes his identification with the Algerian cause the more impressive. But generationally, Fanon was closer to the Commandant of the Army of National Liberation who knew Voltaire, Sartre and Camus, than he was to those uneducated Fellaheen that he spoke for. Indeed, Fanon formulates his idea of race discrimination with reference to Sartre's *Critique of Dialectical Reason*.[44] What Fanon takes from Sartre is an idea of the irreconcilability of colonialism and the natives, 'the union of all against the natives', as Sartre has it, or 'the principle "it's them or us"' in Fanon's version. As we have seen (in Chapter Three) Fanon applies Sartre's anti-Hegelian logic of otherness to the relation between Algeria and France. 'The two zones are opposed, but not in the service of a higher unity [as would be the case in Hegelian dialectics]. Obedient to the rules of pure Aristotelian [i.e. non-Hegelian] logic, they both follow the principle of reciprocal exclusivity.'[45] Here Sartre's theory takes up into itself the empirical content of the Algerian revolution, as articulated by Fanon, for its verification. In the face of the spurious unity proposed by the French right, a 'universalism' in which one party has no rights, or the 'Union Française' that the PCF wishes to negotiate (with whom, exactly?), the 'Aristotelian' opposition appears to make sense. Between European and Algerian, Sartre's 'Reef of Solipsism' is a more compelling reality than it is embodied in a sulky couple in a Left Bank cafe.

Furthermore, in his introduction, Sartre recognises his own themes in Fanon's work. His embrace of Fanon is – ironically, given its substance – the mutual recognition of a fellow proponent of the critique of humanism. 'Chatter, chatter, chatter: liberty, equality, fraternity', Sartre writes in his introduction, 'all this did not prevent us from making speeches about dirty niggers, dirty Jews and dirty Arabs'.[46] Sartre understands that on the solid ground of Fanon's exposure of the pretensions of French democracy, he can say those things that in other circumstances would be over the top. 'In the notion of the human race we found an abstract assumption of universality which served as a cover for the most realistic practices', he wrote, parodying Western humanism: 'On the other side of the ocean there was a race of less-than-humans...in short we mistook the elite for the genus.' Armed with this exposure of the lie of humanism, Sartre can be bold: 'With us there is nothing more consistent than a racist humanism since the European has only been able to become a man through creating slaves and monsters.' Here, 30 years before Phillipe Lacoue-Labarthe wrote it, is the basic argument that 'Nazism is a humanism'. The point is that France only achieved its humanity, by denying the humanity of the Arab.

In the consideration of the Algerian war, reality is stood on its head. Oppression takes on the cloak of universalist humanism, and liberation is made into a polemic against such humanism. This angry polemic against humanism is what fascinates Sartre. The war illustrates the exhaustion of humanism, its reduction to an ideological cover. Sartre is drawn to the way that the war corrodes the claim of universal humanity. Sartre did not only write an introduction to *The Wretched of the Earth* in 1961, but also, in 1958, a long review in *L'Express* of Henri Alleg's *The Question*, an account of his tortures. In that essay, too, we can see Sartre picking away at humanism and its claims. Of the torture he writes: 'if patriotism has to precipitate us into dishonour, if there is no precipice of inhumanity over which nations and men will not throw themselves, then, why, in fact do we go to so much trouble to become, or to remain, men? Inhumanity is what we really want.'[47] In the struggle between the torturer and his victim,

Sartre suggests that a new situation has emerged, in which common humanity is impossible. 'Man has always struggled for his collective or individual interests. But in the case of torture, this strange contest of will, the ends seem to me to be radically different: the torturer pits himself against the tortured for his "manhood" and the duel is fought as if it were not possible for both sides to belong to the human race.'[48] Having discussed in academic terms the dialectic between master and slave, Sartre is here confronted with a real-life equivalent. And, in this version, the Hegelian resolution of mutual recognition and respect is unimaginable. The abstraction 'humanity' cannot contain both Alleg and Massu. In the conflict between native and Frenchman, Sartre recognises the force that challenges the most cherished values of European humanism. 'They asked for integration and assimilation into our society and we refused....When despair drove them to rebellion, these sub-men had the choice of starvation or of re-affirming their manhood against ours. They will reject all our values, our culture, which we believed to be so much superior.'[49] Three years later in Fanon's *Wretched of the Earth*, Sartre found the rejection of 'all our values, our culture' poignantly expressed. Jean Christianson, though, remembers that Sartre was not always so drawn to the purifying violence of the oppressed. Around 1955, 'he always used to say to me: "Oh, your Algerians are violent people, they're violent!"'.[50] Cornelius Castoriadis describes Sartre's relationship to Fanon perceptively: 'What was specific to Fanon, and what Sartre emphasised in his preface to *The Wretched of the Earth*, was obviously not the anti-imperialist struggle but Third World messianism and the virtual obliteration of political and social problems, over there as well as over here.'[51]

It should be said that Fanon's own work is one thing, and its reception amongst French intellectuals another. Fanon does polemicise against the hypocrisy of a humanism that accompanies inhumanity. With great subtlety Fanon shows that even the values of the Enlightenment can become inverted to be carriers of oppression. In *L'An Cinq de la Révolution Algérienne* Fanon writes perceptively about 'the campaign of Westernising Algerian women': 'Servants under the threat of being fired, poor women dragged from their homes, prostitutes, were brought to the public square and symbolically unveiled to cries of "Vive l'Algérie Française!"'.[52] As Fanon astutely says the colonialist's 'methods of struggle were bound to give rise to reactionary forms of behaviour on the part of the colonised',[53] in other words the defence of the veil. However, Fanon does not endorse this rejection of women's equality. Rather he hopes that it can be overcome in the struggle against the occupation. Similarly Fanon explains sympathetically the Algerian distaste for 'immodest' French radio shows, as a rejection of that Western culture and technology that was associated with the occupation. But when the FLN starts its own broadcasting station, he notes, the dislike of this technology vanishes. Rhetorically, Fanon rejects humanism, specifically where it has been reduced into a defence of French interests. But his active and future-oriented sense of building a new society cannot be accomplished in the name of the Other. Rather, Fanon aims to 'start a new history of Man' and even 'try to set afoot a new man'.[54]

In the European (and American) reading of Fanon, though, there is a kind of inversion of his meaning. Where Fanon is concerned to initiate a new humanism, that is free of the hypocrisy to which humanism had been reduced in the mouths of the French occupiers, his interpreters have read something else. For them, Fanon, and the Algerian revolution, is the disproof of the claims of humanism as such. So, for example, Lyotard's (contemporary) assessment of the Algerian conflict is ambiguous. He wrote in 1961 'those who have been objects in world politics, in the history of humanity have achieved subjectivity'.[55] On face value, this is a wholly positive statement of the new emergent subjectivity. However, its context is a disappointment with the role of the 'French working class [which] has not in all honesty fought against the war in Algeria', suggesting that 'the solidarity between the proletariat and the colonised remains [a] sacred cow'.[56] In this respect, Lyotard, supporter of the Algerians, stands on the same ground as Laurent Casanova of the PCF, who refuses to support the Algerians. For both, the starting-point is the presumed failure of the working class to make common cause with Algeria. Like Sartre, Lyotard makes the Algerian revolution into a bonfire of old certainties and illusions. This is an attitude that the European leftists Lew and Garnier describe well: 'The lyrical power of Fanon's *Wretched of the Earth* – and the title as well – is a perfect expression of the pathos of an inverted universalism, of the belief that the East was going to enlighten the West. It also expresses the desire for a new historical subject to replace that of the socialist tradition, with its belief that a new liberator would come from a humiliated world that had become a storm zone.'[57] Fanon here is cast in the role of the exterminating angel who blasts all the pretensions of a tired European humanism away. And, as Lew and Garnier wisely suggest, the dramatics cover up an underlying disappointment with the possibilities of a more mundane advance.

A surprising number of France's leading intellectuals were in some sense connected to Algeria and the Algerian war. Some like Sartre chose the connection. Lyotard was a teacher in French Algeria, who sided with the Algerians. Pierre Bordieu did anthropological field studies there. Others, like Louis Althusser, Jacques Derrida and Albert Camus (who played in goal for the Algerian football team) came from French-Algerian stock. The war was a seismic shock for France's humanist tradition, and the beginning of its involution. The intellectuals were the focus of that involution of humanism only because it was a tradition that was founded upon the intellect, since the Enlightenment and its Encyclopaedists had first enthroned reason in France. In Britain, a comparable conflict, the war with Ireland had different consequences, wrecking English traditions of liberty, of the presumption of innocence, habeas corpus, free speech and the right to silence. Such principles were difficult to sustain in the face of internment without trial, and a succession of miscarriages of justice. The central pillar of France's special claim was its rationalist tradition and it was this that suffered most by the repression and eventual revolt of Algeria.

That said, the conflict was by no means restricted to the realm of ideas. On the contrary, the conflict threatened to tear French society apart. Right-wing students seized government buildings in Algiers on 13 May 1958. The French Algerians and the army colluded in the creation of a military regime in Algiers, forming a Committee of Public Safety. General Massu joined it (later he said he had been coerced).[58] The French government dithered, and General Salan, the Algerian Commander-in-Chief called for de Gaulle to take power. The army was threatening a coup d'êtat and on 24 May seized control of Corsica, installing a military governor. When the government ordered its immediate recapture, the navy mutinied.[59] Communist Rajani Palme Dutt, wrote that 'the war against the Algerian people with half a million troops has now rebounded against French democracy'.[60] The Socialists voted De Gaulle into power.

Once De Gaulle realised that the only solution was withdrawal, he was faced with an unenviable conflict with the settlers and their supporters in the French military. General Massu publicly criticised the betrayal of French Algeria. Unwilling to accept defeat, elements of the military calling themselves the OAS launched a terrorist campaign. De Gaulle took advantage of the situation to propose a new constitution with sweeping presidential powers to face down the challenges to the state. The right was humiliated, the army purged and the establishment rocked by crisis. The enhanced authority of De Gaulle shocked the left. Looking back at the creation of the Fifth Republic, the PCF realised too late that they had missed an historic opportunity to change the course of events.

> 'While the conflict continued at anything like peak intensity – which it did for another three years – the Left, like the rest of France, was mainly conscious of the sheer fact of crisis and the terrifying possibility of civil war which lurked behind it. This in turn produced a certain ambivalence on

the Left towards De Gaulle's new regime. The PCF had been thunderstruck by the events of 1958. A revolutionary situation along classically Leninist lines had existed – the ruling class had been unable "to live and rule in the old way" – and the revolution had duly taken place. But it had been De Gaulle's revolution, not theirs – indeed, everything had taken place almost as if the Party had not existed. For a few months the PCF tried to rally the masses in defence of the fallen Fourth Republic, but quickly gave up as it realised that that cause was now for ever lost.'[61]

As the subject of revolutionary change, the PCF had unquestionably missed its moment.

Chapter Seven

ALTHUSSER AND THE DEATH OF THE SUBJECT

The Algerian conflict gave rise to a crisis in the state in which all sides were wrong-footed. De Gaulle came out on top, but hardly through any decisive resolution of the problems of French society. A decade later the conflict broke out again, but this time in France as first protesting students, then striking workers clashed with police. For a few brief weeks in May 1968 it seemed as if the French state would collapse.

Fearing revolution De Gaulle had planned to leave the country. His old comrade Massu, promoted to the role of general d'armée in 1966, recalls De Gaulle and his family arriving, with all their luggage at his headquarters in Baden-Baden. 'De Gaulle was tired and indecisive, and he seemed to have had enough. I told him it was better he should be killed in Paris than stay here. He asked me to keep talking, and I was able to convince him that he must not resign. I also told him that, having just amnestied all those imbecile students in Paris, he could at least let my comrades out of prison, who had done little more than fight for French Algeria.'[62]

If De Gaulle's nerve faltered, the effect on the Communist Party was strikingly similar. Rather than taking advantage of the crisis, the PCF once again reacted conservatively. The independent initiative of the students and their willingness to go directly to workplaces to demand support all threatened the PCF's monopoly over organised labour through the union federation CGT. In a repeat performance of 1958, the PCF demonstrated that it was a conservative force in French society. It was the PCF's defensiveness and evasion of responsibility that was the substance of the intellectual retreat from subjectivity. This is perhaps most clearly expressed in the intellectual development of Louis Althusser, and his repeated motif of the 'Death of the Subject'. Althusser's intellectual stamina was impressive, but his thinking was prone to running on autopilot in a given direction without taking a wider view. He inspired his collaborators and students with what appeared to be a daring research programme around the themes of anti-humanism, social and ideological structures, and the 'Death of the subject'. As it turned out the literally fatal flaw in Althusser's attitude was a moral cowardice that reflected the paralysis of the official Communist movement.

Althusser's first intervention into party life was imaginative. As described in Chapter Two, Althusser challenged the official party line of 'socialist humanism'. The intellectual policy of socialist humanism was a formalised version of a long-standing claim of Marxism. Since Marx, the left inspired by him had laid claim to the best of the bourgeois society that it aimed to replace. The rationale for socialism was that the old society, having run its course, had become a fetter on productivity and human development. Revolution, by implication, was necessary to save the best of capitalist civilisation from its own tendency towards barbarism. Hence, the official Communist Parties had a cultural 'policy' that was summarised as socialist humanism, meaning that the left would inherit the humanism that bourgeois society could no longer defend. And, as we have seen, such a possibility had certainly arisen in Algeria, where the establishment had made humanism into the mask for its opposite: inhumanity.

Althusser saw it differently. Socialist humanism was, as he strongly hinted, a compromise with the status quo. The policy was a forced attempt to make peace with the old order, not a strategy for fighting it. Socialist humanism was little more than a reflection of bourgeois ideology within the Communist movement. There was a grain of truth in what Althusser said. Once Stalin adopted the policy of 'peaceful coexistence' in 1924, the tendency was for the parties of the Communist International to seek out points of compromise with other sections of society, including intellectuals. The capitals and universities of Eastern Europe were used to stage grand conferences for writers and intellectuals on whatever danger was facing humanity, from fascism to nuclear war. The 'socialist humanism' ideology was the formalisation of that strategy. In discussion with the chairman of the PCF, Waldeck Rochet, Althusser challenged, 'You who are in touch with the workers, do you think they are interested in humanism?'. 'Not in the slightest', Rochet replied, 'they couldn't care less'. 'Then why do you put so much emphasis on humanism?', Althusser continued. Rochet replied: 'Well you see we have to speak the same language as all those university people and socialists....We have to do something for them, otherwise they'll all leave.'[63]

In this telling, Althusser, the professor, is transformed into the champion of the honest toilers, while the agricultural labourer Rochet is sucking up to intellectuals. But Althusser's alternative was not really a break with the ruling ideology of capitalist society. Rather, what Althusser was doing was breaking with the old ruling class ideology, in favour of the emerging form of elite thinking, antihumanism and the death of the Subject. In fact Althusser was well-placed as a teacher at the prestigious École Normale Supérieure to keep abreast of the very latest intellectual developments in which, indeed, he was a key player. Alongside Althusser, Foucault, the psychoanalyst Jacques Lacan and Jacques Derrida were developing an analysis that was anti-humanistic and anti-Subjective. Althusser's real argument with Rochet was that he was out of date. If you wanted to suck up to intellectuals, you had to be with Derrida and Foucault, not Sartre and DeBeauvoir.

It would be wrong, though, to say that Althusser was merely keeping Marxist ideology up-to-date with the latest intellectual fads. That would be to miss out on the extent to which Althusser's own intellectual development was at the forefront of these ideas. Furthermore, his own ideas rationalised two strands: the left's, and in particular the PCF's, own retreat from the field of struggle, and his own personal evasions. The Death of the Subject was a drama that was re-played successively, and with increasing intensity within Althusser's own personal and political life. The Subject in question, the Subject that Althusser put to death was the historical Subject of the working class, symbolically represented, tragically, by his wife Hélène; but ultimately it was his own Subjectivity that Althusser destroyed in a bizarre deal with the courts.

Hélène Rytmann, a Parisian Jew whose family had come from Poland, was the kind of communist militant that Althusser hero-worshipped. From humble origins, she was 10 years older and more experienced than he, she had been active in the party since the thirties and served in the resistance. Hélène in turn admired her intellectual lover, whose Marxist books 'showed the "true worth" of the working class'.[64] 'He felt an obvious admiration for this "real fighter", Hélène, especially since she continued as a sociologist to work in the field, "among the masses", unlike him who was closeted in his study', wrote an acquaintance.[65] However, life as a militant in the PCF was full of double-dealing and backstabbing. During the war, Hélène had clashed with a number of people over tactics, and the rumour was spread that she had been a German informant and she was expelled from the Party. After the war Hélène resumed work with the local committee of the Peace Movement. Recognised as the wartime 'informant', a hearing was called to decide her fate at which Althusser was part of the committee. Party discipline demanded that the original decision be upheld, and, though he plainly did not believe the charges, Althusser describes the vote: 'everyone raised their hand and, to my shame and astonishment, my own hand went up. I had known it for a long time: I was indeed a coward.'[66]

Althusser's relationships to his wife and to the party were complex. It was out of admiration for people like Hélène that he wanted to be in the party. It seems from his own account that his sense of inadequacy made him willing to subordinate his will to the greater will, even relishing that surrender of responsibility. But here the party was demanding that he betray Hélène, the archetypal party militant. Party discipline drew its authority for Althusser from heroic figures like Hélène but the underlying source of authority was his own willing subordination. For that reason, Althusser was bound to choose the party over Hélène. His admiration for her came from a similar wellspring as his loyalty to the party, the isolated intellectual's desire for assimilation into a cause that was greater than he was. Althusser's colleague Foucault describes a similar, though less personal, experience in the PCF (which he later left) in the 1950s, the debate over the 'Doctor's Plot': 'A little while before the death of Stalin, the news spread that a group of Jewish doctors had tried to kill him. André Wurmser held a meeting in our Communist student cell in order to explain, in effect, how the plot was to have unfolded.' Foucault goes on to describe the psychology of this perversion of the truth: 'No matter how unconvinced we were, we still forced ourselves into believing what they told us. This was part of an attitude – I'd call it disastrous, but it was mine and it was my way of staying in the party – of being obligated to sustain the opposite of what's believable; this was part of that exercise of the "dissolution of the self" and of the search for a way of being "other".'[67] Here Foucault is explicit in relating the strategy of the 'dissolution of the self' with the lies perpetrated by the Communist Party, which begs the question why he should later have embraced the same strategy as a positive goal.

These two experiences of party discipline, Althusser's and Foucault's, could be interpreted to mean that all collective action necessarily embroils one in deceit and 'the dissolution of the self'. However discipline is not necessarily a bad thing. What is problematic in both these cases is that discipline was at the service of an unworthy goal, as both Althusser and Foucault were aware. But rather than challenge the goal, both willingly endorsed a course of action that they knew to be false. That was the dissolution of the self, but in Althusser's case it was also the betrayal of his wife, his militant conscience, Hélène. Transformed into an essentially conservative institution, the Communist movement constantly replayed this ugly drama: real militants were subsumed under a supposedly greater cause, which had in fact long since ceased to be such.

Althusser's second betrayal of Hélène came in 1980. This time he strangled her to death. This fact at least is not in dispute, if the meaning of it is. Hélène, Althusser acknowledges, was his harshest critic over the events of 1968. 'Only Hélène asked me what the hell I was doing in a party which betrayed the working class in '68 and she was quite right', he wrote.[68] Not only had Hélène judged Althusser harshly in 1968, but she had held that judgement of him for the 12 years subsequent, until her death, when he was 60 years old and she 70. Althusser's despair over his own status and role took a pointedly self-destructive turn. Already subject to fits of depression, Althusser 'wanted to destroy not only myself but also destroy all traces of my existence: in particular by destroying every one of my books, all my notes, by burning down the École as well and "if possible", while I was at it, by getting rid of Hélène herself'.[69] In the event, he did not kill himself, but only Hélène. But why did his self-destructive urges focus on Hélène? Before he could see through this fantasy Hélène took control. 'She told me with a determination that terrified me that she could no longer live with me....She then made practical arrangements which I found unbearable; totally ignoring me, though I was still there.'[70] Here was Hélène making the judgement on him that he had made on himself, except that now it was externalised. He was not going to kill himself, she was going to leave him, but 'deep down I knew she could not actually leave me'[71] – words that proved to be all too true.

From this point on we find Althusser furiously denying his own responsibility for her murder, as if it just happened. 'Then one day, to cap it all she simply asked me to kill her myself',[72] he writes. Is this believable? Possibly, but surely such a statement would not be acted upon, nor even cited as an argument, not by someone who truly loved his wife. And yet, talking to a psychotherapist after the killing, Althusser says 'I remember putting forward the hypothesis that Hélène's murder was "suicide via a third party"'.[73] In his account of the killing itself, Althusser writes in the passive construction, as though he had no part in the killing. 'I found myself standing at the foot of the bed...with Hélène stretched out before me, and with me continuing to massage her neck....Then I realised, without knowing why...that she was dead....My fate was sealed.'[74] One might have concluded that it was Hélène's fate that was sealed, but Althusser's mind was already on his own future.

The meaning of the murder is contained in Althusser's judgement that 'for a long time Hélène had been right when she claimed that the Party, if not directly then indirectly, had "betrayed the working class" which it claimed to serve'. But Althusser was loyal to the end. He did leave the Party, but not because of its faults. Rather he left to save the party from association with himself. 'I have not renewed my membership since Hélène's murder in 1980. During that whole painful period the Party and *L'Humanité* treated me very decently....I did not want to burden the Party with a dangerous "murderer".'[75] It seems likely that Althusser's self-loathing arose out of the very judgement that Hélène had made on him – that he was supporting a Party that had betrayed the working class. Though he could not deny it, the judgement was awful nonetheless, as it negated his own purpose in life. As the bearer of these bad tidings, Hélène, always his conscience, became the target of his frustration. He assassinated the very woman who represented the spirit of militant activism that had drawn him to the Party, just as she was forcing him to understand that it had failed. In his wife, Althusser killed the personification of historical subjectivity that he sought to eliminate in his theoretical work. Hélène embodied the judgement that Althusser, and the Party, had failed at the crucial moment, and held back.

At the same time as he was killing Hélène, Althusser sought to efface his own subjectivity as author of this act. He succeeded in avoiding imprisonment by having himself declared 'not to be responsible in juridico-legal terms'.[76] In that way his treatment was a mental health matter, rather than one of criminal law. The authorities were no doubt delighted to acquiesce to Althusser's insanity plea, and in 1981, the election of the Mitterand government and the accession of the new justice minister Robert Badinter led to Althusser's release from the asylum. In his memoir Althusser complains bitterly that the insane are 'sentenced for an indefinite period' and 'considered lacking in sound judgement and therefore deprived of the right to speak in his own name'.[77] By contrast, he moaned, 'the ideology of the "debt" and the debt paid" to society is loaded in favour of the convicted person who has served his sentence and, to an extent even protects the criminal who has been set free'.[78] 'I want to free myself from the murder and above all from the dubious effects of having been declared unfit to plead, which I could not challenge in law or do anything about', he stresses. 'I had to survive and learn to live beneath the oppressive weight of that declaration. Which was a wall of silence, or as if I were dead in the eyes of the public.'[79]

The 'Death of the Subject' in Althusser's theoretical writing had a ghoulish reality in his life. Three times did Althusser forsake the Subject. He oversaw the Party's betrayal of the historical Subject of the working class, both personally in the show-trial of his wife Hélène and politically in the failure to act in May '68. He eventually killed his own wife when her honest appraisal of his own role in that betrayal became too much to bear. And finally, evading legal responsibility for the killing, he had himself declared not to be a Subject. The evacuation of subjective agency from his life could not be more complete. The Althussers' personal tragedy in its own peculiarly sordid way simply sounded the actual evacuation of human subjectivity from the French left. Althusser was left a figure without rights or standing, a hollow mockery of the very 'process without a subject' that he saw as history.

Cornelius Castoriadis wrote about the influence of Althusser's structuralism and its coincidence with the events of May '68:

> 'It is precisely at this point that structuralism became the dominant fashion. An era of inanities on the death of man, of the subject, of history etc; of empty discourses on "scientificity" and "the economy" (without Marxo-Althusserian "science" ever producing a single statement saying something about the actual economy); of the denunciation of the idea of alienation as "Hegelian"; of the continued cover-up of the bureaucracy and of Stalinism by silence pure and simple, or by imputing concentration camps to Stalin's "humanism" – whereby Althusser attained the distinction of acting more dishonourably than [Louis] Aragon which is no small feat....While a new contestation was developing, while people were searching for, and beginning to create, new attitudes, norms values, the accent was placed on "structures" so as to evacuate living history.'[80]

Castoridas' pungent summary of the meaning of Althusser's philosophy is all too accurate. However, Castoriadis' counter-position only begs the question of why the apparently revolutionary events of May '68 were theorised as an evacuation of the subject from history. It is apparent that the morally bankrupt traditions of Gaullism, and the

PCF could not advance a new humanism. Instead they produced a degradation of the humanist tradition in France. But the flowering of opposition movements in the student and workers militancy of May '68 might perhaps have become an alternative source of agency. And yet there is precious little trace of any such new humanism in the intellectual products of that time. It is to that paradox that we turn next.

Chapter Eight

THE AGENCY DEBATE

It is hard to remember today that for 60 years radical thinking was dominated by the influence of a conservative, bureaucratic elite in the Soviet Union. The great movement of social change in the early twentieth century embraced a combative European labour movement, the intransigent women's suffrage campaign, and an anti-colonial revolt that stretched from Ireland to India and from Indo-China to the Caribbean. The containment of the Russian Revolution in the years following 1917, though, had a profoundly limiting effect upon the prospects for social revolution. The defensiveness of the new caste of military-political officers in the Soviet Union led them to consolidate their regime with a policy of 'peaceful coexistence'. Between Stalin's seizure of power in 1921 and his death in 1954, the Soviet Union's influence reached its apogee as a consequence of the defeat of the

Nazi empire in Eastern Europe and the alliance with Mao-Tse Tung's national revolution in China. Despite the appearance of dynamism within the Soviet bloc, it is now clear that Stalinism was a conservative social system, which simply expanded to fill the vacuum caused by the internal collapse of the European empires.

Appearances though, were decisive. The geographical existence of the Soviet bloc, and more, its expansion, seemed to indicate the negation of the capitalist system. Radical opponents of capitalism within the Western world allied themselves to the Soviet Union, with profoundly demoralising consequences. Though the public face of official communism was combative, the opportunist strategy of the Soviet leadership was to compromise with the West wherever possible. In practice that meant that the Communist parties in Western Europe and the nationalists in the developing world were subordinated to the Soviet Union's strategic defence. Time and again, the Soviet leadership used its radical credentials to counsel compromise. The conservatism of the Communist parties also led to a resurgence of reformist parties. Reformism as a labour-movement strategy had been briefly eclipsed by the revolutionary wave of 1916-23. But once the Soviet Union sought peaceful coexistence with the capitalist world, it was predictable that the reformist parties of the Socialist International would consolidate their influence within Western Europe. By the time of the Sino-Soviet split in 1963, however, the high tide of Stalinism was beginning to ebb. The disintegration of the Soviet bloc was gradual, as first economic sclerosis in the seventies, and then the burden of a renewed Cold War in the eighties took their toll. It was this internal collapse of Stalinism that gave rise to a debate over who was to be the agent of change.

The debate over agency is often loosely described as the emergence of the New Left, a loose association of disparate groups and individuals, largely centred on the student activism of the sixties, in many different countries. These student radicals went on to be active in anti-war campaigns, especially over Vietnam, campaigning for civil rights for black Americans (as well as for Northern Ireland's oppressed Catholic minority), on the fringes of the Black Power movement, in the foundation of the women's liberation movement, and also of Gay Liberation. Later, such activists were to be found in the emerging environmentalist campaigns in Germany and California in the seventies, the squatters movement in northern Europe, as well as the clandestine terrorist groups, the Red Army Faction in Germany, the Red Brigades in Italy, and the Weathermen in America. The defining characteristic of all of these movements, however, was that they were outside the official Communist parties, and as a consequence, largely peripheral to the Communist and Socialist-dominated official labour movements. The New Left was self-consciously opposed to the 'old left', meaning the Communist parties, the reformist parties and, largely, the trades unions. The paralysis, and eventual disintegration, of the Soviet bloc and the official communist parties that were tied to it, forced the pace of the New Left. Important figures on the New Left were often dissident intellectuals who had broken with Stalinism in disgust at such events as the Nazi-Soviet pact of 1939, or the Soviet invasions of Hungary in 1956 and of Czechoslovakia in 1968. Figures like Herbert Marcuse, author of the critical *Soviet Marxism* (1958), labour historian EP Thomson who founded the *New Left and Universities Review* and the Hungarian dissident Marxist Georg Lukacs, who put his own prolific output down to 'house arrest', were the adopted stars of the new radical students' movements. Later, they developed their own stars, like student radical Daniel Cohn-Bendit, Black Power leader Stokely Carmichael, radical feminist Shelia Rowbotham and Green Petra Kelly.

[margin note: NB There must have been more than anti-C ie hostility to agency.]

The Stalinist and reformist leaders of the official labour movement in Europe were deeply hostile to any challenge to their authority. Anyone who wanted to influence working-class politics in a new direction had to run the gauntlet of rulebook obfuscation and straightforward physical intimidation. The norm was that trades unions discussed only economic issues, while political matters were referred to the party affiliate, Socialist or Communist. Where rules and regulations were not enough to dissuade dissident opinion, violence would do. Delegates to the Liaison Committee for the Defence of Trade Unions who disagreed with the Communist Party of Great Britain's strategy for fighting the Industrial Relations Act were beaten up. In Japan, Trotskyist candidates for the National Students' Union were assassinated, as were anti-Stalinists in Turkey. In America, the problem was somewhat different. There the leadership of the CIO was fiercely anti-Communist and patriotic. The prospects for a radical intervention into the American labour movement were equally testing. The new generation of radicals did not, as a rule, challenge the official leadership of the trade unions, but side-stepped the organised working class altogether, to find new constituencies and fields of activism. Taking the path of least resistance, these radicals took their struggle elsewhere.

It was, perhaps, predictable that the activists and intellectuals loosely called the New Left would begin to develop a theoretical justification for their non-labour orientation. There were two components to this theory: first came the identification of new agents of social change; and then, after the event, theories were developed to justify the circumvention of the working class, namely that the working class was in fact a conservative force. Ultimately these were two sides of the same coin. But the order they came in was important. In the flush of the *événements* of May '68 the sober conclusion that the working class was a reactionary force was not made explicitly, rather the more positive embrace of what came to be known as the new social movements characterised the New Left's appeal. It was only later, when the radicalism of the sixties gave way to a more sombre era of the late seventies and eighties, that the labour movement was declared dead – by which time the prophecy had realised itself. This order of events meant that the debate over agency was disguised. It appeared to be an optimistic embrace of new sources of change. In content, though, it was the opposite. The search for new sources of *deus ex machina — an unexpected active agent—*

agency was merely symptomatic of the new radicals' narrow social base. Though this New Left was very self-consciously opposed to the old Stalinist movement, it did continue certain established features of the old radical intelligentsia. Most characteristically, it shared the wish that change would come about through the *deus ex machina* of some external agent. Where the old radicals looked to Moscow for deliverance from the capitalist yoke, the New Left was excited by events in China, the Third World, and amongst the wretched of the earth. The question of agency was posed in terms that were at odds with any real sense of responsibility. Instead the quest was on to find a ready-made vanguard, whether amongst the peasantry of the Third World, or in black ghettos. The difficult task of convincing other people of the need for change was imaginatively circumvented in the identification of sections of society who were already revolutionary, without any need of political persuasion. It was the desire for a magical solution that drove the debate over agency, not a realistic strategy to take control of events.

As we saw with Algeria, the attraction of Third World conflicts was that they seemed to break out of the framework of the old left. While the first world had stabilised after the war, the putches and coups of Third World revolutionaries were often more dramatic. Radicals in the West embraced a variety of nationalist revolutions. The conflict between Stalin and Yugoslavia's Marshall Tito seemed to offer new possibilities in the non-aligned movement, while the Sino-Soviet split invigorated student radicals with its more militant, peasant-led version of Maoist communism. The somewhat isolated revolutionaries of the Trotskyist Fourth International dreamed of 'the fundamental dynamics of the Latin American revolution...developing into a socialist revolution without intermediary stages'.[81] This was essentially a dream that a Latin American Santa Claus would deliver socialism under the Christmas tree without any need to work to achieve it. These same revolutionaries could not help but be impressed by the events of May '68, and promptly set about developing a theory of a 'New Youth Vanguard'.

'All these student movements, despite their social composition and their political and theoretical contradictions, have developed an anti-capitalist and revolutionary consciousness on a broad scale', they wrote.[82] The wish was father to the thought. If only we could find ready-made revolutionaries, there would be no need to do the dull business of winning people to the cause. And the advantage of the presumed 'New Youth Vanguard' was that it was outside of the influence of the traditional labour movement, avoiding the need to challenge the old left. 'The revolutionary upsurge of May 1968 confirmed both the qualitative change in the relationships between the new vanguard and the traditional organisations as well as the considerably expanded opportunities for work by the revolutionary Marxists within this vanguard.'[83] It was clear why the 'Fourth International' needed the students, but not so clear why the students needed the Fourth International. After all, if they already were fully-formed conscious revolutionaries then they would create their own future, as, in a sense, they did.

Writing about the emerging youth culture and its radical dimensions Tom Nairn said 'youth' 'can for the first time assume an other than biological meaning, a positive social meaning, as the bearer of those pressures in the social body which prefigure the new society instead of the reproduction of the old one'.[84] John Clarke and his associates at the Birmingham University Centre for Contemporary Cultural Studies parodied Lenin with the suggestion that 'youth was the vanguard party – of the classless, post-protestant consumer society to come'.[85] But the difficulty was precisely that social change was reduced to a biological meaning in the cult of youth. There is nothing intrinsically revolutionary about youth. In the pages of the Communist Party journal *Marxism Today*, Don Milligan reproduced the statistical evidence of young people's political affiliations – Young Conservatives 100 000 members, Young Liberals 15 000, Young Socialists 15 000, Young Communists 5000 – and commented caustically: 'here we can see the unadorned evidence – the real situation is that the reactionary section outnumbers the progressive section by four to one'. Milligan accurately interpreted the much-celebrated protest songs of the sixties as more cynical than revolutionary.[86]

In the United States a yet more potent argument was made for a new agent of revolutionary change: black Americans. The organisation of the Black Panther Freedom Party drew together a number of black militants from the civil rights organisation, the Student Nonviolent Coordinating Committee, the Democratic Party and the civil rights movement. Eldridge Cleaver and Bobby Seale had worked as administrators in Lyndon Johnson's War on Poverty programme. Stokely Carmichael of the SNCC had raised the slogan 'black power' in 1966, as well as organising the Lowndes County Freedom Organisation out of the delegates of the Mississippi Freedom Democratic Party, refused accreditation at the 1964 Democratic Convention. The Black Panthers raised the slogan of armed self-defence, and, citing their constitutional rights, openly carried rifles. The stage was set for an all out conflict with a nervous FBI. Many Black Panthers were assassinated or wounded and imprisoned in a year-long military campaign of armed raids and frame-ups. The revolutionary reputation of the Black Panthers left white radicals awe-struck, as Tom Wolfe parodied in his essay 'Radical Chic', a description of Leonard Bernstein's fund-raising dinner for the Panthers.

The militancy of the Panthers contrasted unfavourably with the generally conservative outlook of the white American working class. According to the League of Revolutionary Black Workers, only if white workers followed the lead of blacks, whose 'liberation struggle...is moving at a quickening pace', could they shed their 'white skin privilege' and join the worldwide revolution.[87] Leonard Harris and Cedric Robinson argued the case that the revolutionary subject was now the black race, not the 'white' working class.[88] So Harris writes, citing Robinson, that 'Marx's model of the working class, to the extent that the working class is pictured as a historical subject...is misguided'.

'The radical nationalism of African people', by contrast, 'is a historical form of subjectivity'.[89]

The revolutionary élan of the Black Panther Party was indeed impressive. But the very confidence with which the Black Panthers made their case tended to disguise their precarious situation. While radicals applauded them from afar, they were being killed off and jailed. At the high-tide of sixties radicalism, the Panthers' seized the moment, but their tactical creativity was indicative of a relatively narrow and precarious social base. Once underground they were isolated. Worse still, the ebbing tide of sixties radicalism left the remaining members of the group hunted and alone, in the face of a murderous FBI campaign. Radicals were impressed by the militancy of the Black Panthers, but the truth is that black militancy was born of desperation. They had been rebuffed by the Democratic Party and beaten by the Chicago police. Taking up arms was a sign of having very little to lose. The paramilitary defeat of the Black Panthers following the return of a hostile Republican administration in 1968 added to the demoralisation of black America.

The lauding of the black vanguard said more about the frustrations of radicals with the greater part of the American working class, and its apparent indifference to the political agendas of the radicals.

New Social Movements?

The outcome of the debate over agency is often described as the emergence of the New Social Movements, as in the late Ralph Miliband's tribute to the 'quite outstanding contribution which feminist, ecological, anti-racist and other "new social movements" have made'.[90] But the existence of the new social movements has often proved difficult to pin down. The German social scientist Claus Offe's examination of the role of the new social movements is cautious. 'Even enumerations aiming at completeness are rare in the literature' he says, before recommending Alberto Melucci's list of 'the student movements, feminism, sexual liberation, urban movements, ecology struggles, the mobilisation of consumers and users of services, of ethnic and linguistic minorities, communitarian and counter-cultural movements, the struggles around health-issues, and others'.[91] The difficulty in enumerating the new social movements is often short-circuited with a guilty 'etc', as in Roger Harris rushed typology 'socialist political parties, trade unions, feminist, environmental, etc, movements'.[92] This 'etc' tells us that Harris is building a movement in his head, as surely as if he had said 'and Uncle Tom Cobbley and all'. Ralph Miliband's 'and other "new social movements"' is only slightly less obvious. Martin Heidegger wrote of the homogeneity of modern society that there was a 'boundless etcetera of indifference',[93] but this is the boundless etcetera of difference. It is the bad infinity of the endless sequence that can always be expanded by the addition of another forgotten or excluded social movement.

The ambiguity of the new social movements does not end with definitions. In fact the new social movements themselves are in their nature amorphous, as Offe explains. 'The process by which multitudes of individuals become collective actors is highly informal, ad hoc, discontinuous...they have at best rudimentary membership roles, programs, platforms, representatives, officials, staffs, and membership dues. The new social movements consist of participants, campaigns, spokespersons, networks, voluntary helpers and donations. Typically, in contrast to traditional forms of political organisations, they do not employ the organisational principle of differentiation in either horizontal (insider versus outsider) or the vertical (leader versus rank-and-file members) dimension.'[94] The organisational ambiguity of the new social movements is presented here as an advantage over the old organisations. But is it? With officers elected by members, the rights of the members to challenge policy or leaders are clear. In an informal network, decisions cannot be tested, nor members held accountable for their actions. The environmentalist campaign Greenpeace has had considerable success intervening in the meetings of industry shareholders to protest over genetic modification and pollution. It is pointed that Greenpeace itself could never be the target of such an intervention. The organisation has a tiny staff, and an unelected board. The millions of Greenpeace subscribers who pay standing orders to Greenpeace have no rights over policy.

However, it is a mistake to assess the new social movements in terms drawn from more traditional organisations. The formula 'new social movement' is something of a misnomer. What are called new social movements are not really social movements at all, in the meaning that the words suggest. The debate over agency should not be taken at face value. In the first flush of the New Left, these groups borrowed the language of the old left, of 'vanguards' and revolutions. As first expressed, the debate over agency was about the emergence of new agents of social transformation. But the appearance of the debate was deceptive. The real meaning of the 'new social movements' is a move away from the idea of an agent of social transformation altogether. The novel forms of organisation are a break with the idea of collective agency.

Alberto Melucci, the Italian sociologist who has done most to theorise the rise of the new social movements makes this very clear. 'Social movements cannot be represented as characters, as subjects endowed with an essence and a purpose within a pièce whose finale is knowable', he writes.[95] 'Many analyses start from the implicit... assumption that the actor exists: in other words, that there is a "workers' movement", a "women's movement", a "youth movement", an "environmental movement", and so on.'[96] What is wrong with this approach? Melucci explains: 'the image of a movement as a character is inadequate.' 'These "movements" reveal conflicts' but 'these conflicts do not have a subject'.[97]

What Melucci is trying to say is that the new social movements are not agents of change and not historical subjects. That would be to see them in terms of the old social movements. What then is the positive effect of the 'new social movements'? 'The allegedly "anti-modern" character of "movements" in fact consists in their proclamation of the end of linear progress', he writes, thinking, one imagines, of environmentalist and other defensive campaigns against unwelcome changes. Melucci thinks this is what is needed: 'the central problem of complex systems is the maintenance of equilibrium.'[98] Not social change then, but its opposite, the maintenance of equilibrium in the face of an unwelcome 'linear progress' is the concern of the new social movements. Reluctantly, Claus Offe agrees that the new social movements are essentially conservative in their character. 'These movements often strongly emphasise the preservation of traditional communities, identities and social as well as cultural environments.'[99] Also, new social movements are 'abandoning the idea of progress and perfection in favour of tenaciously defending present values and identities'. As defensive and even traditionalist organisations, the new social movements simply do not fit the model of an agent of social change, or a historical subject. That would imply a future-orientation and strategic intent that is alien to the underlying nature of the new social movements.

Instead of acting as historical subjects, the 'new social movements' are primarily concerned with 'rendering power visible'. 'Power which is recognisable is also negotiable, since it can be confronted and because it is forced to take differences into account', Melucci adds.[100] The strategy of bringing out into the open the 'powers-that-be' and negotiating with them is a long cry from the transformative action of historical subjects. It is, as Melucci perceptively explains, a process that leads to 'the selection of new elites'. 'In many Western countries during the 1970s, for example, collective action produced certain changes in left-wing or progressive political organisations (such as political parties and trade unions) and, above all, resulted in the emergence of a new generation of skilled personnel in the key communications media, advertising and marketing sectors of the "information society".'[101] Offe agrees that the new social movements 'are rooted in major sections of the new middle class'.[102] Offe claims that the new middle class is often allied with 'decommodified' or peripheral groups, such as middle-class housewives, students, the retired and the unemployed. But the excluded sections are essentially in a subordinate relation to the new middle class, as Offe hints. 'These two segments also sometimes share institutional environments, as in the cases of teachers and their students, social workers and their clients and so on.'[103]

The transition from the radical rhetoric of the New Left to the elite-building middle-class politics of the new social movements needs to be accounted for. Where early on the talk was of revolutionising sexual relations, race and society, in more recent times the preoccupation is with negotiating power, managing change and maintaining equilibrium. Most pointedly the relationship of advocate to social group has degenerated into that between professional carer and client group. The explanation for these changes is not something that can be fully understood within the inner life of the new social movements themselves. Rather, it is in their relation to the central historical subject of the twentieth century, the collective subject of organised labour, that all of the limitations and possibilities of the new social movements have played themselves out. Throughout the literature of the New Left and the new social movements the central attainment that is cited as the turning point in the history of these movements is this: the understanding that the new social movements will not take a subordinate role to organised labour, and, in consequence, that the exploitation of labour by capital will not be seen as the overriding contradiction in modern societies. Using the terminology of the Chinese Communist Party in its breach with Moscow, the new social movements rejected the hegemony of the organised working class.

The irony is that in truth, the decisive influence on the course of the new social movements has been the fortunes of the labour movement. As long as organised labour was strong, the New Left was essentially peripheral, and in its character radical. With the decline of the labour movement, the new social movements revealed their character as vehicles of a conservative, middle-class outlook. The debate over agency took the form of a search for new social subjects, but the underlying trend that provoked that debate was the defeat of the historical agency of the working class. In Russell Jacoby's account of the emergence of the movement 'the intensification of subjectivity is a direct response to its actual decline'.¹⁰⁴

Intriguingly the other aspect of the new social movements is their growing disappointment even with the alternative agents of social change identified by the New Left in the sixties. The new social movements have turned their attitude to Third World nationalism through 180 degrees. Whereas solidarity movements uncritically embraced third world nationalism in the sixties and seventies, increasingly activism on Third World issues is coming to mean vilifying Third World regimes for their presumed human rights abuses. According to human rights lawyer Geoffrey Robertson, the 'movement for global justice has been a struggle against sovereignty'.¹⁰⁵ 'The great play of sovereignty, with all its pomp and panoply, can now be seen for what it hides: a posturing troupe of human actors, who when offstage are sometimes prone to the chorus.'¹⁰⁶ Radicals who would have been defending Vietnam against American intervention in the 1960s were cheering Nato's bombardment of Belgrade in 1999. Not just Third World nationalism, but nationalism amongst the black populations of the West is viewed with much greater anxiety than it was. The growth of the Nation of Islam in the USA caused serious heart-searching amongst American radicals. Feminists were appalled by Louis Farrakhan's million-man march, as they were by the Promise Keepers' movement. Even looking back the romance has drained from black militancy and Stokely Carmichael is today remembered more often for his statement that 'the only position for women in the SNCC is prone', than he is for coining the phrase 'black power'.¹⁰⁷ In Britain the National Union of Students imposed a ban on Islamic groups for their opposition to homosexuality, and the gay activist group Outrage organised a campaign around the 'special problem' of gay-bashing in the black district of Brixton (Outrage has also targeted Zimbabwean president Mugabe, once a star of radical Third Worldists, for anti-gay laws in his country).

Of course it is true that many Third World nations have illiberal social policies, as it is that black men are not necessarily anti-sexists, or that women often collaborate in unequal relationships. But whoever thought that that was not the case? Only the New Left's powerful illusions in their chosen 'vanguard' groups created the conditions for this embittered sense of disappointment. A more realistic approach would have understood that there are no spontaneously radical social groups, and political change comes as a result of convincing people, it does not fall out of the sky. This experience of disappointment, though, meant that the new social movements are qualitatively different in their attitude to the focus of their actions than was the New Left. Rather than advocating on behalf of given social groups, the new social movements have become interested in speaking up for those who by definition have no voice. The mode of advocacy is – at least in appearance – altruistic rather than representative. In the ecology movement this is most striking. The subject of the ecology movement is necessarily amorphous. The subject is 'nature', which cannot speak. Or, if that appears too awkward, the subject is the future generations who will inherit the Earth from us. Similarly, many feminists have gravitated to advocacy on behalf of abused children, who, in the words of Beatrix Campbell's book have suffered 'Stolen voices'.[108] Rather than solidarity with mass nationalist movements, Third World activists have agitated on behalf of small national minorities, like the Ogoni in Nigeria, or indigenous peoples in Latin America. The characteristic feature of these campaigns is that there is little chance that the target of the beneficence of such campaigns will disappoint by failing to go along with the strategy. In fact the relationship has changed from one in which the subject of the campaign is itself an agent of social change, to one where victims become the mascots of altruistic campaigners.

The agency debate began looking like the invigoration of the left, with the identification of new subjects of historical transition. But the underlying motivation was a disbelief in the possibilities of building a popular movement out of the mass of working people. In its eventual conclusion, the development of the new social movements reveals these not to be social movements at all. Rather the underlying dynamic was always conservative and elite politics, though that could only finally gain full expression with the defeat of the organised labour movement in the eighties.

Chapter Nine

'THERE IS NO ALTERNATIVE'

Market theorists like Hayek and Popper strongly associated the free Subject with capitalism. That association was an ideological one. In the 1980s it was put to the test. The result ought to have demonstrated that the market by no means guaranteed subjective freedom. In the event, though, it was not the market that was blamed for the problems of the 1980s, but individual freedom itself. The communitarians criticised subjective freedom because they took on face value the claims of the Thatcher and Reagan governments to represent individual freedom. Their response was ultimately a conservative response to the socially corrosive effects of market policies. But because the argument that there was no alternative to the market had been won, the culprit identified for the problems of the eighties was the selfish individual.

In the 1980s in Britain and America, a campaign to put the individual first was inaugurated from the highest echelons of the government. The elections of Margaret Thatcher as prime minister in 1979 and Ronald Reagan as president in 1980 engaged a comprehensive distaste for big government. As Reagan, who first stepped into politics with a speech for the radical right-wing candidate Barry Goldwater in 1964 said, 'government was not the solution, it was the problem'.[109] Reagan's election appealed to a sentiment that was expressed in the campaign around Proposition 13 in California, commonly called the 'Tax Revolt', in which Californians voted by 65 to 35 to reduce property taxes.[110] Resentful of big government, voters turned to Ronald Reagan's promise to give the country back to the people.

Margaret Thatcher's Chancellor Nigel Lawson recalls that 'Margaret instinctively realised the need to regain the moral as well as the practical initiative from collectivism. In this she was strongly fortified by the writings of the economist and philosopher Friedrich Hayek'.[111] Thatcher, like Reagan appealed to a sentiment that saw big government as a barrier to individual freedom. Thatcher's popular reforms included offering tenants of government housing the right to buy their homes, as many did. She also sold off government-owned companies like British Telecom and British Gas to small shareholders in a move sold to the public as 'popular capitalism'.

Retrospectively such reforms have been tarnished by the later problems faced by these administrations. But it would be wrong to imagine that the appeal of the opposition to big government was limited to the right's core constituency of the propertied classes. Historian Eric Foner argues that in America left-leaning radicals gave the ground of freedom to the political right, by virtue of their own preoccupation with state power, and in particular their orientation towards the Supreme Court. 'As the social movements spawned by the sixties adopted first "power" and then "rights" as their favoured idiom, they ceded the vocabulary of "freedom" to a resurgent conservatism....The very fact that "rights" were being protected and invented by the most undemocratic branch of government [the Supreme Court] opened the door for the rise of populist reaction, which fed on the argument that bureaucrats in Washington were riding roughshod over local traditions and prejudices.'[112] In Britain, too, statism was more distant from the people than ever. Even for the Labour government's core constituency of organised labour the experience of the government's attempt to use the law to constrain wage rises provoked demands for 'free collective bargaining', free of state regulation, that is. In office, the Keynesian state was a disappointment to the very people it purported to help, the poor and the working class. It is unlikely that many union activists voted for Margaret Thatcher, but she did win support from enough working class voters to carry the country. The success of neo-conservatism in winning some working class support provoked the left to theorise about the 'reactionary' character of the working class. British leftist Andrew Gamble characterised Thatcherism as an 'authoritarian populism', that appealed on an atavistic basis to the working class. Americans like Theodore Allen and David Roediger developed theories of the 'white skin privilege' over black Americans that US workers enjoyed.'[113] These analyses were ingenious, but ultimately they told us less about the working classes, than they did about these leftists' alienation from ordinary people, whom they wrote off as reactionary and racist.

With the left in retreat, the theory of the free market revolution was tested to the full throughout the 1980s. Margaret Thatcher said that now at last the government would be 'restoring people to independence and self-reliance'.[114] The free market theory that Thatcher and Reagan had been taught by Friedrich Hayek and Milton Friedman said that by dismantling the government regulations that held people back individual enterprise would be set free.[115] Rolling back the collectivist state would reveal a healthy individualism underneath. The dependency culture, in which people were artificially propped up with government money would be kicked away so that we could stand on our own feet. In the event things turned out differently.

The Thatcher and Reagan governments did not roll back the state. State expenditure continued to increase. In America federal outlays rose from $509.9 billion in 1980 to $979.9 billion in 1986. Federal debt soared from $914.3 billion to more than $2 trillion.[16] In Britain General Government Expenditure grew from £85,729 million in 1979 to £515,000 million in 1989.[17] Despite a policy of handing nationalised industry back to the private sector, the British government continued to subsidise. The privatisation of British Aerospace, for example, was sweetened with an injection of £110 million of government funds. The government sold Royal Ordnance to BAe at a cut-down price of £190 million, though its landholdings alone were worth £500 million. Later the government sold Rover to BAe at the knockdown price of £150 million with a cash injection of £547 million. On top of these disguised payments, the government paid straightforward subsidies, such as the £700 million start-up cash for the European Airbus project. It seemed that British industry was not about to be left to stand on its own two feet, but was instead sheltered in a dependency culture of government largesse.

More directly demoralising of course was the tremendous growth in the numbers of those unemployed and reduced to dependency upon the state. Closing down heavy industries like steel, shipbuilding and coal did not lead to the growth of jobs in more competitive industries in sufficient numbers to absorb those thrown out of work. Unemployment rose to three million before falling back to over one million. Even then the political pressure the government faced over unemployment led it to disguise the numbers by changing the way that they are calculated. Eventually 60 changes were made in the way that the government calculated the unemployment figures. The fall in unemployment at the end of the eighties did not represent a reduction in those reduced to dependency upon welfare by the downsizing of British industry. Social security spending rose by 31.8 per cent between 1979 and 1989.[18] Far from setting individuals free from the welfare state, the Conservative government oversaw the greatest expansion in the numbers of those dependent upon state welfare payments in the postwar period.

Not just government expenditure increased, but also government regulation increased. Ironically it was the policy of privatisation that led to the growth of government regulation of industry. Government bodies were created to regulate the newly privatised industries, like Ofwat, for the water industry, Oftel, for British Telecom and Ofgas.[119] Furthermore, those industries that are nationalised have been subject to much greater regulation. Economists Thompson and Kay wrote that 'detailed scrutiny by government of day-to-day activities of nationalised industries has tended to increase rather than diminish, and their autonomy in investment and planning decisions, and in industrial relations, has been steadily eroded'.[120] The Conservative government introduced ever more institutions for regulating the public sector, such as the Office of Standards in Education, created special ombudsmen and Citizens' Charters to regulate public services. Whatever the policy was, it was not one of letting the market decide. Indeed, one of its effects was a far greater web of regulation of private economic activity. This growing regulatory framework was a consequence of the government's own anxiety that it was losing control of privatised industries.

Beyond their own core constituency, the free market revolutionaries were strangely reluctant to extend much in the way of personal choice. In fact the Thatcher government, despite promising slimmed-down government, massively increased the burgeoning 'quangocracy' of 'quasi-autonomous non-governmental organisations'. These quangos were a prime target of the Conservatives when they were out of office, but strangely they multiplied ever more rapidly after 1979. A survey in 1985 showed that 22 important quangos employed more than 44 000 people and spent somewhere in the region of £1,777 million. Appointees to these were often Tory Party members, company directors and landowners.[121] By 1994 there were discovered to be 5521 quangos responsible for spending £48.1 billion a year, or one sixth of the total government expenditure.¹²² There are now almost three times as many people serving on quangos as there are elected representatives in local and county councils and the House of Commons: 70,000 as against 25,600. Between them quangos spend more than local authorities.¹²³ There is nothing inevitable about the growth of the quangocracy, as is sometimes claimed.¹²⁴ The reason that the quangocracy grew under Margaret Thatcher is quite straightforward. She extended the role of appointed bureaucracy in direct proportion to the reduced influence of elected government. 'We had grappled with the problem of bringing more efficiency into local government', wrote Margaret Thatcher of her first term of office, 'but the Left's redoubts in the great cities still went unchallenged'.¹²⁵ 'Thatcher decided not to revive city government but drastically to reduce its scope and power', wrote *Times* columnist Simon Jenkins.¹²⁶ The quangos, especially the Urban Development Corporations and Enterprise Zones were expanded as an alternative route for cash to the regions, by-passing local government, and, creating a new layer of bureaucracy. In Jenkins' account the tendency of the government to mistrust any governmental institution outside of its control led to a 'Tory Nationalisation of Britain', with direct rule over schools and other formerly independent institutions. The free market philosophy was always uncomfortable with elected government, which it artificially opposed to individual liberty. But even individual rights were to suffer under the Conservatives.

'Trade union reform' was the policy that most clearly found the government of freedom at odds with civil liberties. Trade unions as independent organisations of workers were an anathema to the right. As collective organisations, trade unions were at odds with the narrowly individual interpretation of rights. The rights of trade unionists to freely associate were largely unintelligible to Conservatives. 'The cloth-capped colonels of the TUC use their industrial power for political ends', the future employment secretary Norman Tebbit fulminated against strikers at the Grunwick and George Ward plants. 'If Ward and Grunwick are destroyed by the red fascists, then, as in 1938, we will have to ask, whose turn is it next?'[127] This was the point at which the right's bias towards business could not be contained by the neutral language of liberty. In the collective action of trade unionists, the Conservatives could only see intimidation on the one hand, and the undue influence of monopoly power on the other. Trade union reform took away the rights of trade unionists to demonstrate outside workplaces and imposed restrictive limits on strike action. In place of the rights of workers to organise, the Conservatives raised a dubious 'right to manage' – a late addition to the canon of democratic rights. On her first term, Thatcher reflected that 'we had cut back union power; but still almost 50 per cent of the workforce in employment was unionised'.[128] The campaign against collectivism became a war against the 'Enemy Within' as striking trade unionists were subjected to violent and oppressive policing.[129] Ironically it was this most oppressive element of the Conservative Party strategy of the 1980s that was the most successful. The organised labour movement was already at an impasse, and the government's successive victories over it gave the appearance of forward movement. But in fact it was this dismantling of the collective organisations of the working class that did most to destroy individual initiative and enterprise amongst British people.

The collective organisations like trades unions, and the affiliated parties of the left, Labour and Communist, never recovered from the sustained attacks of the neo-Conservative right. On the free market theory of Hayek and Friedman the defeat of these collectivist institutions ought to have led to a flowering of individualism. But that judgement was based on a misunderstanding. The right counterposed collective organisation and individualism in too mechanical a way. In fact collective organisations are not a barrier to individual self-assertiveness. On the contrary, most people use such collective bodies as an arena in which their personal ambitions are advanced. Far from being opposites, collective and individual are mutually supporting.

The British Conservative Party, establishing a model for the political right at the end of the eighties, became a victim of its own success. The slogan 'There is no alternative' summed up Thatcherism, and was shortened to the acronym TINA, by critics of the government.[130] In the first place TINA seemed like a statement of adamantine purpose, like Martin Luther posting his proclamation at the Diet of Wurms, saying 'here I stand, I can do no other'. But in time, as the Tory government lost direction under Thatcher's successor John Major, it sounded more like a counsel of despair. The palpable truth underlying the slogan was that the political alternative, the state socialism of the Labour Party was mortally wounded, and incapable of providing a challenge to the government. Moreover, the oppositional movement of organised labour in the trade union movement was by 1985 effectively finished as a social force. The government had committed itself to more than taking its turn in office. It had committed itself to finishing off socialism, and it succeeded. The Tories' single biggest achievement was the transformation of the Labour Party into a second conservative party. Without any principled opposition in parliament, the House of Commons debate declined into personalised name-calling, and was no more than a rubber stamp for government policies.

For two centuries the character of English life had been shaped by the contest of left and right in the Commons. More than that, the wider society, too, had been shaped by the contested character of politics. The nineteenth century contest between Tory and Liberal parties had motivated both to build up their electoral bases. Electoral reforms in 1832 and 1870 enlarged the electorate, and forced the political parties to woo the public. To contemporary eyes, this electioneering appears somehow corrupt, and indeed it often was. But it also put a tremendous premium upon the importance of ordinary people. The political elite was forced to articulate its goals in terms that a greater mass of ordinary people could not only understand, but also identify with. The contest of Liberal and Tory parties also engendered the creation of the third great political party, the Labour Party. Frustrated at the choice 'between plutocrats and aristocrats', working people put up their own candidates. The growth of the Labour Party moderated those ambitions to suit the bourgeois respectability of the House of Commons. At its height in the 1950s the system of political contestation between left and right embraced nearly three million members of the Conservative Party, a million Labour party members and more than 10 million associated trade unionists, and even a quarter of a million members of the British Communist Party, not to mention an electorate of more than 30 million. The greater or lesser involvement of all of these people depended upon the political contestation of the major parties at the tip of the pyramid, to make sense of the loyalties of the serried ranks below. But if there was no alternative, then these loyalties too, were redundant.

With no great hope represented by the Labour Party, the party membership withered. Trade unions too had proved inadequate in the defence of the members' jobs and livelihoods, and atrophied. The wave of political apathy spread from the left to the right. The first to experience the disillusionment was the far left, but before long the mainstream of the Labour Party and the trade unions, too were demoralised by their apparent lack of purpose – a lack underscored by successive failures at the polls. After the Labour Party lost its way, the peculiar effect upon the Conservative Party was that it too tended to decline. The Conservative Party is Britain's oldest mass membership party. It was created as a counterweight to the electoral mass of trade unionists affiliated to Labour. But it depended on provoking middle class resentment against the rise of organised labour. Without the old enemy to motivate the grass roots, the Tories' middle class supporters became more attuned to the way that the government had failed to defend their livelihoods and left the party in droves. The average age of the Conservative Party in 1992 was 62 and there was little sign of new recruits. Membership fell into a precipitate decline, falling from 756,000 in 1995 to 350,000 in 1998. Not just the Conservative Party declined, but all of those other institutions that were loosely associated to it lost members. The impact of the assault on mass political organisations had an intriguing, knock-on effect on other kinds of collective activity. Membership of mainstream Christian churches fell by more than a million from eight million in 1975 to 6,720,000 in 1992. The National Federation of Women's Institutes, The Mothers Union and the National Union of Townswomen's Guilds have all seen their memberships fall by nearly half since 1971. The Red Cross Society, the British Legion, the RSPCA, the Guides and the Boy Scouts all suffered major falls in membership over the same period. In fact, almost all major public institutions from the National Farmers Union to the Green Party were affected by the decline in popular participation.[31]

Not just organisations of political representation, or of wage bargaining, but cultural and voluntary organisations were affected by the disaggregation of mass politics. On the Thatcherite model, this transformation ought to have led to the liberation of healthy individuals, freed from the constraints of collectivist corporatism. Of course, the opposite turned out to be the case. Without the mediating links of club, party, union or Women's Institute, individuals were more isolated from society. A solipsistic individuation of society, in which people retreated from public life and social engagement, was created, rather than a healthy, self-assertive individualism.

Fear and loathing

Social atomisation gave rise to moral panics. Isolated from ordinary social solidarities, individuals were susceptible to inflated fears and anxieties. The clearest expression of this tendency is the intense fear of crime. The British Crime Survey inaugurated by the Home Office in 1982 surveyed people's perception that they had been the victims of crime. The BCS reported a 14 per cent crime rise between 1987 and 1992 and burglaries alone rose by 88 per cent between 1982 and 1992.[32] However, the BCS figures continually outstripped the police's own record of notified offences by five times. The personal perception of victimisation was far higher than the numbers of offences that people felt it to be worth acting upon. Defenders of the BCS insist that the survey is a more accurate measure, but in great part it was measuring the increase in the public perception of crime, and of the fear of crime.[33] A Metropolitan Police report noted in 1986 that 'fear of crime' is 'a pervasive problem'.[34] The *British Social Attitudes* survey also noted a rise in the fear of crime that was not necessarily related to crime rates: 'whichever measure of fear is used, strong links exist between fear and social attitudes which have little to do with crime'.[35] Anxiety about social breakdown was projected as a heightened perception of criminality. Much of the anxiety centred upon the perceived danger of violent offences, as well as the more prosaic experience of burglaries. Some anxieties were concentrated upon muggings and drug-related offences that were associated in the public imagination with immigrant communities. These were particularly prone to exaggeration and panic. In some cases there were panics over crimes that simply did not exist. In 1990 Nottingham Social Services were investigating cases of ritual Satanic child abuse, under the influence of their Deputy Director of Social Services Andy Croall, who turned out to be a Christian fundamentalist 'on a mission from God'.[36] Press reports of Satanic child abuse reached such a fever pitch that the government commissioned a report by Professor Jean La Fontaine, 'The Extent and Nature of Organised and Ritual Abuse', in 1992, that concluded there was no such thing. Nonetheless, the willingness of people to believe that child abuse was pervasive increased without any apparent proof. In this case the perception of crime and social breakdown was a psychosocial response to increased isolation and individuation. Willing to think the worst of one's neighbours was a consequence of not knowing them.

The perception of growing criminality and breakdown arose out of the disaggregation of collective organisations and more informal forms of social solidarity. With fewer shared experiences and common ambitions, isolation increased, giving rise to fear. Isolation was the fruit of the neo-conservative campaign against collective organisation. In their struggle to regain control over society after the militant challenge to the status quo in the seventies, the establishment was dismantling the very social institutions on which their authority rested. All of the transmission belts between government and people were being removed. The remaining popular sentiment that the government could relate to was fear – the very fear that its own policies had engendered. Thoughout their period in office the Conservative government promoted a repressive policy under the rubric of law and order.

The law-and-order campaigns were the evil twin of the Conservatives' appeal to freedom. Alongside the rhetoric of liberalisation, the real change that was taking place in legislation was the incremental move towards a police state. The important pieces of legislation were: the 1981 British Nationality Act that removed the rights of British passport holders overseas to come to Britain;[137] the new powers under the Prevention of Terrorism Acts (1984 and 1989) that greatly extended the rights of the police to detain without trial those they deemed terrorist suspects;[138] the Public Order Act of 1986 gave police new powers to ban marches, demonstrations and pickets, as well as being able to dictate the time, duration and size of them;[139] the Criminal Justice and Public Order Act 1994 removes the suspect's centuries-old right to silence, creates new police powers of 'stop and search' and limits the disclosure of police evidence to defence lawyers. As well as these major new powers, the Conservative government legislated against so many trivial aspects of life from 'dangerous dogs' to the banning of 'video nasties', that the book of British statutes has grown more since 1979 than at any other time in its history.

On top of the new legal prohibitions, the government introduced other kinds of regulation. Around 30 000 Neighbourhood Watch schemes have been set up by the police, where civilians are encouraged to spy on their neighbours. Breaking a major taboo about collecting evidence on citizens, the government pioneered the introduction of more than one million Close Circuit Television Cameras operated by local authorities, private companies and the police – fulfilling George Orwell's prophecy of Britain in his dystopia *Nineteen Eighty-Four*. The number of social workers increased by two thirds between 1976 and 1986.[40] The 1989 Children Act formalised the Social Services 'At Risk' register, which contained the details of 43 200 children in 1990, grew to 45 300 in 1991, vastly increasing the number of families under surveillance and at risk of being broken up.[41] And, in a remarkable innovation in wealth redistribution, the government's Child Support Agency imposed orders on fathers to maintain their abandoned children according to a means test. Whatever the social justification, this was an unprecedented intervention by the state into the organisation of personal finances and relationships. The CSA was often opposed, not only by fathers, but single mothers, too, because it reinforced their financial dependency on often hostile ex-partners, and was undertaken to remove welfare benefits. Of her growing intervention into personal lives, Margaret Thatcher wrote that 'only the most myopic libertarian would regard' the family 'as outside the purview of the state'.[42]

Political assessments of the Thatcher era are confused in taking at face value the Conservative claim to have been the party that stressed individual liberty. The very opposite proved to be the case. Starting from an instinctive hostility to the collective organisations of the working class, the Conservatives showed an instinctive hostility to civil liberties across the board. Most pointedly the Conservative governments fed on the politics of fear that they themselves had created. If there had been a decisive opposition to these attacks on liberty, the price would not have been so enduring. But the opposition party, Labour, retreated in the face of Thatcher's law-and-order campaign. Part of Labour's recovery as a vehicle for the elite was its wholesale adoption of the Conservatives' law-and-order policies, even to the point that Labour attacked Thatcher's legacy for its excessive concentration on individual liberty! This adaptation to the Thatcher agenda tended to obscure the intense restrictions upon individual freedom that occurred in the 1980s. The opposition's failure to expose the Tories' attack on freedom had a peculiar impact upon assessments of the period. It ensured that the legend of the selfish individualism of the eighties was entrenched, and the accepted reaction to the eventual failure of the Conservative government was to restrict individual rights even further. The absence of an alternative could not be made more forcibly.

The end of the Cold War

In Britain the Thatcher government's defeat of 'the enemy within' signalled the exhaustion of the neo-conservative programme. In the United States Ronald Reagan also faced down internal foes. The arrests of the air traffic controllers' union leaders and the sacking of the entire membership of the union early in the presidency signalled a willingness to get tough with trade unionists. The Democratic Party was humiliated in much the same way as the Labour Party was in Britain, reduced to its big city redoubts, and facing the prospect of unelectability. However, in the United States there was no socialism to roll back, only 'big government'. Organised labour in the US was not so heavily entrenched into public life as in Britain. In America, the defining political purpose of the neo-conservative revolution was the enemy without, the Soviet Union, which the president dubbed 'the Evil Empire' in March 1983.

The Cold War of the 1950s was a defining moment for American domestic politics and for the system of international relations established after the Second World War. Its meaning is heavily overlaid with ideology – the central plank of the Cold War was an ideological struggle against Communism – which obscures the real relations taking place beneath the rhetoric. The ostensible reason for the Cold War was the Soviet threat.[41] In the 1950s the appearance of a Soviet menace was underlined by the extension of Soviet power first into Eastern Europe and later into China and South-East Asia. But even in the immediate postwar period, the Soviet threat was used ideologically as the justification for a new Pax Americana in Europe and the world. The permanent siting of US troops in Europe was justified by the presence of the Soviets.'⁴⁴ In the Far East, too, the extension of America's military reach was justified by the alleged Soviet expansionism.'⁴⁵ Over and above the creation of a system for regulating international relations, the Cold War also transformed America's domestic politics. The Cold War at home was the mechanism that integrated a commitment to the 'free market' with the emergency powers of the state to regulate 'UnAmericanism'. The Cold War made it possible to suppress dissident opinion in the name of defending the Free World. J Edgar Hoover's Federal Bureau of Investigations kept an eye on the civil rights movement, trade unions and even the Kennedy presidency, all in the name of fighting subversion.

The Cold War was also the basis on which the new right began to reorient itself. While much of the right had been isolationist on foreign policy in the years before the Second World War, the Cold War laid the basis for the integration of conservatism with an interventionist foreign policy. The conservatives around William F Buckley's *National Review* in the fifties developed a policy of 'fusionism' between conservative and free market themes, described by the future Reagan adviser Donald Devine as 'utilising libertarian means in a conservative society for traditional ends'.'⁴⁶ The integration of these two wings of the right, the conservative and the libertarian free marketeers was reconciled in the rhetoric of the Cold War. Right winger Frank Meyer described the conservative position in the following way: 'In their devotion to Western civilisation and their unashamed and un-selfconscious patriotism, conservatives see Communism as an armed and messianic threat to the very existence of Western civilisation and the United States...they see the defense of the West and the United States as the overriding imperative of foreign policy.''⁴⁷ Barry Goldwater's campaign for the presidency in 1964 was massively defeated but became a rallying point for many of the conservatives who would become the core of Ronald Reagan's republican administration. Goldwater's aggressive Cold War rhetoric was seen as losing him the election, once Lyndon Johnson's campaign team had Goldwater 'branded a bomb-dropper'.[48] Goldwater's tub-thumping was defeated by its own underlying theme: fear. It was not until 1980 that Ronald Reagan managed to re-package the Cold War rhetoric into a more successful theme.

The important thing about the Second Cold War inaugurated by Ronald Reagan in 1983 was just how different it was from the first.[49] The principle difference was in the relative strength of the Soviet Union. In 1949 the Soviet Union was at the apex of its influence. But by the 1970s the inertial limits on Soviet economic growth had become apparent throughout the Soviet bloc. By comparison to Stalin, Brezhnev was a paper tiger. The real drive behind the Second Cold War was the politicisation of relations among world powers. Radical critic Andre Gunder Frank protested that 'the Soviet threat is an instrument to blackmail Western Europe into accepting US economic conditions and to prevent Europe from liberating itself economically from the USA'.[50] It is true that the Cold War bent Europe to American interests. For our purposes, though, it is the domestic Cold War that is important. Battling the 'evil Empire' invested Reagan's government with a higher purpose at a time when harsh economic measures were kicking in. At that time Reagan had to ask Americans to 'stay the course'.[51] But with some deficit spending on armaments the US economy picked up. Americans saw the projection of patriotism and their own personal well being as linked. More than anything else it was the Republican Party's monopolisation of patriotism that ensured its ascendance in the eighties.

The militarisation of international relations in the eighties brought Soviet Premier Gorbachev to the negotiating table. The burden of a new round of military spending was devastating an already paralysed Soviet economy. Colin Powell recalled the negotiations: 'The more he talked and the more we listened, the more we understood. I recall one meeting were I can best describe my unspoken reaction as "my God, he is serious!"."[52] It seemed that Ronald Reagan had won the Cold War. (Though British diplomat and MP George Walden observed that 'the belief that Thatcher and Reagan brought down communism, like the walls of Jericho, with a joint blast of their trumpets is another fond illusion. The truth is that the system was rotting from the inside'.)[53] The Soviet Union was withdrawing from Eastern Europe. Strangely, the triumphalism that ought to have ensued was muted. Reagan's successor George Bush, with the support of Margaret Thatcher, warned that German unification must be gradual.[54] James Schlesinger, former secretary of defence and CIA director, wrote that 'with the end of the Cold War...the United States has lost the magnetic north for calibrating its foreign policy'.[55]

Even more dramatic was the loss of purpose domestically. As the man on whose watch the collapse of the Soviet bloc took place George Bush ought to have enjoyed the reflected glory. But the effect was quite the reverse. The coherence of the government's support depended upon the politics of the Cold War to give it a higher, integrating purpose. Without a moral mission, Republican Party politics reduced to the Oliver Stone parody in the film *Wall Street*, where downsizing corporate raider Gordon Gekko announces 'Greed is good'. The party's core supporters, mid-Westerners, white suburbanites, 'Reagan Democrats' were increasingly alienated from a government that under George Bush just looked like old money Wasp America. In the 1991 contest for the Republican nomination the old conservative coalition was falling apart. Reagan speechwriter Pat Buchanan revitalised American isolationism in a pointed criticism of a president who seemed to spend more time abroad than in the USA, under the slogan 'Come home America'. Kevin Phillips, who, as a strategist for Richard Nixon had developed the strategy of winning Middle America for the Republican Party, wrote a bestseller attacking the Reagan record. *The Politics of Rich and Poor* which countered the claim that wealth would 'trickle-down' to the poorest if the rich were left to create wealth.[56]

The collapse of the Republican coalition found many conservatives ruing the day that they had signed up for the free market measures of the libertarians. Such an emphasis upon individual rights, they feared, was insufficiently authoritarian to instil any sense of moral duty to the state. Conservatives striving to emphasise tradition were stymied by the fact that America's mainstream tradition was, well, liberal. It was based upon the rights of man proposed by John Locke and the founding fathers. They struggled to invent a version of American tradition that was not premised upon a Lockean individual rights approach, but provided a more solid argument for social cohesion. JGA Pocock's *Machiavellian Moment* sketched an alternative American history that derived its civic republicanism from renaissance Italy.[57] Conservative scholar Allan Bloom had an unlikely bestseller with his jeremiad *The Closing of the American Mind*, which bemoaned the loss of discipline consequent upon a rights-culture and dumbed-down rock music. A student of the conservative scholar Leo Strauss, Bloom influenced the Education Secretary William Bennet who wrote his own version of the defence of Western civilisation, *To Reclaim a Legacy*.[58] Bloom also taught Francis Fukuyama, a foreign policy specialist at the Rand Corporation, who had a surprise hit with his article on the end of the Cold War, 'The End of History'.[59] Fukuyama's initial article in *The National Interest* was an optimistic, even triumphalistic account of the victory of the free world. But by the time he came to write up the book, Fukuyama had become more downbeat about the end of history, wondering whether citizens untested by the challenge of conflict might not prove to be 'the last men'. Fukuyama became positively hostile to the liberties that you might have thought the Cold War was defending: 'The rights revolution is simply a legal expression of a broader cultural problem which is a kind of celebration of individualism which in my view amounts to a certain kind of selfishness. What the rights revolution has done is to give a moral language with which to legitimate what is ultimately a kind of selfish and asocial behaviour. I think it's something that's been happening in the United States for 30 or 40 years now.'¹⁶⁰

Of course the idea that the United States had been at the centre of a great flourishing of civil liberties in the 1980s is as hard to sustain as it would be of Britain. The extraordinary measures undertaken in the so-called war against drugs have seen the prison population increase to one and a half million – three time greater than it was in 1980.¹⁶¹ In Los Angeles and New York oppressive police regimes were created in the name of breaking gangs and zero tolerance of street crime.¹⁶² But in Fukuyama's eyes, social breakdown makes talk of individual liberty redundant: 'You have a class of people that are extremely violent...it's not just middle-class fantasies of sedition', he warns darkly. 'I mean, these are poor people that have to live in basically a kind of state of nature situation, with gunfire in their hallways every night.'¹⁶³

In 1980 Ronald Reagan had mobilised an anti-government sentiment represented by the Californian Proposition 13 Tax Revolt. Reagan's was a strange balancing act. He appealed to a sentiment that wanted the state out of people's lives. But in the defence of the free world the state became a more powerful force than ever. Cold War patriotism squared the circle. To defend a free society, special measures were required. But once the Cold War was over, the justification for a strong state was exhausted. Having mobilised popular hostility to big government, and big spending government, the Republican Party found that that sentiment played against them. At its most cranky, elements of the old Republican majority came to see their own government as an instrument of foreign occupation, the 'Zionist Occupation Government', and even took up arms against the state, at Waco and Oklahoma. But more prosaically, frustrated Americans simply got mad with the politicians, whether by supporting Ross Perot's Reform Party, or simply withdrawing interest.

In America the disintegration of the Republican coalition followed the end of the Cold war. On a grand scale the end of the Cold War concentrated the same loss of direction that in Britain was summarised in the desperate proposition 'There is no alternative'. In the nineties the conservative political project degenerated and collapsed. The Conservative and Republican governments' claims to advance the rights of the individual were ideological claims that masked an unremitting hostility to individual freedom as much as to collective organisation. Unfortunately, those ideological claims were never tested. The right was never challenged on the political plane. It just collapsed from the internal incoherence and exhaustion of its programme. The regimes that followed after were the inheritors of the demobilised and increasingly regulated societies that were created in the 1980s. In fact, in so far as Reaganism and Thatcherism were criticised, their claims to stand for individual liberty were accepted, and the perverse conclusion drawn that society needed a greater degree of regulation.

To re-establish control over society in the face of the working class militancy of the seventies, the elite had undertaken a sustained assault on collective institutions. To their surprise, these very collective institutions were not only the rallying point of their enemies, but also the basis of their own social order. The disaggregation of society led to a crisis of legitimacy from which the establishment never truly recovered. At the same time, the dissolution of those collectivities was debilitating for the development of independent subjectivity. The experience of working-class defeat was not enervating, but demoralising. Rolling back state-socialism did not reveal healthy individuals, but exposed people to an atomised and uncertain existence, in which the possibilities of confident self-assertion were minimal.

Chapter Ten

THE THIRD WAY: A PROCESS WITHOUT A SUBJECT

'We are at the end of an epoch, the epoch of opposed systems.'
Achille Ochetto, 25 November 1988

In an interview published in 1970 Georg Lukacs talked of 'twin crises', meaning the crisis of the left, deformed by the influence of Stalinist methods and policies on the one hand, and of the capitalist system, beset by militant opposition.[64] Twenty years later the 'twin crises' had resolved themselves. The left had first become paralysed in the face of the onslaught of the neo-conservatives and then imploded with the collapse of the Soviet Union. However, the immediate perception that the twin crises would be resolved to the exclusive benefit of the right proved deceptive. No sooner had the triumph over communism been announced than the right itself was seen to have lost its way. First George Bush was voted out, then, the British Conservative Party lost office for the first time in 18 years and soon after Helmut Kohl in Germany and the Gaullists in France were out, too. In a series of speeches in 1993, British foreign secretary Douglas Hurd speculated that the right had lost its way politically because it lacked an opponent against which it could galvanise its forces. It was as if the political right were the victors in a tug of war contest, who celebrate the collapse of the opposite team by all falling over themselves. In 1994, in his book *Beyond Left and Right*, professor Anthony Giddens, soon to become an adviser to the British prime minister wrote, 'the terms right and left no longer have the meaning they once did, and each political perspective is in its own way exhausted'.[165] Perry Anderson suggested that left and right are mutually defining, as one declines, so must the other.[166]

The declining importance of the left/right distinction came about principally because of the success that the right had in the 1980s in dismantling the left. Under the weight of successive defeats, parties of the left began to adopt more and more of the programme of the right. Retiring education minister John Patten wrote that 'The opposition has paid the Tory Party the ultimate compliment of erecting its total political platform on our foundations'.[167] Certainly it seemed by around 1990 that the left would simply disappear as a distinctive force in politics, and indeed in many ways it did. Patten though did not fully understand that the ramifications of the transformation of politics wrought by the neo-conservative administration he had been a part of would not affect just the opposition party, but also his own. The parties of the right discovered that they were only one pole of the opposition between left and right. With the organised left demobilised, there was an opportunity for a new political outlook to transcend the framework of left and right altogether.

In America and later in Britain the initiative came from within the dilapidated shells of the old parties of the left. Forced by years of defeat to think hard about how to frame their politics, these parties underwent a transformation, revising their old political programmes to suit new circumstances. In America, it was the Democratic Leadership Council, on the right of the party that became the springboard for the creation of the 'New Democrats', and eventually Bill Clinton's successful leadership campaign. In Britain, successive Labour leaders struggled to jettison the party's distinctive welfarist policies, but it was only with the emergence of a party leader largely unconnected with the old labour movement, Tony Blair, that the party could reinvent itself as New Labour. The revisionist project of the New Democrats and later of New Labour was summarised by President Clinton's political adviser, Dick Morris:

> 'Triangulate, create a third position, not just in between the old positions of the two parties, but above them as well. Identify a new course that accommodates the needs the Republicans address but do it in a way that is uniquely yours.'[168]

Triangulation is a good explanation of the way that the New Democrats tried to transcend the deadlock that kept them out of power in the eighties. What the New Democrats were grappling with was the apparently intractable barrier to success presented by a political debate that had been won by the right. As long as the Democrats meant 'tax and spend', 'soft on crime' and 'weak on defence', then the Republicans would always win. Clinton strategist James Carville understood the intrinsic weakness of the Democratic Party campaigns of the eighties saying 'Whenever I hear a campaign talk about its need to reenergise its base, that's a campaign that is going down the toilet'.[169] The way to win was to redefine the issues, not be forced onto the same ground, struggling to turn out your core supporters, he was saying. British Labour Party leader Tony Blair, under pressure to explain his 'Big Idea', extended the strategy into a fully blown political philosophy, the Third Way.

The Third Way has become the topic of international seminars of left-wing political party leaderships as far afield as South Africa and Brazil. Prime minister Blair has written his own pamphlet explaining what it means, and Anthony Giddens has written two books on the Third Way. But despite this extensive exercise in clarification, most people are still confused about what the Third Way means. Linguistics expert Norman Fairclough analysed the new language of New Labour – as the party now calls itself. Fairclough says that one judgement of the Third Way is that 'it allows the party to have it both ways'.[170] Amongst the Clinton White House staff, too, the charge was made that '"triangulation" was just a fancy word for betrayal'.[171] Doubtless there are many traditional Labour and Democrat party supporters for whom the Third Way means just that. But in itself, that is an assessment that misses the key points about the emergence of the Third Way. Even Fairclough, generally an insightful analyst sees the Third Way as first and foremost an adaptation to the right, missing out the extent to which the terms of the debate have changed. Concentrating upon the deliberate crafting of triangulated politics, the critics underplay the extent to which the Third Way is an idea that mirrors social realities.

In the introduction to his pamphlet prime minister Blair describes the Third Way: 'My vision for the 21st century is of a popular politics reconciling themes which in the past have wrongly been regarded as antagonistic – patriotism and internationalism; rights and responsibilities; the promotion of enterprise and the attack on poverty and discrimination.'

The binary counterpositions put together here are, mostly, those of left and right. Norman Fairclough accurately describes the way that 'the phrase "not only…but also" pervades the political discourse of New Labour in a variety of expressions (eg, "enterprise yet also fairness", enterprise as well as fairness", "enterprise with fairness", "enterprise and fairness"), which both draws attention to assumed incompatibilities and denies them'.[172] According to Fairclough, 'New Labour seeks to reconcile in language what cannot be reconciled in reality'.[73] Here, though, Fairclough's judgement is flawed. His belief that aspirations of social justice and a global market cannot be reconciled rests on a sense of those oppositions as they are given content by social movements. At a time when organised labour was pressing for the restraint of the international market in the interests of 'social justice', then it was not possible to combine the two rhetorically in the way that Blair does. The mutual exclusivity of the terms is not just a matter of logic, but of the wider social contestation of these two visions of justice, the justice of the market versus social justice. The phrase 'social justice' bears a meaning for Fairclough that is derived from the socialist movement, who made it the banner of the demand for welfare. But that movement has ebbed, and the meaning of social justice has been redefined along with the rest of New Labour's politics, not least in the several hundred page report of the Social Justice Commission.[74]

The ease with which Tony Blair maps out a Third Way, a way that appears to be contradictory to those of us schooled in the old political terminology, arises out of the real world minimisation of the social conflicts around left and right. So, in 1994, Gordon Brown, later to become Blair's Chancellor, could say that 'markets and the state should no longer be seen as counterposed. The old battle of public and private has been superseded'.[75] Brown's assessment contains the essential component of the latterly elaborated Third Way. Where the left organised around the state and the right around the market, the contrast between those two aspects of social organisation was politicised. With the massed ranks of the labour movement lobbying for the extension of the welfare state and the middle classes railing against taxation, then the differences seemed to be absolute. But as the hostilities ebbed, the intellectual room for a Third Way opened up. 'The change we must make isn't liberal or conservative', said governor Bill Clinton announcing his candidature: 'It's both and it's different'.[76] 'People out here don't care about the idle rhetoric of "left" and "right" and "liberal" and "conservative" and all the other words that have made our politics a substitute for action', Clinton continued. For one generation this kind of language appears to be just waffle, but for another emerging generation for which the contrast of left and right was a bore, the Third Way – insofar as they are interested at all – seems like common sense.

The advantage of Fairclough's linguistic analysis is that it shows up some of the less conscious parts of the Third Way creed that are betrayed in the choice of words. Looking at one passage of a government document, Fairclough points out that 'grammatically, these are passive sentences without agents'.[77] When you construct a sentence passively, you leave out the subject, or agent. As Fairclough notes, New Labour spokesmen often leave the subject out. His other example is the way that the speechwriters talk about change, as if it was a noun, something, instead of a verb, an action that is done to something. The effect is to take the subject out of the process of change: 'The absence of responsible agents further contributes to constructing change as inevitable.'[78]

Curiously, the New Labour politicians have reproduced Louis Althusser's conception of change as a 'process without a subject'. This is more than just a trick of the language. New Labour is predisposed to see itself as the product of a process without a subject, for the reason that it is the outcome of the defeat of working class subjectivity. The 'heroic' vision of socialism as overcoming the enemy of the capitalists is precisely the one that New Labour has abolished. In the old narrative 'coward's flinch and traitors sneer' but 'we'll keep the red flag flying here'.[79] Revising the party programme cast the modernisers as the cowards and traitors, departing from the path of righteousness. Not surprisingly, they were reluctant to face that kind of judgement. Where the old party motivation drew upon the forward march of the movement, New Labour saw itself as the inevitable response to changed circumstances. In some senses that was right. They were the beneficiaries of a process that they never initiated. The defeat of the organised labour movement on the part of the right was one precondition for New Labour, the exhaustion of the right in fulfilling that programme was another. Blair inherited a political scene made by Margaret Thatcher's government. Of course, New Labour could hardly acknowledge that it was the talentless heir of a government it despised. But the intimation that they were not the authors of their own destiny could not help but be reflected in their thinking. Over and over again, the passive construction in New Labour's language betrays the underlying sense of the Third Way as a process without a subject. The development of two of the core themes of the Third Way, globalisation and modernisation tell us as much.

Globalisation

> 'The growth of increasingly global markets and global culture. Not only does money cross frontiers within the Western economies faster than ever before, but competition exists on an international scale that has never been known. Products are increasingly made by extended networks threaded across the globe rather than within single organisations.' Tony Blair, *The Third Way*

The extensive economic jargon surrounding 'globalisation' is mostly impressionistic, and generally deceptive. The world market in consumer goods dates back to the sixteenth century. Finance was internationalised in the latter part of the nineteenth century, when Europe's surplus capital was invested first in American industry, and then in extractive industries in the colonies. In the postwar period, the 1970s saw the most enduring upturn in capital export – and that generally for negative reasons, where investors preferred speculation to productive investment. Most importantly, though, nation-states remain the basic political form in which capital operates. The much-heralded transnational corporation generally has a head office in one country and investments in others. That companies seek to avoid paying tax by misrepresenting their international structures is one of the more banal insights of globalisation theory.[180] The impression that we live in a world that is more hectic and internationalised, arises from an altogether different source.

The elevated status of the world market in globalisation theory has nothing to do with the intrinsic strengths or weaknesses of that market. It reflects instead the restricted ambition towards national economic policy. With the perception that the market is uncontrollable, the wish is father to the thought. As Keynesian national strategies have fallen out of favour, the belief that national economic policy is unattainable has hardened into a dogma. The underlying meaning of the theory of globalisation is that national economic policy is self-defeating and undesirable. A paper prepared by the Prime Minister's policy unity suggests that 'institutions are lagging behind' globalisation. 'Public sector institutions, domestic and international, are not yet equipped to deal with globalisation.' 'In most countries', the policy wonks moan, 'economic policy is still focused on domestic developments and regulation'.[181] Anthony Giddens explains the point in this way: 'Globalisation "pulls away" from the nation-state in the sense that some powers nations used to possess, including those that underlay Keynesian economic management, have been weakened.' He means that high tax regimes can be avoided by companies that invest internationally, so as to undermine attempts at managing investment in a national economic strategy.

It is of course true that companies seek to maximise their profits. But did we really need globalisation theory to tell us that? The conclusion that national economic strategy is impossible is the cause of the perception of an all-powerful global market, not the other way around. Once the political transformation of the Labour Party was undertaken, the arguments against national economic strategy were marshalled in inner party debate, and the conviction that reform would be undermined by the global market hardened. Until then only the Conservative Party had sought to argue against state spending on the basis of competitiveness on the international market. New Labour took the Conservatives' argument for national competitiveness, renamed it 'globalisation' (to appeal to an internationalist sentiment), and thereby adopted the case against the old policy of nationalisation of industry. What was an act of triangulation on the part of the policy writers became the subordination of policy before a process without a subject – globalisation.

Modernisation/change

The promise of 'Modernisation' is a key part of the Third Way. It is a word whose meaning is suitably broad. Within the Labour Party the supporters of Tony Blair called themselves 'modernisers', indicating their strategy to change the party. Shedding policies that marked the party as a socialist party on the European model of social democracy was called modernisation. The loosely pacifistic appeal of unilateral nuclear disarmament was dumped by the modernisers, along with a commitment to repeal the Conservative government's anti-union laws. The set-piece act of modernisation, though, was the revision of the party constitution's 'Clause IV', the commitment to bring private industry into national ownership.[182]

Modernisation in the party has been something of a moveable feast. When Labour was suffering in the polls because of a perception that it was in thrall to the trade unions that funded it, 'modernisation' entailed the removal of the block vote cast by union leaders in policy-making and the selection of electoral candidates, to be replaced by 'One Member, One Vote' (OMOV). But subsequently, the modernising leadership of the party has avoided OMOV in the choice of candidates for the Welsh Assembly leader and the London Mayoral candidate. Instead they used the old union block vote to try to stop candidates that did not fit the party's profile. Clearly 'modernisation' means different things at different times.

At the 1999 party conference, Tony Blair developed the theme that the country would have to be modernised just as the party had been. The Prime Minister identified the 'forces of conservatism' on both left and right which were holding back the modernisation of Britain. Blair said the twenty-first century would not be about 'the battle between capitalism and socialism' but 'between the forces of progress and the forces of conservatism'. Expanding, he said 'The Third Way is not a new way between progressive and conservative politics – it is progressive politics distinguishing itself from conservatism of Left or Right.' Demotically, the Prime Minister collapsed the differences between his left-wing opponents and those reactionaries outside who resisted the modernisation programme. Addressed to wider society, that programme includes a great deal of government reform, with the creation of national assemblies in Wales, Scotland and Northern Ireland, reform of the House of Lords, as well as reform of such established institutions as the British Medical Association, the police and the judiciary. The first thing to note is that modernisation is a process that rises above political contestation of left and right. Once the debate has been recast as one between progress and the forces of conservatism it is no longer a matter of choice. Nobody would willingly choose to be part of the past. The correctness of the modernisation programme is put beyond debate. The political choice has been taken out of the equation, and opponents thrown onto the defensive. Reposed as modernisation, the party's political programme assumes an inexorable purpose that transcends simple political huckstering.

There are precedents for the 'modernisation' discourse, some expected and some surprising. In the original strategy of modernising the Labour Party, the modernisers won the debate once they had recast the debate. They threw off the character of the party's moderate wing and became modernisers. In so doing, they re-cast the left, like Transport and General Workers Union secretary Ron Todd, as 'dinosaurs'. There is, though, a more distant precedent for the strategy of depoliticising a conflict by re-casting it as a struggle between modernisers and reactionaries. In the 1960s Harold Wilson secured the leadership of the Labour Party with the support of the left, by opposing a proposal to dump Clause IV by the party revisionists of his own day. However, Wilson overcame his own identification as a left-wing leader by rewriting Labour's policies in terms of modernising Britain. Wilson promised that under Labour 'Britain is going to be reforged in the white heat' of the technological revolution.[183] 'We are living in the jet age, but we are governed by an Edwardian establishment mentality', warned Wilson, 'in science and industry, we are content to remain a nation of gentlemen in a world of players'.[184] In this way Labour's appeal in the 1960s rose above the partisan debate connecting directly with youthfulness and progress. The critique of the establishment as an historical throwback was incorporated into radical thinking.

Perry Anderson along with Tom Nairn developed the idea that the United Kingdom was an arrested development, 'the product of the defeat of the English Republic in the seventeenth century'.[185] Echoing Wilson, Anderson argues that 'the archaic mainframe of the Ukanian [sic] state itself' explains why 'the civil service and financial system of the United Kingdom have been so unsuited for economic reconstruction'.[186] This became known as the 'Nairn-Anderson' thesis, that Britain had never successfully completed the democratic revolution characteristic of other liberal republics, and was held back by a parasitic class of aristocrats.[187] An unlikely convert to the Nairn-Anderson thesis was the Tory prime minister Margaret Thatcher. Like Nairn and Anderson, Thatcher painted her opponents as mired in a feudal past, holding the country back with their restrictive practices. Using the language of liberalisation, Thatcher's programme of modernisation began with an attack on the Tory Party Grandees and their corporatist policies, before taking on the Trade Union barons who were holding the country back. Later Conservative administrations took on other vested interests like the educational establishment, the civil service and the medical profession. From FA Hayek, Thatcher borrowed the argument that socialism was a 'road to serfdom'. Repackaged as modernisation, the policies of the right were presented as simply commonsensical and the only way to reverse British decline.

Labour's modernisation programme shares some of the features of those that went before it. It is a programme that rises above political differences. Modernisation assumes a relentless force that can be slowed or accelerated, but not reversed. Casting opponents on the left as well as the right as 'forces of conservatism', Blair puts his own strategy beyond debate.

The essence of the Third Way, as reflected in its language, is the depoliticisation of government, its transformation into a technical matter of administration. Norman Fairclough describes it thus: 'the government's policies are sold as merely technical solutions to what is assumed to be an agreed problem.'[188] Taking the politics out of social administration leads to a change in the idiom of policy, but more important is what that change reflects: the removal of government from any realistic political contestation. When trade and industry minister Stephen Byers was challenged in the House of Commons about his failure to act to prevent the closure of the Rover car plant, he responded angrily that his opposite number should stop 'playing party politics'.[189] A one-time radical, Byers would have relished the opportunity to campaign against job losses, but as a minister in Blair's government, the threat to thousands of jobs is wholly outside the political process.

Depoliticisation

The contestation of positions between left and right has clarified political choices since 1789. Since the 1980s, though, the struggle between left and right has become dulled, so that the differences mean less. The effect upon political discourse is marked, and the ascendance of the Third Way is only an extreme expression of it. Increasingly government has been discussed in curiously bloodless, denatured language. Winning political slogans of the last 15 years have included President Mitterand's re-election slogan 'Avec le President', the Australian Labour Party's 'It's time',[190] Bill Clinton's 'New Covenant' in 1992, and his 'Bridge to the twenty-first century' in 1996 ('you were going there anyway', joked comic Rory Bremner). Those who fail to understand these cryptic phrases are enjoined to 'get with the programme', 'stay on message', or simply to stick with the (unspecified) 'project' or 'agenda'. All of these vacuous statements are attempts on the part of speechwriters to overcome the problem that George Bush Snr once dismissed, bemusedly, as 'the vision thing'. 'Where there is no vision, the people perish', his opponent in the 1992 American election Bill Clinton quoted the scripture.[91] Wise words. Unfortunately Clinton's own presidency suffered from precisely that fault. Clinton told his adviser George Stephanopoulos four months into the presidency that 'we don't have a core vision'.[92] By May of the following year Clinton was complaining 'I'm president. I need to be for something'.[93] Of course Clinton was in a better position than the modernising leader of the British Labour Party Neil Kinnock who, when tackled over a confused message in a newspaper interview, replied to his adviser, 'I don't know what I've said in there. It's all words to me. Words, just words'.[94]

The contestation of left and right was once more than just words. The opposite poles of public life create the framework within which political loyalties and social identities have been shaped. That framework, though, has collapsed. Geoff Mulgan writes:

> 'For this generation politics has become a dirty word. Our research finds that they are less likely to vote, to join a party or to be politically active....Similar trends of disconnection are apparent in other countries, where they have prompted a far more serious reaction than in the UK. Political disconnection also leads to social disconnection: just 49 per cent of 18-34 year olds say they would be willing to sacrifice some individual freedom in the public interest compared to 61.5 per cent of 35-54 year olds. Over a third of 18-34 year olds take a pride in being outside of the system.'[95]

It might seem as if the end of left and right is a distant matter of elite politics. But with the democratisation of public life in the twentieth century, political choices have had a far greater span than the clubbish atmosphere of the major constituent assemblies. The greater part of society was enjoined to understand its own ambitions through the prism of the politics of left and right in the mass democracies of the twentieth century. As the political machines have been demobilised, the participation of the greater mass of people in the questions that shape their lives has been cut off. The first effect is that the compass of political debate has narrowed. The mass of working people have a far less direct relation to political life than they did when they were indirectly affiliated to European Social Democratic Parties through unions, or mobilised as ethnic blocs in the Democratic and Republican parties. 'The bosses and their machines were rooted in soil that has long since disappeared', writes George Will about Tammany Hall in New York and Mayor Daley's Chicago.[196] Robert Reich reports the analysis of the US census Bureau on who voted in November 1994's elections: 'The rich are voting more. People on the bottom half of the economic ladder are voting less. And those at the very bottom are hardly voting at all. Sixty per cent of Americans with family incomes over $50 000 said they voted last November, up from 59 per cent in 1990. By contrast, just 27 per cent of those with incomes under $15,000 said they voted, down from 34 per cent in 1990.'[197]

The effect is to set the mass of working people back to a state something like the eighteenth century, when politics was largely the preserve of the upper classes. For the working classes public life looks more like the modern equivalent of following court gossip and watching public hangings. Our relationship to power is largely tangential and voyeuristic, as we follow the celebrity powerful; conversely, we are presented with the spectacle of public hearings over bizarre murders and other crimes. High-profile public events in recent times have an archaic feel – the funeral of Princess Diana, whose public support mirrors that of the Prince Regent's snubbed bride Princess Caroline; the humiliations of public figures accused of sleaze, like Helmut Kohl or even the US president – are all reminiscent of eighteenth-century politics, if not of court life. The masses of ordinary people are represented in public life either as consumers or as the objects of middle-class charity. The difference between then and now is that the masses in the eighteenth century had never been a part of public life, and its institutions were not made for them. By contrast the contraction of the public sphere at the close of the twentieth century comes after a hundred years of widening public participation. All institutions and representative bodies that were designed assuming that level of participation have tended to fall in on themselves, lacking that popular content.

Constituent assemblies have lost authority, as the political process that they once housed has become sclerotic. 'The adversarial culture is hostile to good government', said Callum Macdonald, Member of Parliament for the Western Isles of Scotland. 'The public is offended by the tribal rituals of Parliament. They might enjoy it as daytime soap, but they do not respect it as policy-making.'[98] In Washington similar reactions against the gridlocked Congress can be heard, as too with many of the European constituent assemblies. As the political process becomes less responsive to popular pressure, the need for consultation diminishes and political leaders have streamlined their administrations by bypassing the party in favour of political advisers. 'The first cabinet meeting in months', recorded US Labor Secretary Robert Reich on 18 February 1994, adding 'it suddenly strikes me that there's absolutely no reason for him – or any other president – to meet with the entire cabinet'.[99] Similarly at Number Ten Downing Street 'Thursday cabinet meetings' are 'rarely longer than 30 to 40 minutes', one civil servant told historian Peter Hennessy, and 'though there was a formal agenda, the Prime Minister did not stick to it'.[200] The reason that cabinet government has declined in importance is that policy is increasingly generated not through debate between elected representatives, but by pointy-headed policy wonks appointed to dream up new initiatives. George Stephanopoulos describes the scene at Camp David in January 1993 when 'about 40 of us – the Clintons, the Gores, the cabinet, and several consultants and staff – were going to spend a day "setting goals" and "getting to know each other"':

> 'The aluminum easels sealed it. A pair of them stood at the front of the room, holding giant pads of blank white paper just waiting to be filled with our objectives, goals and feelings. Two sensible-looking middle aged ladies with Romper Room smiles on their faces and jumbo Magic Markers in their hands completed the picture. They were "facilitators", brought in by the vice-president to help us bond. This weekend was Gore's baby, an amalgam of management science and New Age sentiment'.[201]

Robert Reich took a note of the objectives decided by this 'team-building, brainstorming, hierarchy-flattening, group-groping management-by-discussion': 'Restore jobs, reform welfare, reform health care, restore the environment, improve educational standards, give people new skills, reform social security, reform campaign finance, reinvent government, convert from defence to civilian production, complete the NAFTA and GATT treaties, reduce the deficit, bring jobs to poor cities and rural areas, create a national service corps for youth, achieve peace in the Middle East.'[202] Real political processes are problematic and demanding, but as Reich notes, 'making lists in the woods is exhilarating'. In Britain, too, the numbers of policy wonks doubled from 38 before the 1997 election to 74 in 1999, just as their budget increased from £2 million to £3.9 million.[203] The creation of the Social Exclusion Unit, a Policy Unit, a Forward Planning Unit and an enhanced Press Office operating out of Number Ten raised questions about a politicisation of the civil service.

Different branches of government have increased in authority as the legislative branch has declined. The American Supreme Court and the European Court of Human Rights have adjudicated on matters that once would have been the preserve of the constituent assemblies, such as abortion rights, freedom of information and civil liberties. Increasingly the political representatives themselves have come under the scrutiny of quasi-judicial bodies, such as the Parliamentary Commissioner for Standards in the UK and the Special Investigator into the Office of the President in the USA. Though such moves to subordinate elected representatives to judicial control have meshed with a mood of distrust for politicians, the danger of creating a power higher than the democratic will of the people has largely passed unnoticed. In the absence of a plausible mechanism of democratic accountability, the role of 'auditors' and 'ombudsmen' overseeing government has increased in the United Kingdom under both the Blair administration and the previous Major government.[204]

The impact of depoliticisation upon policy-making itself is the most poignant demonstration of the loss of the decision-making process. In Britain and America in the early nineties the intermediate administrations of the right, John Major's and George Bush's, were predisposed to minimise the pressure for new political initiatives. By contrast the incoming Democrat and Labour governments of Bill Clinton and Tony Blair are marked by a degree of legislative incontinence.

Bill Clinton's programme Putting People First compensated for its lack of an overarching vision by a flurry of specific policy proposals. The sheer number of these gave the impression of a sense of political purpose. As proposals though, they are curiously precise, from proposals to 'develop new natural gas applications' to creating a 'child care network'.[205] In the place of a unifying theme, Clinton made specific promises, in what we might call 'micro-politics' as opposed to macropolitics. Similarly, New Labour, though wary of making uncosted promises, gave a specific list of five pledges to the electorate: reduce classroom sizes, reduce National Health Service waiting lists, jobs for young people, fast-track punishment, and tough rules on government borrowing and spending. Campaign manager Phillip Gould recalled 'They worked because they connected immediately to people's lives;

because they were relatively small, which gave them credibility; because they were costed and because they were an explicit contract between the voter and Tony Blair.'²⁰⁶ These pledges are not recognisably part of any political ideology, but just practical measures. As specific promises on the part of the Labour leader that 'connect immediately' they are designed to bypass the complex process of politics, with its parties, representatives, mandates and programmes. Instead a direct promise from the leader over the heads of all political intermediation.

The trend towards practical proposals set the scene for the legislative activism of the Clinton and Blair governments. On top of that, and despite the lack of a coherent vision, there was a remarkable sense of responsibility and expectation amongst the incoming policy teams. Clinton aide George Stephanopoulos recalls the sentiment of the incoming team: 'Now we had work to do, lots of it. Sure, it wouldn't be easy, but we'd waited a long time – the country had waited a long time – for our chance to change America, and we were going to do it all in 100 days, just like FDR.'²⁰⁷

New Labour, too, was preoccupied with the sense of historical destiny, in being the first Labour government in nearly 20 years. Ambitious plans were undertaken. New Labour instituted referenda for constituent assemblies in Scotland and Wales, and for an assembly in Northern Ireland, mandated to create a power-sharing executive between Catholics and Protestants. Reform of the House of Lords was undertaken. The Bank of England was made independent of government and the European Convention on Human Rights was made law. The Clinton Administration was struck with a similar impetus to change. Reform strategies were set out from reforming healthcare to reinventing government, no less. Policy-making activism was characteristic of both administrations. This activism arose out of a sense of the need to make historic changes. But ultimately the very ambitious nature of the drafting of reforms and constitutional amendments was indicative of the political vacuum at the heart of these Third Way administrations.

Stephanopoulos' comparison between Franklin Roosevelt's New Deal administration and Bill Clinton's New Covenant is instructive. Roosevelt changed the face of America with government reconstruction of industry and agriculture. The New Deal, though, did not spring like Pallas-Athene from the heads of speech writers. It was based upon the upswell of urban immigrants, under-represented in the political process, who had rehearsed their irruption onto the political stage with Al Smith's 1928 Democratic campaign. The New Deal was violently tested in the political clashes of the time, as an ideology of ameliorating the effects of the Hoover slump. The New Deal had a cadre of southern and Eastern European politicos and lawyers, as well as a mobilisation of the CIO, and ethnic blocs in the Northern cities. Roosevelt himself, as has often been noted, was in many ways in the rear of the reform movement that he led. By contrast the Clinton administration was based on a small handful of professional political advisers. It related most directly to the liberal intelligentsia, but its electoral base was passive. The policies were drafted not by elected politicians or even officials, but party advisers, aping the grandeur of reform.

New Republic editor Andrew Sullivan describes the outcome of Hillary Clinton's health reform 'as the national government disgorged 268 boxes of papers from her taskforce on healthcare': 'They wanted a total overhaul of the system according to the dictates of what a small group of experts deemed rational. They wrote memos and they wrote memos about memos. They had meetings and meetings about meetings. They generated "cluster-groups" and "toll-gates", dozens of working groups and countless position papers. They felt powerful and philosophical.'[208]

In the event Congress simply smothered the reforms with so many qualifications that it collapsed. Hillary Clinton tended to blame the insurance companies for their advertising scare campaign. But for all their self-serving motives, the insurance companies at least knew that to win they had to galvanise a following amongst the public. The

Healthcare taskforce was drafting plans but in truth it was not making policies. Policies are not the product simply of good ideas, but the outcome of a political struggle. As such real policies secure adherents and supporters. Amongst each other the taskforce thought their ideas were good, but the tragedy was that they had so few friends to advise them that they were off the wall.

The problems of the Hillary Clinton health taskforce are characteristic of the incontinent legislative programmes of the Third Way governments. In fact these are neither policies nor even legislation in any real sense. To become laws in the proper sense of the word, their legitimacy would arise from the will of the public, however represented. But in the first place much of the public has abandoned the electoral process. Furthermore, the legislative democratic process has been bypassed in Westminster, as the government announces its reforms first at the television studios and only later at the Houses of Parliament. Proposals that arise out of no discernible political process are not policies at all, but simply statements of intent on the part of the administration, largely untested by any real public debate.

Characteristic of these non-policies were the Labour government's constitutional changes. Before the election in 1997, opposition to the Conservative government often took on a regionalist focus. Scots protested their unhappiness at being slighted by the largely southern-based Conservatives by calling for independence. A wise observer would have understood that regionalism was only the form of the protest, but that its content was anti-Tory. However, the intellectuals around New Labour theorised this trend as a substantial demand for regional representation. Referenda for the Scottish and Welsh assemblies proved to be damp squibs. In Wales less than a quarter of those qualified voted for the new assembly, and in Scotland, the majority for the assembly was compromised by a poor turnout. Labour even instituted a London Mayor on just a 30 per cent turnout. Before it knew what was going on the Labour government was juggling with fractious and thinly supported regional assemblies. Northern Ireland's veteran politicians bluntly faced down the prime minister's demand for a deal, while the Welsh scuppered the Labour Party's candidate for first secretary Alun Michael and the Scots elected all kinds of rebels and Scottish nationalists. The Blair administration had failed to understand that a constitutional change premised upon a minority of the vote is not any kind of constitution. The attitude of the Scots to their assembly is one of indifference. In fact it is not in any practical sense the constituent assembly of the Scottish people, because it does not arise out of their own determination, but exists instead as a layer of local government. The unwillingness of the Scottish MPs in the House of Commons to stand for the new body says as much. All the government succeeding in doing was to create a talking shop for every self-important malcontent in the regions, unrestrained by any popular expectation that might have given rise to a more adult debate.

In the Clinton administration the First Lady understood the basic difficulty, though she was unable to escape it herself. Bob Woodward describes the scene:

> '"Six months into it", she said in bewilderment, "the American people know nothing of our plans?" All of them were there to help the president communicate his policies and philosophy, and yet the country knew nothing. [Adviser James] Carville could see she was at the end of her rope. Her husband, she said, had become the "mechanic-in-chief", tinkering instead of being the president with a moral voice, a vision.'[209]

The politics of the Third Way do indeed transcend the opposition of left and right. But in doing so they transcend also the activist formation of the political will, that Rousseau called the general will. The realm of subjectivity that is politics is shrunken and diminished.

The politics of fear

In terms of social vision the parties of the Third Way have failed to connect with the public, but that does not mean that there is no connection. If they have failed to appeal to a collective vision of the future, both the Democrats and New Labour have managed to relate to a more atomised electorate, by playing upon its fears. New Labour's campaign adviser Phillip Gould developed the following analysis while working for the European Socialist candidates, in a document called 'Fighting the Fear Factor' in February 1994.

'Modern electorates are insecure, uncertain and anxious. They "are more afraid of things getting worse than they are hopeful of things getting better". This mood of anxiety about the future allowed the right to use the tactics of fear, enabling them to dominate politics for the 1980s and early 1990s. To defend against attacks rooted in fear, progressive parties had to respond instantly when challenged...'[210] Gould is coy about the fear factor, insisting that only the right would use the politics of fear. But the logic of his argument is that, to win, Labour must create its own fear factor, one that will work for them.

For Labour he proposed 'connecting with the populist instincts of voters through policies that are tough on crime' and were for 'social cohesion versus social disintegration'.[211] Here Gould is developing the argument that will re-pose the question of fear so that it works for New Labour, in a way that it worked against old Labour. Instead of challenging the fears cranked up by the Tories, Gould proposed that New Labour should connect with them, by talking tough on crime. But as his own analysis shows fear is not so much a product of crime as one of social disaggregation. By posing the problem as one of 'social cohesion versus social disintegration' New Labour was beginning to pin the blame for crime on the Tories.

Gould distilled his political message looking back over the 1997 election: 'fear will not diminish as a factor in modern politics. Modern societies and modern economies mean more change, less continuity, and, inevitably, insecurity and anxiety will increase. Electorates will be less certain, more anxious, more fearful about the future.' What is fascinating about this account is that Gould plainly understands that fear is not directly a product of crime, but of social change.

Actually he tends to naturalise social change, as if it were simply a fact of life. It would be more accurate to say that the loss of continuity and increase in anxiety is a consequence of the collapse of the political process, and the resultant social atomisation. Gould goes on to explain how the 'fear factor' has worked for the right:

> 'In general over the last two decades, the right has campaigned on a basis of fear, the left on hope. Almost inevitably fear won. Fear is a more compelling emotion, more easily provoked. Reagan in 1984, Bush in 1988, Thatcher in 1987 and Major in 1992 all used fear shamelessly as a weapon: fear of taxation, fear of communism, fear of crime.'

Gould is reluctant to spell it out, but he is far too cynically honest a political adviser to miss the point. If the left is to win, then it must use the fear factor. And to do that it must repose the question of security so that it is more amenable to the left. Fears over taxation and extremism have to be neutralised, because they tend to lead to conservative conclusions. But the modernising left can create its own fear factor, as Gould all but acknowledges. 'Progressive parties have learned to...connect directly with the insecurities of working families', he writes. And they have to do so because 'in an increasingly fast-changing world, insecurity is likely to grow, and with it the basis for fear-based campaigning'.[212]

In the event, New Labour did create its own fear factor. In the first place it reformulated the crime panic so that it was more amenable to a centre-left interpretation. As shadow Home Secretary, Tony Blair raised the issue in his Labour Party conference speech in autumn 1992. 'When the Tories create a creed of acquisition and place it alongside a culture without opportunity, when communities disintegrate...then it takes not a degree in social science, merely a modicum of common sense to see that in the soil of alienation, crime will take root.'[213] Blair was managing a careful re-interpretation of the problem of crime. He knew that he could not be seen to be saying that the criminal is not responsible, and so he emphasised that there needed to be punishment. But he did seek to identify the individualism of the Tories' free market society with rising crime. As a point in fact, recorded crime rates in the early nineties were falling, but this is a speech designed to attach to fear of crime, not really to deal with crime itself.

In an interview for BBC Radio 4's *The World this Weekend*, on 10 January 1993, Blair finessed the point, with a now-famous soundbite: 'I think it's important that we are tough on crime and tough on the causes of crime too.'[214] In this way Blair identified himself with strong punishment but also identified the government with crime, saying that 'The Tories have given up on crime'.[215] In that way, Blair reconciled the irreconcilable.

The following month, Blair's opportunity to ram home the association came with a freak killing of a toddler James Bulger by two young boys, Jon Venables and Robert Thompson. It was a crime that shocked the nation, and connected to a sense of anxiety about the state of Britain. In a speech at Wellingborough on 19 February 1993, Blair said 'the news bulletins of the last week have been like hammer blows struck against the sleeping conscience of the country, urging us to wake up and take an unflinching look at what we see'. He talked of 'disintegration', of a 'moral chaos which engulfs us all' and 'the importance of the notion of community'. 'We cannot live in a moral vacuum', he said.[216] The meaning was clear enough. Blair was turning the fear factor on the Tories. The hapless Venables and Thompson, themselves just boys of 11 and scarcely able to understand what they had done, were made into scapegoats not just for the killing but also for the nation's collective angst. Realising that they had struck a chord by cranking up fear over crime, New Labour in power have done exactly that, targeting the weakest sections of society for punishment, be they 'squeegee merchants', beggars or gypsies seeking asylum from persecution.

Playing upon the fear factor, New Labour proposed itself as the resolution of the problem. At the Labour Party conference in autumn 1995, Blair reflected on his generation: 'We enjoy a thousand material advantages over any previous generation, and yet we suffer a depth of insecurity and spiritual doubt they never knew.'[217] The identification of the symptoms is accurate. But the disease is a product of the depoliticised and disaggregated society that New Labour was a part of. But rather than arguing for a political engagement, Blair simply reposed the problem of disaffection as an exhortation to community. In June 1996 Blair wrote a memo outlining his policy for Labour: 'a set of values based around a belief in society and community...a strong and cohesive society'.[218] This really is just the problem, alienation represented as the solution, community. The memo was rewritten as a document Change and National Renewal launched on 23 June, in which the blame for alienation is pinned on the right-wing opposition. The Conservatives failed, according to Blair, because 'they saw all forms of social cooperation as inherently wrong, fit not for reform but for demolition'. The result of this was 'to tear apart the social fabric and encourage a narrow view of self-interest which was both selfish and ultimately self-defeating'.[219]

Former Tory leader Margaret Thatcher was moved to protest that Tony Blair was exaggerating the problem of crime. 'Crime and violence are not the result of the great majority of people being free – they are the result of a small minority of wicked men and women abusing their freedom.'[220] Given Thatcher's reputation for playing on the fear of crime her comments are remarkable. But they do illustrate a profound difference in the mobilisation of the fear factor in British politics. The British Conservatives under Thatcher rendered the problem of criminality as one that was external to society, on its margins. In effect they criminalised black and immigrant communities.[221] But the criminalisation under the Tories was a strategy that emphasised the boundary between the minority, lawless communities and the majority lawful population, with the implication that the latter were English and white. Tory criminalisation was a vicious policy, but it never went as far as Blair did in holding the whole of society to be responsible for criminal behaviour. Even Margaret Thatcher balked at that.

Blair was drawing upon the communitarian critique of the selfish eighties. (According to Philip Gould, Blair adviser David 'Miliband and I drew heavily on Francis Fukuyama's *Trust*').[222] But as we have seen, the eighties were not really a time when individual rights were increased, or even one in which individuals pursued their own interests with vigour. There was an individuation in the sense of an atomisation and dismantling of social solidarities. But this hardly amounted to an outburst of selfishness. If anything it was a barrier to self-assertiveness, undermining the confidence of individuals to take control of their lives. Blair's appropriation of the fear factor from the right meant that he too would be advancing his own cause by playing upon anxiety. Rather than seeking to reverse the trend of individual uncertainty, New Labour's community politics aimed at accelerating the fear factor, by turning it to their own advantage.

The Third Way connected with the electorate, not on the basis of their collective purpose, but instead playing upon their individuation and the anxieties that arose from it. The voters were no longer represented in the polity as the collective subject of the democratic process. Instead they were recognised by the state as the isolated and persecuted victims of events beyond their control.

Therapolitics

In 1993, Hillary Clinton told a crowd in Austin Texas that 'all of us face a crisis of meaning' and that 'signs of alienation and despair and hopelessness' can be seen 'popping through the surface'. We need a system, she argued that 'gets rid of micromanagement, the regulation and the bureaucracy, and substitutes instead human caring, concern, and love'.[223] Basing the authority of the state upon love seems a little far-fetched, but it is a proposal with a purpose. Where the classical republican state derived its authority from the will of the people, that model of legitimation for state power is closed due to a restriction of the public sphere of political contestation. The ruling elite seeks new sources of legitimation, and a distinctive idiom for expressing them.

In the classical model of the republic, right is the determining principle. Government is exercised by virtue of the people's expression of their will. Where the people are no longer constituted through the political process as a people, but remain instead atomised individuals, the state cannot represent the general will. In such conditions modern elites relate to the electorate on a more personal basis, in which circumstance, the expression of love is more appropriate.

In his analysis of the *Therapeutic State*, James Nolan quotes this opinion piece from the *Washington Post* by William Schneider following the terrorist bomb attack upon government buildings in Oklahoma City in May 1995: 'It took a tragedy to remind Americans of what they like about Bill Clinton. Remember all those jokes about how Clinton "feels your pain"? Well, we were all feeling pain after the Oklahoma City bombing. The president expressed the country's pain eloquently at the memorial service. Clinton showed empathy and compassion – exactly what he does best.'[224] Offering therapy to the nation is the way that the politicians of the Third Way have squared the circle of relating to a fragmented electorate outside of the ordinary political process. Of course to some extent these politicians are simply drawing on the belief systems of their generation. George Stephanopolous recalls that the president invited 'New Age self-help gurus Tony Robbins and Marianne Williamson to a secret session up at Camp David'.[225] During a bout of illness, Hillary Clinton, Healthcare reformer sent Stephanopoulos 'a carton of homeopathic cures'.[226]

In March 1995 key New Labour figures such as Mo Mowlam and Patricia Hewitt met with leading psychotherapists and academics at a conference at the Tavistock Clinic, Britain's most prestigious psychoanalytic institution. The contributors self-consciously counterposed the values of 'attachment' and 'identity rooted in belonging' to the notorious Thatcherite dictum that 'there is no such thing as society'.[227] Developing a kind of 'therapolitics' New Labour was learning how to relate to the inchoate expression of public sentiment. Tony Blair got the opportunity to try out his therapolitics following the unexpected death of Diana, the Princess of Wales and estranged wife to Prince Charles, the heir to the British throne. Diana was herself adept at the art of appealing to popular emotions, playing the role of victim of the manipulative royal family. Her death sparked an atavistic public reaction of mass mourning more characteristic of rural catholic Europe than urban Britain. Forewarned by the psychologists of the importance of this public mourning, Blair seized the moment with a speech designed to appeal directly to the emotional state of his subjects. 'I feel like everyone today – utterly devastated', Blair said. 'Our thoughts and prayers are with Princess Diana's family – in particular her two sons, two boys, our hearts go out to them.'[228] Blair's elegy blurs the personal and the formal. He interrupts the formal description 'her two sons' with the personal 'two boys', as a side commentary, to remind us that these are ordinary people. He is like us, not motivated by political concerns, but sharing in our grief. Of course there is a massive illusion at work here, in that none of the mourning public knew Diana Spencer at all, and it is doubtful whether Mr Blair travelled much in her circle either. This is a spectacle for public consumption that assumes the form of private intimacy. That way the prime minister attaches himself to ostensibly personal motives in his audience. Blair's demotic ennobling of the 'People's Princess' is as schmaltzy as her own desire, expressed in Martin Bashir's BBC interview to be 'Queen of people's hearts'. The language of emotional ties – even fictitious ones – substitutes for the political process in connecting the government to the people.

American commentator Jedediah Purdy suggests that 'therapeutic politics is politics' capitulation to a culture withdrawn from politics'.[229] That is right, but it is also a contributory factor. The more that therapeutic modes of addressing the public substitute for the political process, the more reinforced the redefinition of the public becomes. No longer 'we, the people', the collective subject of the Republic, but rather the fragile and persecuted victims, owed a duty of care, but not respected as authors of their own destiny.

APATHY BECOMES A MATERIAL FORCE

Human subjectivity is diminished in theory, but as laid out in Part Two, it has also been diminished in fact. In the first place it is in the realm of politics that we can see the retreat from agency. For France, as the country that made the rights of man its own, the denial of these same rights to Algeria was a disaster not just for Algeria, but for French humanism, too. The struggle for liberation ought to have strengthened humanism, but instead the French left as much as the establishment refused to recognise the Algerians' claim. In the realm of philosophy, the Algerian struggle became a struggle against the idea of a common humanity. Already predisposed to elevate otherness over universalism, radicals like Sartre found their ideas vividly realised in the conflict. The involution of French humanism came home to Paris in the structuralist theory of the death of the subject. For theory, the appeal of a 'year zero' like uprooting French humanism was more than intellectual. It found its verification in the paralysis of the French Communist Party in the events of May 1968.

May 1968 marks the emergence of an intense debate over agency that looked very promising at first sight. The authority of the old political system collapsed, opening up a wide range of possibilities. But in the event the debate over agency was fuelled by a reaction against the collective subjectivity of the working class. The politics of the New Social Movements have proved to be a disappointment – more conservative than at first appeared, and more fragmented than its initial appeal supposed. In the end, the New Left was not an alternative to working class agency – just as the politics of identity that flowed from it proved to be a retreat from subjectivity, not an alternative to it. The New Social Movements recoiled from universalism into particularism because they were implicitly opposed to the era of mass politics.

In the 1980s the return of the right in Britain and America seemed to offer another alternative – the freedom of the market place and the subjectivity of the entrepreneurial individual. If only the bureaucratic constraints could be removed, argued the neoconservatives, a healthy individualism would emerge. But it did not work out like that. The Hayekian individualism championed by the right was not really a call for freedom. On the contrary, it was an ideological battering ram against the collective rights of organised labour. Instead of relaxing the regulations, the right clamped down on individuals as much as on collective organisations. Instead of lifting the culture of dependency, the right increased the numbers dependent on the state. The right's mistake was in thinking that individual subjectivity existed in inverse proportion to collective organisation. That was a false counter-position. In fact collective organisations like trade unions, clubs and churches are the mediating bodies within which individual subjectivity is engendered. The right's programme of rolling back collective organisation meant the defeat of individualism, not its advance. Its programme exhausted in the victory over the left, the right had nothing positive left to offer, and collapsed.

The politicians of the Third Way, in America and Britain, are the inheritors of the left's retreat from, and the right's destruction of, collective organisation. The end of left and right as political alternatives has narrowed the sphere of public debate. The political process is all but closed off, or at least embraces far fewer people than it once did. Human agency is diminished by the absence of political alternatives, lacking a realm in which it can be expressed. The perception that we are at the mercy of processes outside of our control, like globalisation, expresses that closure of political agency. Policy options, it is argued, are limited because of the global economy. Furthermore, political advance itself assumes the character of an inexorable process: modernisation. In the opposition between the forces of conservatism and those of modernisation, political debate is superfluous. Only managerial-technical decisions seem to remain. But even this model of apolitical regulation is marked by the loss of control, as ruling decisions lack the authority of a substantial political process. The governments of the Third Way have succeeded in relating to wider society not through representational politics, but through fear, and emotionalism. The people as collective subject of the political process is no longer. Instead we have a victim-support state.

The account of the diminished subjectivity laid out here might appear to be unduly political in its character. One might be tempted to ask what were the underlying social processes that preceded the political transformations that lead from May 1968, through the neoconservative reaction to the Third Way. Certainly there are no end of accounts of underlying social trends that give rise to today's fragmented and individuated society. My emphasis, however, is on politics. That is because politics is the realm of subject formation, to an extent that private life never could be.

It would be easy to illustrate the background social trends behind the political conflicts described here. One could point to the economic recession that prevented France from absorbing Algeria's surplus labour, providing the human material of the 'wretched of the Earth'.

One could point to the growing middle class in Europe and the expansion of higher education that preceded the events of May 1968, and the relative decline of manual labour as a proportion of the workforce. One could point to the recession of the early eighties to explain the return of the right, as representatives of the 'dictatorship of capital'. And if one paid too much attention to the sign on James Carville's War Room in Little Rock Arkansas, one might be persuaded that 'it's the economy, stupid' that explains Bill Clinton's election victory.

All of these elements are present in the conflicts described – but they are not decisive. Instead they provide the background to the final determination of the course of events. How one reacts to recession, or boom, what effect that changes in the social composition of a country will have – these are factors that are decided eventually in the realm of political disputation. Will recession provoke resistance or apathy? Will the new middle classes ally themselves to the labour movement or oppose it? These are questions that turn on the state of human subjectivity. Of course one can sketch a version of history in which subjectivity is unimportant, or proves to be simply an effect of underlying processes – but that is exactly what is being disputed here.

[Margin note: Responses to crises are determined politically]

On the contrary, the question of subjectivity demands that we take seriously the self-determining realm of political contestation. Furthermore, the diminution of subjectivity can become decisive. As Theodor Adorno said, inverting Marx, 'apathy too becomes a material force when it grips the masses'.

The question of society, though, is important – not so much as a determining factor, but because social organisation, too will be shaped by the diminishing of subjectivity. The whole of social organisation depends upon the way that human individuals constitute themselves as subjects – subjects of contracts, laws, relationships and so on. If human subjectivity fails so to constitute itself, then that will have a knock-on effect throughout society. Thomas Hobbes elaborated a theory of society starting from its basic building block, the individual, whom he imagined as an appetite-driven animal.

Hegel developed that approach in his *Philosophy of Right*, wherein he derives the whole political and legal superstructure from the initial postulate of the Will. Today one would have to reverse the process and start with the diminished subject, as the atom from which contemporary society is made.

Part Three

Chapter Eleven

THE RETREAT OF THE ELITE

The political retreat of the elite from its own subjectivity in the Third Way is matched by its defensiveness in the cultural and intellectual life of society.

Sixty years ago Jose Ortega y Gasset wrote *The Revolt of the Masses*, a book that charged the masses with selfishness, hubris and indifference to culture and society. In his last book the late Christopher Lasch, American history professor and social critic, reversed Ortega's accusation, turning the tables on the elites that he says have betrayed democracy through indifference to society and self-obsession. His description of the way that the new elite has cut itself off from the wider society which it vilifies as Middle America is precise. Lasch describes an elite that lives apart and thinks and behaves differently from the majority of Americans: 'The thinking classes are fatally removed from the physical side of life – hence their feeble attempt to compensate by embracing a strenuous regimen of gratuitous exercise.' Pouring scorn on Bill Clinton's labour secretary Robert Reich who coined the term 'symbolic analysts' to describe the new elite of advertisers, administrators and movie stars, Lasch charges that 'the thinking classes have seceded not just from the common world around them but from reality itself'. 'They live in a world of abstractions and images, a simulated world that consists of computerised models of reality – "hyperreality" ', which explains, 'their belief in the "social construction of reality" – the central dogma of postmodernist thought'.¹ Another American critic, Mike Davis, describes the geographical retreat of the elite in his book *City of Quartz*: 'new luxury developments outside the city limits have often become fortress cities, complete with encompassing walls, restricted entry points with guard posts, overlapping private and public police services, and even privatised roadways.'²

It is as if the elite had physically recoiled from society. But since elites only exist in relation to society, the retreat of the elite actually represents a retreat from the purpose of its own existence. The status of an elite as the leaders of the nation is called into question by its retreat from the nation.

Retreating socially and geographically from wider society, elites have also retreated from the productive economy. Financial journalist Doug Henwood describes the revolt of the shareholders: 'Not satisfied with one of the great long-term bull markets in US history, they continued to whine about "unlocking shareholder value" hidden in the crevices of corporate America.'³ The demand for greater and greater returns on investments is a consequence of the stalled investment plans of large corporations. As funds accumulate in their accounts, rather than being turned to new production, they become the targets of shareholder activism. William Greider describes how the American

Federal Reserve and the German Bundesbank in the early nineties imposed a regime of slow growth that redirected surpluses into financial speculation, so that rentiers made money by withdrawing funds from production. Adding to the high cost of capital funds was the growing insistence of investors on insurance against risk.[4] One might have thought that entrepreneurialism was all about risk, but the growing weight of the insurance industry, as well as the importance of hedges indicates that contemporary capitalists are more interested in protecting their assets than taking risks.

One predictable effect of slow growth rates, meaning limited demand for labour and high returns on investment, is the much-noted tendency to increasing social inequality. Andrew Hacker shows how between 1975 and 1995 the richest 20 per cent of American households saw their share of all incomes grow from 43.2 per cent to 48.7 per cent, while the poorest 20 per cent saw their share fall from 4.4 per cent to 3.7 per cent.[5] In Britain, income inequality increased in the first two years of the New Labour administration.[6]

The retreat from wider society and from productive investment is indicative of the failure of the elite to act as an elite. Unlike their Victorian forebears, the modern leaders are reluctant to give a lead. The starkest expression of that retreat from leadership is the emergence of an elite anti-capitalism. In April 2000, Mark Brown, heir to Britain's Vestey family fortune was accused of being a ringleader of the previous June's Carnival Against Capitalism. The 35 year-old former public schoolboy shares a £27 million trust fund from which he draws an estimated £44 000 a year.[7] In the same month Lord Peter Melchett stood trial for his attack on genetically modified crop trials. Eton-educated Melchett is the great grandson of Sir Alfred Mond, the industrialist who founded Imperial Chemicals Industries, and for whom my grandfather, John Patterson, worked as an electrician for most of his life. A former cabinet minister and now organic farmer in Norfolk, Lord Melchett headed the environmental group Greenpeace, and warns against the growth of profiteering agribusiness. The late financier Sir James Goldsmith dedicated himself to opposing the destructive effects of free trade and the global market towards the end of his life – a case that he put in his book *The Trap*.[8] Sir James had been known as a stock market predator, raiding companies and breaking them up for their assets – one of the buccaneers who broke the mores of London's 'respectable' stock exchange. Sir James' fortune financed many environmentalist groups, with a pointedly anti-business slant, including the magazine edited by his brother Edward Goldsmith, *The Ecologist*.

The emergence of the anti-capitalist capitalist is a morbid expression of the elite's retreat from its own subjective role as social vanguard. The very thing to which they owe their own success, the market and business now strikes them as problematic. Feelings of success have given way to those of guilt.

In 1991, Kevin Phillips recognised that there was a new mood, quite distinctive from the happy celebration of the free market in America under Ronald Reagan. 'Many conservatives', he wrote, 'including President George Bush himself, were becoming defensive about great wealth, wanton moneymaking and greed'.[9] According to Richard Brookhiser, 'as Wall Street withdrew from political responsibility, government drew away from Wall Street'. The effect was that 'industry was detached from civic-mindedness'.[10] International currency speculator George Soros also attacked the international financial system in his book *The Crisis of Global Capitalism: Open Society Endangered*. 'I was struck by the irresponsibility of foreign investors', he writes. 'I was fully aware that the robber capitalist system was unsound and unsustainable and I was quite vocal about it; nevertheless I allowed myself to be sucked into the Svyazinvest deal' in Russia.[11] Soros warns that 'truth be told, the connection between capitalism and democracy is tenuous at best....In capitalism it is private interests, in democracy it is the public interest'.[12] 'The trouble is that...exchange values may well come to replace intrinsic values', he adds.[13] And 'profit-maximising behaviour follows the demands of expediency and ignores the demands of morality'.[4] Amongst his many dubious financial deals, Soros' speculation against sterling in 1992 forced it out of the European Exchange Rate Mechanism. Like Sir James Goldsmith his distaste for the dirty business of making money is reconciled by his philanthropy, through the Soros Fund, which reputedly consumes half his income in educational and other charitable activities. The subjectivity of the capitalist entrepreneur is paralysed with guilty self-doubt.

There have always been sons and daughters of the ruling class who have reacted against their own. And there have always been businessmen, like George Peabody or Andrew Carnegie, who, dissatisfied with the dirty business of making money, have thrown themselves into good works. The contemporary mood of distaste for capitalism, though, is distinctive. Its context is a loss of nerve on the part of an elite that is no longer confident of its ability to lead society. In one sense it matters less that such authoritative figures disparage the capitalism that has sustained them, since there is no decisive opposition movement of the lower orders to take advantage of these self-doubts. But that is also part of the problem. Negotiating the challenge of the working class in the nineteenth and twentieth century gave a coherence and purpose to the ruling classes. Without that challenge, their relation to wider society is less clear, and a source of greater anxiety.

Increasingly, the values that were associated with free enterprise are seen as problematic. The success of environmentalism is that it has made industry synonymous with pollution. Heavy industry is forever 'dirty' in the minds of the public. In 1996 the British Schools Curriculum and Assessment Authority organised a National Forum on Values to decide on a consensus as regards what values should be taught. On the panel were representatives of the major religions and other moral leaders, and the SCAA refused to release the statement until all were agreed on its content. Interestingly the core values of the document were 'Society' and 'Environment'. However 'there are omissions', according to educationalist John Beck: 'there is nothing explicit on the values of enterprise, competition, wealth creation, self-sufficiency.'¹⁵ That is not surprising since the business class itself is so apologetic about such values.

The growing importance of the environmental critique of industrialism looks like a popular movement to restrain big business. But the surprising thing is just how much big business is involved in subsidising the environmentalists. Bemused, Ron Arnold of the American Enterprise Institute recorded some of the links between business and the environmentalist groups that were criticising them: World Wildlife Fund (annual budget $60,791,945 in 1993), major donors: Chevron, Exxon, Philip Morris, Mobil and Morgan Guaranty. Nature Conservancy (annual budget $278,497,634 in 1993, net assets $885,115,125 in 1993), main backers: Rockefeller Trust, Mellon Trust. National Wildlife Federation (annual budget $82,816,324 in 1994), contributors: Arco, Du Pont, Ciba Geigy. National Audubon Society (annual budget $40,081,591 in 1992), contributors include: Bank of Boston, The Ford Foundation, General Electric, HJ Heinz Co, Monsanto, New York Times, Proctor & Gamble. Environmental Defence Fund (annual budget, $17,392,230 in 1993), contributors include: Carnegie Corporation of New York, The Ford Foundation, the Fund for New Jersey, Richard King Mellon Foundation, Rockefeller Family Fund, Rockefeller Foundation.¹⁶ Corporate support for environmental campaigns indicates a degree of self-doubt on the part of big business. In the back of their minds is the nagging suspicion that they are part of the problem.

The American philosopher Sydney Hook described a comparable situation in 1941, which he characterised as 'a new failure of nerve in Western civilisation'. Hook outlined symptoms of that failure of nerve that seem strikingly similar to today's symptoms of the collapse of elite subjectivity, 'a flight from responsibility, both on the plane of action and on the plane of belief'. Hook outlined some of the characteristics of that failure of nerve: 'the recrudescence of beliefs in the original depravity of human nature; prophecies of doom for Western culture...dressed up as laws of social-dynamics; the frenzied search for a centre of values that transcends human interests; the mystical apotheosis of "the leader" and elites; contempt for all political organisations and social programmes...together with the belief that good will is sufficient to settle thorny problems of economic and social reconstruction; posturing about the cultivation of spiritual purity...a concern with mystery rather than problems, and the belief that myth and mysteries are modes of knowledge.'[7] It would not be difficult to find contemporary equivalents for each of these symptoms which Hook identified in that crisis period just before America entered the Second World War.

The retreat from leadership on the part of the elite is not a small matter. On the contrary, it calls into question all social relationships that are based upon authority and purpose. The degradation of subjectivity is a process that begins at the top, and runs down throughout society. As the saying goes, the fish rots from the head.

Two of the most important problems associated with the retreat of the elite arise in the intellectual spheres of cultural and scientific advance. Both high culture and science are in their nature elitist. There cannot be a high culture if all culture is equally valid. Similarly there cannot be scientific truth without the distinction between reason and opinion. The development of both arts and sciences becomes problematic if the elite acts in denial of its own role as elite. The subjective retreat of the elite has objective consequences for both high culture and science, effects that are expressed in the debates over 'dumbing down' in culture and the 'precautionary principle' in the sciences.

Dumbing down

'Dumbing down' are not words that media pundits and the culturati want to hear. 'The accusation is the final gasp of an upper-class male elite and their co-optees', spits columnist Madeleine Bunting.[18] Broadcaster Peter Bazalgette dismisses the charge as typical of a 'lazy, old, unthinking, miserable brigade' who 'hark back to a so-called golden age of broadcasting that never was'.[19] 'That's enough about "dumbing down"', says critic David Goodhart, damning those that make the charge: 'they're just nostalgic elitists.'[20] The anger of the commentators was provoked by a handful of books and public speeches by figures such as novelist VS Naipaul and artist David Hockney charging that the culture was being 'dumbed down'. Defending, British novelist-turned-broadcaster Melvin Bragg rubbished the 'foolish senior citizens of culture puff-puffing in'.[21]

Quantifications of acculturation are by no means straightforward, making the 'dumbing down' thesis difficult to prove, either way. Certainly what evidence there is seems to weigh against the dumbing down thesis, whether in rising literacy levels, educational qualifications or increased sales of books and broadsheet newspapers. On the other hand, many of these scales themselves are suspect, book sales representing falling production costs, or, more pointedly, as it is alleged, increasing educational qualifications themselves indicating falling standards. Polemics against the dumbing down thesis will point out that the charge of falling standards is a perennial one, that is most often associated with the pessimistic outlook of reactionaries who deplore the spread of democracy.

What is novel, though, is that the defence of the culture against the charge of dumbing down that is often made today is that excellence itself is a questionable virtue. So Melvin Bragg, announcing a new series of his South Bank Show argued that 'the old distinctions' – between 'high and low art' – 'are not only less and less relevant to what is actually going on, but increasingly the refuge of the merely snobbish – a champagne-and-canapé view of the arts'.[22] Bragg is doing more than resisting the accusation of dumbing down, he is insisting that it is irrelevant, because the distinction it is based upon, that between high and low art, is itself irrelevant. Coming from a respected populariser of high culture, this is most damning. It is a defence that works by abandoning the battlements altogether.

'Keep your high culture', Bragg is saying, 'those grapes are sour anyway'.

Reporting the results of its own survey of 18-24 year-olds, the *Guardian* newspaper conceded that they were 'measurably "dumber" than older age groups' not knowing who Winston Churchill was, or William Caxton or John Milton. But, the *Guardian* editorialised, maybe they do not need to know, in 'a world of information overload'. Commenting on the reported ascendancy of low culture over high, the *Guardian* leader writers took refuge in the same ploy as Melvin Bragg, pretending that the differences did not matter that much anyway: '"high" and "low" categories are, if not outmoded, then usefully antagonistic', they suggested. Again, the underlying response to the accusation of dumbing down is not to rebut the charge, but to suggest that maybe intelligence is overrated anyway.

Eliding the distinction between high and low culture is a manoeuvre that was first popularised by the French critic Roland Barthes. Barthes' short critical essays dwelled on elements of popular culture, like wrestling, striptease and soap-powder with a seriousness that had only previously been dedicated to high art.[4] Deploying the dispassionate mode of investigation of semiotics, Barthes saw no great distinction between popular and high culture, since both were codes to be cracked. Barthes' influence called into question those critics who put a special premium upon high art – and that included not just the traditionalists, but the avant-garde too. At a conference at the Institute of Contemporary Arts in 1985, Jean-François Lyotard announced that 'the big movement of avant-gardism is over'.[5] Like its close cousin in politics, vanguardism, avant-gardism implied a struggle against the traditional order. But what the avant-garde shared with the high culture it attacked was a desire to raise itself above the everyday. As the distinction between high and low culture was called into question, the avant-garde lost its special claims. Popular culture, not the avant-garde, provided the new icons of the intelligentsia.

The contemporary trend to 'dumb down' describes a failure of nerve on the part of the elite. It is their loss of belief in the merit of the cultural values entrusted to them. The manifestation of that loss of belief is expressed in the relation between the elite culture and the mass. Once elitism was concerned to protect its monopoly over the best that society had to offer. Today's elites by contrast have prostrated themselves before the judgement of the wider public – except that this public exists largely in the imagination of the elite itself. In fact the barbarians at the gate are the same fantastic projection of elite insecurity they always were, but this time the city fathers have opened up the gates and surrendered to the imaginary horde.[26]

Michael Jackson, then chief executive of Britain's left-field television broadcaster Channel 4, gave a speech in March 1999 at the Institute of Contemporary Arts in which he resisted the charge that 'culture generally, and television in particular, is dumbing down'. Jackson's argument against the view that television was dumbing down was made in terms of the humility of the broadcaster before his audience: 'none of us in television any longer have authority as of right. We have to earn it....The audience will no longer listen to us just because of who we are.' The contrast with BBC founder John Rieth's model of broadcasting's higher purpose, or even John Birt's vaunted 'mission to explain' is striking. Jackson is in awe of his audience, questioning whether he has anything to offer. In point of fact, the Channel 4 audience remains a minority audience, something of an advantage for the channel's advertising demographics. But Jackson pursued a mass audience that was largely of his own imagining: in fact it was a projection of his own insecurities.

Former British culture secretary Chris Smith rehearsed the argument that the distinction between 'High Culture' and 'low culture' is misleading at the best of times, and that 'George Benjamin and Noel Gallagher are both musicians of the first rank'.[27] 'Fuck me', said Oasis front man Gallagher, invited to Number 10, 'if the prime minister wants to see me I must be a right geezer!'.[28] In the event it was the Brit-Pop stars who tired of the prime minister first, sensing that they were being flattered, rather than listened to. The political elite's pursuit of the young pop stars said more about their own anxieties than it did about the virtues of Oasis.

What is destructive in cultural life is doubly so in education. Heather Macdonald describes a reluctance on the part of American teachers in higher education to ask too much of their pupils. 'Professors who exempt students from the very standards that governed them when they were in school feel compassionate, noble and powerful.' They are, according to Macdonald, 'willing to overlook spelling, punctuation, and grammatical errors in favour of a "holistic" approach to student writing'.[29] In her book *All Must Have Prizes*, British journalist Melanie Phillips described a similar reluctance on the part of British schoolteachers to teach. 'Since the child's feelings must be paramount, it follows that teachers are reluctant to correct the child's work and say that an answer is wrong.' 'There is ample evidence', she charges, 'that teachers have in great numbers swallowed wholesale the retreat from teaching and the redefinition of knowledge.'[30]

The evidence of falling standards, though, is by no means universally accepted, especially since it runs counter to the evidence that more and more people are staying on to study for higher education and exam pass rates are increasing. Michael Barber at London's Institute of Education confronted with evidence of falling standards of literacy alongside increasing pass rates at General Certificate of Secondary Education ties himself in knots: 'Thus, improbable as it may seem, it appears that we have rising standards and falling standards at the same time. While they are rising for the many, they are low for perhaps 40 per cent and perhaps falling for a significant minority of this group.'[31] The government has used the issue of standards to put pressure on teachers, through more examinations and greater regulation of course content and teaching methods. However, the idea that it is schoolteachers who are to be held responsible for the dumbing down of education misses out on the extent to which the entire culture is reluctant to demand high standards.

This is a problem that starts higher up the food chain than the school staff room.

In fact we find that throughout the elite there is a reluctance to assert the claims of its culture. The ideal of striving for excellence strikes an unpleasant note today, that it would not have done for a Victorian public. To excel, to rise above the norm, seems to be anti-democratic. That sentiment of embarrassment is characteristic of an elite that no longer believes in the superiority of its cultural achievements. All across the board we can see examples of the way that the elite has recoiled from the responsibility of moral and intellectual leadership. As an indication of the inner psychological state of the ruling class, such a failure of nerve is not something you can argue with. If the elite has lost faith in its own ability to lead, then that is their business. But the negative impact of this failure of nerve on wider society is profound and destructive.

Precautionary principle

In the sciences, as well as the arts, the elite has a problem of confidence in its own achievements. The advance of the environmental movement reverses an association between the capitalist class and industrial development that has stood for two centuries. At the Rio conference in 1992, development was systematically problematised as polluting the environment and threatening the atmosphere. Whatever the facts about global warming, the reversal of this identification of the elite and industry is remarkable. The ruling classes of Europe and America have, since the era of democratic revolutions in the late eighteenth century, stood on the solid foundation of industrial and scientific advance. In the nineteenth century, Karl Marx had characterised capitalism's moral imperative 'Accumulate, accumulate, that is Moses and the prophets!'. In Rio, the emphasis was upon development that was 'sustainable'.[12]

For the sciences in particular, this failure of nerve has a name, the precautionary principle. Timothy O'Riordan and James

Cameron explain the precautionary principle in the following way:

> 'As evidence of life-threatening environmental transformation accumulates, wealthy societies at least, and impoverished cultures if they are given the option, are becoming more risk averse. They expect better guarantees of zero discharges or strictly limited damage before allowing change to proceed. This is inevitably shifting the burden of proof onto those who propose to alter the status quo, rather than simply expect victims subsequently to seek compensation.'[33]

Phrased in this way the precautionary principle seems eminently reasonable. Who could object that those who threaten us with pollution ought to justify themselves? However, it is little noticed that the precautionary principle, in 'shifting the burden of proof', places upon the natural sciences a demand that they are incapable of meeting – absolute certainty.

The origins of the precautionary principle lie in Germany's Federal Republic, where it was first known as the *Vorsorgeprinzip*. In 1976 the government stated that 'Environmental policy is not fully accomplished by warding off imminent hazards and the elimination of damage which has occurred. Precautionary environmental policy requires furthermore that natural resources are protected and demands on them are made with care'.[34] The *Vorsorgeprinzip* was adopted internationally through the 1987 Ministerial Declaration of the Second Conference of the Protection of the North Sea at which the participants stated that they:

> 'accept the principle of safeguarding the marine ecosystem of the North Sea...this applies especially when there is reason to assume that certain damage or harmful effects on the living resources of the sea are likely to be caused by such substances, even where there is no scientific evidence to prove a causal link between emissions and effects ("the principle of precautionary action").'[35]

The precautionary principle was enshrined most emphatically in the 1992 Rio Declaration on Environment and Development. 'In order to protect the environment, the precautionary approach shall be widely applied by States according to their capabilities. Where there are threats of serious or irreversible damage, lack of full scientific certainty shall not be used as a reason for postponing' measures to prevent environmental degradation.[36]

Following the Rio summit, industry was being reinterpreted as a source of difficulties and, more strikingly, the claims of scientific reasoning were being called into question. The clamour for regulation of industry at the Rio summit was matched only by a rising impatience with scientific evidence. 'Lack of full scientific certainty' would not be an excuse and, 'even where there is no scientific evidence to prove a causal link', safeguards will be put in place.

It is worth noting that the growing anti-industrial clamour expressed at Rio came from the heart of the establishment. It was in the realm of international summitry rather than science that the 'precautionary principle' took hold. In the first instance, the *Vorsorgeprinzip* was an early foray by Germany into the realm of foreign policy, at a time when that country was constrained by its past. Tackling pollution was a relatively uncontentious issue for Germany to advance on the international stage. In Britain Sir Crisipin Tickell, former Guardsman and Britain's Ambassador to the United Nations was instrumental in winning first Margaret Thatcher to the cause and then John Major to support the Rio Conference.[37] In 1988, in a speech written by Sir Crispin, Thatcher told the Royal Society 'we have unwittingly begun a massive experiment with the system of the planet itself', and that 'fundamental equilibrium of the world's system' was not secure.[38] In the 1970s Crispin Tickell published a book recommending that the independence of small nations might have to be abrogated for the greater good of protecting the atmosphere.[39]

In 1992 opposition to the Rio summit came from the USA and the developing world. The old money in Europe, though, was eager to see the rest of the world's industrial development slowed to its own sedentary pace. Though the Intergovernmental Panel on Climate Change was presented as a scientific agreement, it was obvious that the essence of the matter was decided through international diplomacy. One member of the IPCC, climatologist Greg Easterbrook, resigned, complaining that the bureaucrats were writing the science and that scientists on the panel had only ever been shown separate sections, never the whole draft. According to Easterbrook, climatology was a science so dominated by politics that it was becoming impossible to do science there. Environmental campaigners, frustrated at seeing their issue hi-jacked by the elite, reacted with local protests to try to take the issue back.[40]

The precautionary principle summarised the changed attitude to science on the part of the ruling elite. In the past the elite had imagined itself as at one with scientific advance. Every contingency of the market economy was dressed up as rationality, as unavoidably true as the findings of natural science. In the 1970s the elite Club of Rome report *Limits to Growth* signalled the breach between scientific progress and the propertied elite. '"The God that failed" in the image of technological omnipotence is now revarnished and shown around again under the umbrella of "ecological concern"', wrote the radical critic Istvan Meszaros.[41] With the 'precautionary principle' a founding tenet of scientific rationality was stood upon its head.

The reversal of the onus of proof onto science that it should prove ahead of time that its procedures are safe sounds like common sense but in fact is unattainable. Scientific enquiry produces no absolute certainties, and no scientist could ever demonstrate absolute safety. In fact the founding of scientific enquiry arises out of the differentiation of the absolute knowledge of faith with the merely conditional character of scientific findings. 'Galileo realised that the human mind could not penetrate the secrets of nature unless it abandoned the preposterous claim to exhaustive knowledge', writes the biographer William Shea.[42] The precautionary principle reverses that advance, by demanding exhaustive knowledge of future events, which, in their nature, are not absolutely knowable. The ecological critique of science, though, charges science with having 'begun a massive experiment with the system of the planet itself'. Anyone would think that without technology, the course of natural history was entirely predictable. In truth, though, the reverse is the case. It is not science that introduces uncertainty into human affairs, but nature. The experiment was already taking place, only now its effects are being observed.

The adoption of the precautionary principle by the international ruling elite is a milestone in the interaction between science and society. For two centuries Europe's nascent capitalist classes have identified with the extension of scientific rationality, at times in the teeth of religious obscurantism and political reaction. But with the Rio Summit it is clear that the now ruling capitalist elite has retreated from its identification with scientific progress. The recent debate over genetically modified foodstuffs illustrates the point. The British government's investment in GM technology is extensive, and has been since the 1970s. But in 1998 rising public anxiety over GM food caused the British government to think twice about its support for GM. Brian Wynne, sociologist and government adviser, insists that the lay public's distrust of the scientists cannot be simply rejected as ignorance, but must itself be recognised as another species of knowledge. This knowledge, he says, is just as valid, if not more so, as the findings of science.[4] Like culture, science is dumbed down when popular prejudice is elevated to comparable status with scientific findings. The government backtracked over the licensing of GM foods and supermarkets refused to stock them – despite the absence of one single instance of anyone becoming ill as a result of GM technology.

The elite's retreat from leadership is destructive in its consequences. Without an ideal of excellence to strive for, society loses its incentive to progress. Where the values of competitiveness and enterprise are held in low esteem, the motivation to achieve becomes flattened. Cultural achievements are held lightly and the very ability to judge is compromised. The resistance to elite culture carries the appearance of a plebeian revolt from below. Of course the reduction of Western civilisation into a badge of superiority for a small elite was itself a vulgarisation. But without any higher ideals to strive for, it is not possible to challenge elitism, only to dumb down. At the core of the problem is the collapse of elite subjectivity.

In the sciences, too, the reversal of the elite's identification with scientific enlightenment augurs ill for wider society. Scientific advance is put into question when the most influential members of society value public opinion over scientific findings. The adoption of the precautionary principle by world rulers marks a new turning point in history. Uncertainty is at the core of market societies, and it is peculiarly self-denying for a capitalist elite to aspire to absolute certainty about the future. But applied to science, where the provisional character of knowledge is intrinsic to its development, the demand for certainty is comparable with the victory of religious faith over knowledge. Without a sense of itself as a class that can galvanise wider society, the subjectivity of the elite has lost its purpose.

Chapter Twelve

SYMPTOMS OF DEGRADED SUBJECTIVITY

> 'We are all abused children, injured by the longing for permanence, stability and continuity, whereas our experience is all of separation, dissolution and disruption.' Trevor Blackwell and Jeremy Seabrook [44]

The elite's retreat from responsibility is not merely a matter of concern for its members. It impacts upon the whole of society. Without an ideal of subjectivity to live up to, or to challenge, subjectivity itself is degraded. In this chapter we look at the degraded subjectivity in society. Characteristically the degradation of subjectivity is expressed relatively, in the elevation of some supposedly higher principle than agency or responsibility. In the following we look at three symptomatic expressions of degraded subjectivity, infantilisation, emasculation and the pathologisation of society.

Infantilisation

As an up-and-coming lawyer in the field of family law, Hillary Clinton's 1974 essay 'Children's rights: a legal perspective' proposed a new approach to the question of children's rights.[45] Instead of assuming a child's incompetence before the law, Clinton argued that the system should start from the assumption that children are competent, so that their rights can be recognised. By putting children on a par with adults, capable of expressing their own concerns, they are taken seriously as people with rights of their own. In Britain the 1989 Children Act, which came into force in 1991, has put children's rights at the centre of social policy. In the act, the interests of the child are held to take precedence over the rights of parents. Whether in considering custody between parents, or placing the child in care, the act states that 'the child's welfare shall be the court's paramount consideration' (Children's Act 1989, s1). Under the auspices of Unesco, the World Children's Parliament met in Paris on 21-27 October 1999, and the British National Society for the Prevention of Cruelty to Children has conducted an extensive survey into children's attitudes.[46]

The growing concern with the rights of the child expresses a confusion in society about the boundaries between childhood and adulthood. Superficially it seems as if the extension of children's rights is an example of an increased sense of personal responsibility in societies. Indeed it appears that children's responsibilities are assuming ever-greater proportions. Following the public outcry in Britain over Jon Venables and Robert Thompson, the 10-year old murderers of James Bulger, the *doli incapax* rule was abolished. *Doli incapax*, a law dating back to the Middle Ages was introduced to prevent children from being hanged for simply foolish behaviour. *Doli incapax* put the onus on courts to show that children between 10 and 13 understood the gravity of offences they were charged with before sending them for trial. Since the abolition, Britain now has the lowest age of criminal responsibility in Europe, except for Ireland and Turkey. British courts have seen children as young as 10 stand trial in circumstances that they simply cannot understand. In one trial, the courts gave defendants crayoning books to occupy them, on the understanding that they could not be expected to follow the court proceedings – and yet these were the very proceedings on which their fate hung.

In a recent case an 11-year old boy stood trial for breaking a toddler's leg. The boy had some learning difficulties, and, while he knew that what he did was bad, he clearly had no comprehension of the full gravity of his act. He was taken to trial just 12 days after the abolition of *doli incapax*. Now he has a criminal record. And because his victim was a child, he has been placed on a register of child abusers for the rest of his natural life. This boy is now to be counted among child-killers and perverts, colloquially a 'beast', who must inform potential employers of his record of abuse, and keep the police informed of his whereabouts, for the next 60 or more years.

Since the government decided that it would start prosecuting children, it has taken the next logical step and established jails for children. The first such institution is run by the private security firm Group 4 in Kent. According to a report early in 1999 by social services, staff training, services and conditions are in no way adequate for young children. Staff turnover has been high, and staff have complained of violence against them. Records of violence against the children is a more closely guarded secret – but it is known that staff have often lost control, having to call on Group 4's other security officers to regain control. Resentment at being thrown into cells led children at the prison to riot. The then Home Secretary Jack Straw announced his latest raft of measures against children with a paper bullishly titled 'No more excuses'. Throughout the document Straw poured scorn on the principle of *doli incapax* (which he translates as 'incapable of evil' rather than the more orthodox 'incapable of harm' – indicative of his own pre-modern thinking). To Straw it is simply absurd to think that children should be incapable of 'evil'. This is realism, as Ionesco said, with all four feet firmly planted on the ground. Proposals include more curfews against children, special laws to arrest children and more children's jails. So far a further four jails are planned, bringing the number of places up to 200.

At first it is difficult to understand how a society that cherishes children to the extent of making their interests paramount could at the same time try to imprison them. The explanation is as simple as it is disturbing. The changing attitude to children reflected in the legal changes is not really about children at all, but about adults. The belief that children should be made responsible for the decisions that affect their lives, springs from the same misunderstanding that wishes to see them answer for their actions before the law. The misunderstanding is that children are essentially like adults. Losing sight of the difference between children and adults, though, is not merely a misunderstanding. It is a misunderstanding that arises from a degraded sense of adulthood. Less confident of the virtues of maturity, the society is less clear that is has something of value to teach the young.

Childhood is not a permanent state of existence, but arises out of the cultural and legal differentiation of children from adults. Children as late as the eighteenth century were considered as simply small adults. The social demarcation of children from adults came in Britain with the introduction of compulsory schooling, first to age 11, and then later to age 15. Victorian campaigns against child labour ran alongside the early sentimentalisation of childhood innocence. These attitudes were no doubt replete with all kinds of hypocrisy, but nonetheless they represented a massive leap forwards in social life. The recognition that childhood was a special state, in which children arose from owed a duty of care by their parents and by the wider public, was a wholly progressive advance. The possibilities of such an advance arose from the parallel increase in personal responsibility that the state recognised in householders. The extension of the vote and other civil rights corresponds to the growing recognition that children are not like adults, but human beings whose own sense of personal responsibility is not yet sufficiently matured to assume responsibility for their actions.

In present circumstances, though, the culture is less confident to insist upon the superiority of adulthood over childhood. The British Children Act enshrines that loss of confidence. The underlying assumption of the injunction to make the interests of the child paramount is the false assumption that young children have interests distinct from their parents.

Those adults who take children's choices seriously, whether positively in consulting with children about decisions that they in fact are incapable of making, or negatively in punishing children for behaviour whose import they simply do not understand, are telling us more about themselves than they are about children. Eileen Vizard, consultant child and adolescent psychiatrist told the High Court that the boy Robert Thompson did know right from wrong when he killed James Bulger. However, Vizard, when interviewed on television said she was surprised not to be asked the reasons in the boy's background for his actions.[47] Vizard's comments are telling of her own inability to understand the meaning of culpability. People who know right from wrong can act upon that basis. Those whose actions can be explained by reasons in their background, as opposed to reasons in their consciousness are by definition not culpable, or, as the court has it, do not know right from wrong. Vizard failed to understand that she could not have it both ways, either Thompson knew what he was doing, or he was obeying a motivation that was hidden from him. Her intellectual failure was to distinguish between responsibility and its absence.

Jack Straw's firm injunction 'no more excuses' sounds very impressive, until one sees the blubbing child on the receiving end of his disciplinary regime. Does it enhance Straw's standing that he sets Group 4 security on a crowd of unruly teenagers? It does not. On the contrary, it shows up his own insecure sense of what personal responsibility is. Considering the slim grasp of the rights of adults Straw showed as Home Secretary, it is hardly surprising that Straw cannot distinguish them from children.

In Europe and America the age of majority has tended to be blurred by the extension of further education, meaning that many more young people are studying beyond the age of 18 than used to. In itself, increased educational opportunity ought to be a good thing. But it has led to a greater sense of confusion about the dividing line between childhood and adulthood. Where the legislative rule of thumb tended clearly to demarcate a period of roughly 16 to 18 for rights of voting, sexual activity, working, self-supporting, today their is much greater ambiguity. The reason for the ambiguity is that the distinctiveness of adulthood has been to some extent worn away.

Commenting on the themes developed in amateur manga – Japanese comic books – feminist Ueno Chizuko pointed to the Peter Pan syndrome among the young adult followers of *yaoi* and *rorikon* genres. 'Do the *yaoi* girls and the *rorikon* boys really have a future?', she asked.[48] Official perception is that popular culture is 'vulgarised, feminised and infantilised to the point where it has become "baby-talk"'.[49] Commenting upon the craze for the Japanese cartoon characters Pokemon, 'pocket monsters', *Vanity Fair* columnist Christopher Hitchens wisely suggested that the parents are as gripped as the children – 'this isn't that old story about the commercialisation of children. It's about the infantilisation of adults'.[50] The Peter Pan syndrome jumps out of the pages of Japanese manga, but it is present in the West, too. US columnist Barbara Graham sums up the sentiment when she writes, 'I decided at an early age that I would never grow up....Grown-upness seems to be...a dead-end state populated by a bunch of boring people whose primary obsessions were life insurance and Getting Ahead'.[51] Young British journalist Charlotte Raven expressed some distaste at the growing numbers of 'adultescents', known as 'middle youth', who were crowding out the clubs and dance-hall, in her article 'middle youth ate my culture'.[52] Advertising executive William Eccleshare of Amnirati Puris Lintas explained the use of pre-adult images in promotional material in this way: 'If all advertising seems to be directed at the young, it's because we've found the most effective way to appeal to everyone is to make commercials which embody attitudes associated with youth.'[53]

Perhaps it is not surprising that youth is an ideal, given the deterioration in health associated with ageing. However the attraction of manufactured innocence is more pointed in the popular US television series *Dawson's Creek*, where teenagers hang on the verge of adulthood in perpetuity, or more fetishistically in *Buffy the Vampire Slayer*, where the teenage lead fights off a world of adult monsters that terrorise her schoolfriends. In Britain in 1996 the survey and forecasting organisation Mintel found that 41 per cent of childless men between the ages of 20 and 34 are still living at home with their parents. The *Daily Mail* commented in high moral tone that 'by minimising their financial worries and responsibilities, their ample disposable incomes can be spent on such indulgences as eating out, travel and fashionable clothes'.[54]

Where the ascent to maturity appears to be less distinctive, and even less attractive, what has been called infantilisation is the result. The confusions around the adult-child distinction in contemporary societies are substantially a reflection of this aspect of degraded subjectivity.

Emasculation

> 'Blue-collar men are losing their jobs or fear that they will. Their wages are dropping, and they have to take women's jobs in fast food, retail sales, hospitals and hotels. Their wives have to work harder. They're angry and humiliated....That's it. Emasculation'.

US Secretary of Labor, Robert Reich, recorded floating this theory with Congressman David Obey, who replied 'your either a genius or you're nuts. If I were you I wouldn't share that theory with anyone else'.[55] In fact the view that working men have been emasculated is common coin. It is the vision of men defeated that runs through popular films of the 1990s such as *Falling Down*, in which Michael

Douglas is the humiliated man who can't take it anymore, or, with even less subtlety, *The Full Monty*.

In the United States, unemployment for men and women in October 1999 was the same at around 3.5 per cent. Women's incomes were 54 per cent of men's in 1996 – a shameful difference, but also a great improvement on the 1980's 39 per cent. For England and Wales the news is even more striking:

> 'The new figures from the Office for National Statistics show that women in paid employment outnumber their male counterparts by 12,000....The numerical barrier was officially broken in September last year. Newly revised figures for the period show there were 11.248m women in the workforce against 11.236m men.'[56]

Even more remarkable perhaps is the closing gap between men's and women's pay in the United Kingdom. In 1970 women's hourly pay was 63 per cent of men's, but by 1999 had risen to 80.9 per cent of men's.[57] None of these statistics suggest an end to inequality, but they do indicate a sea change wrought on the sexual division of labour.

What is more difficult to fathom is why the improvement of women's position in society should necessarily be associated with the defeat of the male sex. The radical bulletin, the *Left Business Observer* from which the American figures are taken saw fit to issue the following 'coda/fatwa':

> 'It's unfortunate that such material progress for women...has come amidst a general stagnation of incomes, and a sharp and steady erosion of white men's paychecks....But anyone who uses these figures to promote a Limbaughesque agenda of white guy ressentiment will find himself under an LBO fatwa.'[58]

It is true that the advances in women's pay and employment were thrown into relief by the recession of the early 1990s, but it is not necessarily the case that women's advance is synonymous with male defeat. On the contrary, the recent improvements in the economies of Britain and the USA both find women's position improving within a general improvement in pay and employment. The preoccupation that is found amongst commentators with the problem of male ressentiment is not wholly justified. Rather it is a sign of an increasing tendency to pathologise masculinity.

Masculinity is increasingly seen as a problem, as is reflected in popular culture and advertising. In South Africa the Advertising Standards Authority said a group of men had complained that an advertisement depicted all South African men as rapists. A spokesman said: 'We found the advert to be discriminatory on the basis of gender in contradiction of the constitution.'[59] Britain's Advertising Standards Authority ruled against advertisements for Nissan and Lee Jeans. The Nissan advertisement showed a man holding his crotch as if in pain and was accompanied by the caption: 'Ask before you borrow it.' The Lee advert showed a woman wearing a stiletto-heeled boot resting on the buttocks of a naked man, with a caption that read 'Put the boot in'.[60] In Spain the government itself launched an advertising campaign against the macho culture in September 1998.

Masculinity, so psychotherapist Roger Horrocks reports, is in crisis.[61] The expectations of what it is to be a man today are confused and uncertain, or even held to be a problem. 'Masculine values' like assertiveness, self-possession, comradeship and courage were once seen as traits whose virtue was beyond question. Many of the 'manly virtues' that were once seen as evidence of a healthy natural order, today seem to be interpreted as inherently pathological conditions. According to Horrocks, assertion leads to violence, self-possession, and a kind of autism, and comradeship becomes men's closed-shop against women, while hard courage conceals a want of care. Horrocks argues that 'in becoming accomplices and agents of the patriarchal oppression of women, men are themselves mutilated psychologically'.

The militant form of masculinity represents a considerable self-abuse and self-destruction by men. 'In hating women the male hates himself.'[62] Horrocks gives a personal example of the way that the demands of masculinity can become a burden to men:

> 'I remember my fierce anxiety about being male when I was an adolescent in a Lancashire town, and went around in a gang of lads to pubs, dances and parties. We had a strict code of behaviour and watched each other like hawks to make sure that we all followed it. Any divergence was instantly spotted and ridiculed. For example, the fact that I stayed at school until I was 18 was treated with great suspicion: it wasn't manly.'[63]

According to sociologists J Taylor Gibbs and JR Merighi, these pressures are felt all the more keenly among groups of men who are already marginal.[64] They perceive an assertive machismo in black Americans that they think is both a defensive reaction to racial disadvantage, but also a spur to violent criminality, such as drug-dealing and shootings. What they call pseudomasculinity 'is thus conceptualised here as a mediating factor between marginal social identity and criminality'. Gibbs and Merighi expand: 'that is, the young black males who develop "macho" behaviours as a defensive strategy to counter their feelings of marginality will be at a greater risk for antisocial behaviours than those who deal with marginality with more pro-social adaptive strategies.'[65]

It is odd that Horrocks should accept that certain traits are 'masculine' and others 'feminine'. In this sense, masculinity theory simply takes over the old schematic division of masculine and feminine, except that it reverses the plus and negative signs, holding masculine qualities to be deficient, or pathological, instead of seeing them as the standard. At its root this tendency is not about men and women, but the underlying values that the culture espouses. Those values that were – artificially – associated with manliness are now themselves held in low esteem. This is true whether they are exhibited by men, or by women. Behind the pathologisation of masculinity is a distaste for assertiveness and self-possession. Identifying these values with an outmoded masculine culture is a way of disparaging them. The much-asserted 'crisis of masculinity' turns out to be no such thing, but in content the degradation of subjectivity.

Using the terms of the so-called 'crisis of masculinity', a great many human virtues can be turned on their head and made into vices. Circumspection is reinterpreted as denial, fortitude as an inability to open up, self-possession as an inability to share, determination as intolerance, ambition as selfishness. Rendered pathological as masculine, these virtues are ridiculed and belittled. In the process, truly human qualities are degraded. The pathologisation of human qualities, though, is not just reserved for men. On the contrary, the willingness to reinterpret human behaviour as an illness is characteristic of the tendency to degrade subjectivity.

Pathological society

James Nolan points to the tendency for 'child behaviour once treated as unruly or hyperactive' to be 'given the pathological label of Attention Deficit Disorder' (ADD).[66] Nolan points out that this relatively recently diagnosed syndrome is supposed by experts to be common amongst five per cent of the population. The ordinary treatment for ADD is the drug Ritalin. In Britain, too, the drive to diagnose ADD has led to extraordinary increases in the numbers of children with it. Dr David Foreman of the Abbey Hulton clinic in Stoke has been investigated by the Health Council after it was noticed that 150 children had been prescribed Ritalin for ADD.[67]

The American Supplemental Security Income (SSI) programme was originally designed to give income to disabled people, but amended to give payments to disabled children. Following a legal relaxation of criteria for payment in 1991, the number of disabled children on SSI climbed from 340,000 in 1990 to 900,000 in 1994. Ben

Wattenberg reports the case of an Arkansas child who plaintively asked his teacher whether his 'crazy money' would be cut off if he did well on his test.[68] In Wattenberg's telling this is just a story of social security fraud. In fact it is indicative of something much more disturbing than financial dishonesty on the part of less well-off parents. This is more than the usual story of the dependency culture. There is a much wider trend for parents to try to have their children classed as children with 'special needs'. In Hove in the UK in 1996 the local education authority was moved to clamp down on the numbers of school children classified 'special needs' as numbers climbed into the hundreds. Challenged by parents, the education authority was on the verge of instituting special tribunals to test the cases before their lawyers advised them that the parents would themselves seek legal representation, sending the whole process spiralling out of control.

The problem in both these cases is not so much welfare fraud, as the transformation of social values expressed. The parents involved were happy to see their children declared to be disabled or in special need because this classification would win them greater teaching or financial resources. That represents a considerable reversal of ordinary social norms. Where in the past parents might want their children to be rated as above the average, these parents relished the proposition that their children were at a disadvantage. The marginally generous social welfare policies were rewarding disadvantage – but more problematically the parents' own value scale had been transformed from one of pride in achievement to a pride in disadvantage.

What can be seen at work in schools is also a process throughout society. More and more people are willing to classify themselves as being in need of help, and the reserve that is associated with keeping one's problems to oneself is crumbling. One consequence of this trend is the growth of those seeking some kind of counselling or advice about the problems facing them from professional counsellors. In Britain the numbers of people seeking some kind of counselling has grown immeasurably. The association Counselling, Advice,

Mediation, Psychotherapy, Advocacy and Guidance (CAMPAG) tried to calculate the numbers of working counsellors. In February 1999 they did a 'mapping snapshot' of those in the field for that month. Their calculations found 540,000 advice workers, 5000 advocates, 632,000 counsellors, 44,000 guidance workers (mostly careers advice), 5500 psychotherapists and 4500 mediation workers. In all no less than 1,231,000 counsellors or nearly 10 times the number of policemen and women working in Britain (127,000).

Conclusion

THE SUBJECTIVE FACTOR

Like Mark Twain's death, reports of the 'Death of the Subject' are exaggerated. They have to be. The fulcrum point on which society turns is the freely willing subject. For all of the attempts to imagine a world without subjects, but only processes and objective forces, no developed society is conceivable without rationally choosing individuals at its core. This indeed was the one rational insight of the 'methodological individualists', that the decision-making procedures of a complex society are inconceivable without at least as complex a network of decision-makers. Every day the totality of human interactions sufficient not just to recreate the conditions of mankind's survival but also of its growth are achieved by no other force than us human beings. And yet the evidence, outlined in the foregoing, is that collectively society is recoiling from personal responsibility and choice. Subjectivity is held in low esteem.

The only way to understand this mismatch is that the human subject persists, but in denial of its own subjectivity. Overwhelmed by the sense of powerlessness that grips each of us, we characterise our society in profoundly impersonal, even inhuman ways. Globalisation takes society out of our control. Biological metaphors for human behaviour assume ever-greater force, as anger, desire and jealousy are all traced – improbably – to genetic causes. Cultural explanations, too, predominate as human actions are endlessly reduced to the outcome of environmental influences. Psychology provides further reasons to distance oneself from one's own choices, in the theory that family life determines behaviours. This is the condition that Jean-Paul Sartre characterised as 'bad faith', the recoil from freedom that provides more and more alibis to explain away the meaning of our actions.

The accumulated defeats of the past weigh down upon us, making ambitious programmes for the future seem unattractive, even dangerous, or incipiently dictatorial. But for the most part, younger people are less likely to have experienced those defeats directly, only through the transmission of diminished expectations of the future. More problematically, the retreat from subjectivity assumes an organisational form. Social institutions, like the growing numbers of counsellors, or the reorganisation of welfare and legal systems on the basis of 'children's rights' gives a solidity to the retreat from subjectivity. Now vested interests exist to deny the expression of subjective action.

Despite these difficulties, the subjective factor is by no means eliminated from human society; it merely persists in wilful denial of its own existence and import. Ironically, human endeavour has attained some of its greatest achievements in this period of generally lowered expectations. It is only in recent times that physical hunger ceased to be a consideration for the populations of the developed countries of Europe and America, and the means exist to eradicate it completely, thanks to innovations in agriculture. Improvements in healthcare have brought increasing life expectancy not just to the developed world but to the underdeveloped as well. Technological advances make it conceivable that more of society's available time can be dedicated not just to recreating our animal existence, but to developing our cultural lives, freed from the realm of mere necessity. Communications technologies are making the physical barriers between societies less meaningful, at least in the transmission of ideas and information.

All of these spectacular advances could become the means of sustaining and transmitting a depressed society that is preoccupied with its own powerlessness. But that would be contrary to the real meaning of those advances. Though human subjectivity persists in denial of its own existence, it is nonetheless the single most powerful force at work in society and nature. To attain full consciousness of its own potential would itself increase that potential exponentially.

NOTES
Part One

1. Office of National Statistics, *Britain 2000: Official Yearbook of the United Kingdom*, 1999; Robert Worcester and Roger Mortimer, *Explaining Labour's Landslide*, Politico's 1999
2. A representative of the liberal outlook of the eighteenth century Immanuel Kant writes that the principle of rights is to 'be a person and respect others as persons' (quoted in Avineri, *Hegel's Theory of the Modern State*, Cambridge University Press, 1972, p137) or it is 'the equality of each member with every other as a Subject'.
3. 'It is not from the benevolence of the butcher, the brewer or the baker that we expect our dinner, but from their regard to their own interest.' Adam Smith, *The Wealth of Nations*, Penguin, 1987, p119
4. 'Whoever refuses to obey the general will shall be constrained to do so by the whole body, which means nothing other than that he shall be forced to be free', JJ Rousseau, *The Social Contract*, Harmondsworth: Penguin, 1972, p64. Rousseau's forceful mode of expression alarms more individualistically minded readers, but he only means that if you beat up old ladies you will go to prison, for your own good, as much as anyone else's.
5. See Hillel Ticktin, *Origins of the Crisis in the USSR: Essays on the Political Economy of a Disintegrating System*, ME Sharpe: Armonk, 1992
6. A British National Party slogan of the late 1980s
7. Francis Bacon wrote that 'building in the human understanding a true model of the world ...a thing which cannot be done without a very diligent dissection and anatomy of the world.' *The New Organon*, New York: Macmillan, 1986, Aphorism CXXIV, p113
8. See The Constitution of the United States of America, Article One, 'Congress shall make no law respecting an establishment of religion, or prohibiting the free exercise thereof'.
9. 'Nothing is required for this enlightenment, however except freedom; and the freedom in question is the least harmful of all, namely, the freedom to reason publicly in all matters.' Immanuel Kant, 'What is Enlightenment' in *Perpetual Peace and Other Essays*, Indiana: Hackett, 1983, p 42
10. 'The Inhabitants shall have the right of free association and assemblance', Constitution of the Kingdom of the Netherlands, in Baron Asbeck (ed), *The Universal Declaration of Human Rights And its Predecessors (1679-1948)*, Leiden: EJ Brill, 1949
11. See Habeas Corpus Act, 1679 (Great Britain) 'An act for the better securing the liberty of the subject, and for the prevention of imprisonments beyond the seas' in Baron Asbeck (ed), *The Universal Declaration of Human Rights And its Predecessors (1679-1948)*, Leiden: EJ Brill, 1949
12. '1. That all men are by nature equally free and indpendent, and have certain inherent rights, of which, when they enter into a state of society, they cannot, by any compact, deprive or divest their posterity; namely, the enjoyment of life and liberty, with the means of acquiring and possessing property, and pursuing and obtaining happiness and safety.' Bill of Rights (Virginia) in Baron Asbeck (ed), *The Universal Declaration of Human Rights And its Predecessors (1679-1948)*, Leiden: EJ Brill, 1949
13. See 'Two Concepts of Liberty' in *Four Essays on Liberty*, Oxford, 1969
14. See CB Macpherson, *Democratic Theory: Essays in Retrieval*, Oxford University Press, 1983
15. *The Information*, London: Flamingo, 1995, p129
16. Semiotext(e), 1983, p39
17. Cadava, *What Comes After the Subject?*

18 Slavoj Zizek, *The Ticklish Subject: The Absent Centre of Political Ontology*, London: Verso, 1999
19 *Reason and Faith*
20 *The Postmodern Condition: A Report on Knowledge*, Manchester: University Press, 1989, pxxiv
21 *The Postmodern Condition*, pxxiv
22 *Intellectual Impostures*, London: Profile, 1999
23 *The Undoing of Thought*, London: The Claridge Press, 1988, p116
24 Jacques Derrida indicates the intrinsic nature of difference with his own concept of différance indicating not only differentiation, but also the deferment of the moment of closure that is definition, and hence the perpetual play of difference. 'Différance is the nonfull, nonsimple, structured and differentiating origin of differences.' *A Derrida Reader: Between the Blinds*, Hemel Hempstead: Harvester, 1991, p64
25 *A Derrida Reader*, p65. My thanks to Kenan Malik for pointing this passage out.
26 *A Derrida Reader*, pix
27 *Of Grammatology*, Maryland: John Hopkins UP, 1997, p16
28 *Of Spirit: Heidegger and the Question*, Chicago: University Press, 1991, p40
29 Quoted in Luc Ferry and Alain Renault *Heidegger and Modernity*, Chicago University Press, 1990 p2. I have missed out a second parenthesis, a sideswipe at Stalinism.
30 Michel Foucault, *The Order of Things: The Archeology of the Human Sciences*, London: Tavistock, 1986, p 387. The striking image is drawn perhaps from this fragment of Herakleitos: 'History is a child building a sandcastle by the sea, and that child is the whole majesty of man's power in the world.' *Herakleitos and Diogenes*, trans, Guy Davenport, San Francisco: Grey Fox Press, 1979
31 Michel Foucault, *The Order of Things*, p344
32 Michel Foucault, *The Order of Things*, p345
33 GWF Hegel, *Natural Law: The Scientific Ways of Treating Natural Law, Its Place in Moral Philosophy, and Its Relation to the Positive Sciences of Law*, Pennsylvania University Press, 1975
34 Karl Marx, Tenth thesis on Feuerbach, *Early Writings*, Harmondsworth: Penguin, 1984, p423
35 CB Macpherson, *The Political Theory of Possessive Individualism: Hobbes to Locke*, Oxford University Press, 1964, p197
36 Of course, the coalescence of Hegelians, Marxists and poststructuralists by no means exhausts all possible views about the existence or otherwise of the natural individual. An echo of the eighteenth-century theory of natural right persists in some sociobiological theories, as well as in the free market theoreticians who follow Frederick Hayek and Karl Popper. But even these defenders of individualism offer only an anaemic and truncated support for the Subject (see Chapter 5). A greater sense of the contingency of social arrangements is forcing the pace of the historical relativisation of the Subject.
37 'It is in fact in the life of a people or nation that the Notion of self-conscious Reason's actualisation...that the Notion has its complete reality.' *The Phenomenology of Spirit*, Oxford: University Press, 1977, p212
38 With Engels, *Communist Manifesto*, Peking: Foreign Language Press, 1977, p46, 47
39 Georg Lukacs, 'Reification and the Consciousness of the Proletariat', *History and Class Consciousness*, London, Merlin, 1983
40 Jean Baudrillard *The Mirror of Production*, St Louis: Telos Press, 1975, p47
41 Jean Baudrillard *The Mirror of Production*, p67
42 Friedrich Nietzsche, *Genealogy of Morals*, New York: Vintage, 1989, p45
43 *Being and Time*, Oxford: Basil Blackwell, 1990, p44
44 *Being and Time*, p44
45 Richard Rorty, quoted in Richard Kearney and Mark Dooley (eds), *Questioning Ethics: Contemporary Debates in Philosophy*, London Routledge, 1999 p152

46 Richard Rorty, *Essays on Heidegger and Others: Philosophical Papers*, Vol. II, Cambridge University Press, 1991, p197
47 Richard Rorty, *Objectivity, Relativism and Truth: Philosophical Papers*, Vol. I, Cambridge University Press, 1991, p196
48 Quoted in Richard Kearney (ed), *Questioning Ethics: Contemporary Debates in Philosophy*, p158
49 Richard Rorty, *Objectivity, Relativism and Truth*, p198-9
50 Richard Rorty, *Objectivity, Relativism and Truth*, p199
51 Cornelius Castoriadis, 'The State of the Subject Today', in *World in Fragments: Writings on Politics, Society, Psychoanalysis and the Imagination*, Stanford University Press, 1997, p 168
52 Cornelius Castoriadis, 'The State of the Subject Today', in *World in Fragments*, p 169
53 Cambridge: Polity, 1991, p5
54 J-F Lyotard, *Political Writings*, London: University College, 1993, p122-3
55 J-F Lyotard, 'The Wall, the Gulf and the Sun', *Political Writings*, p 122-3
56 'Posthuman', lyrics by Marilyn Manson / Music by Ramirez, Gacy
57 Much of this imagery was developed in William Gibson's novel *Neuromancer*.
58 In Charles Lemert (ed), *Social Theory: The Multicultural and Classical Readings*, Boulder: Westview Press, 1993, p599
59 In Charles Lemert (ed), *Social Theory*, p598-9
60 See Karl Marx, 'Theses on Feuerbach', in *Early Writings*, Harmondsworth: Penguin, 1978
61 London *Guardian*, 20 March 2000
62 'Ideological State Apparatuses', in Slavoj Zizek (ed), *Mapping Ideology*, London: Verso, 1994, p128
63 'Ideological State Apparatuses', in Slavoj Zizek (ed), *Mapping Ideology*, p129
64 *The Future Lasts a Long Time*, London: Vintage, 1994, p215
65 *The Future Lasts a Long Time*, p218 (Althusser's italics)
66 *For Marx*, Harmondsworth: Penguin, 1969, p221
67 *For Marx*, p221
68 *For Marx*, p228 (Althusser's italics)
69 *For Marx*, p229 (Althusser's italics)
70 *For Marx*, p229
71 'I became obsessed with the terrifying thought that these texts would expose me completely to the public at large as I really was, namely a trickster and a deceiver ...who knew almost nothing about...Marx...I had only seriously studied Book I of *Capital* in 1964.' *The Future Lasts a Long Time*, p148
72 'I had read Heidegger's Letter to Jean Beaufret on Humanism, which influenced my arguments concerning theoretical antihumanism in Marx.' *The Future Lasts a Long Time*, p176. 'The letter on humanism', in which Heidegger denounces Jean-Paul Sartre's humanism is reproduced in the *Basic Writings*.
73 Judith Butler, *The Psychic Life of Power: Theories in Subjection*, Stanford: University Press, 1997, p2-3
74 Judith Butler, *The Psychic Life of Power*, p5
75 Judith Butler, *The Psychic Life of Power*, p10
76 The British Labour MP Tony Wright makes this play on words in the title of his book *Citizens or Subjects* without even realising what he is doing.
77 *Oxford Dictionary of English Etymology*, ed CT Onions, Oxford: University Press, 1985
78 English philosopher TH Green suggests that the different meanings are national. 'English writers commonly call that the subject of a right that Germans would call the object', *Lectures on the Principles of Political Obligation and other writings*, Cambridge University Press, 1986, p180

79 The word 'sovereignty' carries a similar history, where the original exercise of sovereignty was restricted to the Prince, its universalisation suggests to some, like Tony Wright in his *Citizens or Subjects*, that the sovereign power of the elected assembly is simply despotism to the nth power.
80 Beatrix Campbell and Anna Coote, *Sweet Freedom: The Struggle for Women's Liberation*, Basil Blackwell, Oxford, 1987, p227
81 Sally Vincent, *New Statesman*, 19 December 1980
82 'Pornography: The Representation of Power' in Catherine Itzin (ed), *Pornography: Women, Violence and Civil Liberties, a Radical New View*, p93
83 'Pornography: The Representation of Power' in Catherine Itzin (ed), *Pornography*, p93
84 Richard Kearney and Mark Dooley (eds), *Questioning Ethics: Contemporary Debates in Philosophy*, London Routledge, 1999, p260
85 Judith Butler, *Gender Trouble: Feminism and the Subversion of Identity*, Routledge, London, 1990, p5
86 Judith Butler, *Gender Trouble*, p5-6
87 See Burkart Holzner, 'The Construction of Social Actors: An essay on social identities', in T Luckmann (ed) *Phenomenology and Sociology*, Harmondsworth: Penguin, 1978, p291-310, for example
88 TH Green, *Lectures on the Principles of Political Obligation and Other Writings*, Cambridge University Press, 1986, p79
89 TH Green, *Lectures on the Principles of Political Obligation and Other Writings*, p79
90 Michael J Sandel, *Liberalism and the Limits of Justice*, Cambridge University Press, 1982
91 Michael J Sandel, *Liberalism and the Limits of Justice*, p121
92 Michael J Sandel, *Liberalism and the Limits of Justice*, p153
93 Michael J Sandel, *Liberalism and the Limits of Justice*, p150
94 Michael J Sandel, *Liberalism and the Limits of Justice*, p134
95 Amatai Etzioni, *The Spirit of Community: Rights, Responsibilities and the Communitarian Agenda*, New York: Crown, 1993, p25
96 Alisdair MacIntyre, *Three Rival Versions of Moral Enquiry*, London: Duckworth, 1990, p193
97 Michael J Sandel, *Liberalism and the Limits of Justice*, p30
98 Michael J Sandel, *Liberalism and the Limits of Justice*, p33
99 Charles Taylor, *Sources of the Self: The Making of Modern Identity*, Cambridge University Press, 1989, p505
100 Amatai Etzioni, *The Spirit of Community: Rights, Responsibilities and the Communitarian Agenda*, New York: Crown, 1993, p9
101 Charles Taylor, *Sources of the Self*, p506
102 Michael J Sandel, *Liberalism and the Limits of Justice*, p33
103 In Richard Kearney and Mark Dooley (eds), *Questioning Ethics: Contemporary Debates in Philosophy*, London Routledge, 1999, p220
104 Carole Pateman, 'The Fraternal Contract' in *The Disorder of Women*, Cambridge: Polity, 1989, p52
105 Carole Pateman, *The Sexual Contract*, Cambridge: Polity, 1988
106 Carole Pateman, *The Sexual Contract*, pp116-153
107 'The Leveller leaders wanted the vote to be given to "freeborn Englishmen". Unless they had fought for Parliament, servants and those in receipt of alms – that is wage labourers and paupers – were excluded from the franchise, because these two groups were not economically independent. Thinking in terms of small household industrial and agricultural units, these Levellers held that servants – apprentices and labourers as well as domestic servants – were represented by the head of the household no less than were his womenfolk and children.' Christopher Hill, *The Century of Revolution*, Wokingham, Van Nostrand Reinhold, 1980, p111

108 Carole Pateman, 'The Fraternal Contract' in *The Disorder of Women*, p45. Pateman continues evocatively, 'The brothers give birth to an artificial body, the body politic of civil society; they create Hobbes's "Artificial Man, we call a Commonwealth," or Rousseau's "artificial and collective body", or the "one Body" of Locke's "Body Politick".' Despite this hint, Pateman does not extend the critique of the state as male womb-envy.
109 Carole Pateman, 'The Fraternal Contract' in *The Disorder of Women*, p46
110 Catharine Mackinnon, *Toward a Feminist Critique of the State*, Harvard University Press, 1991, p 164-5
111 Catharine Mackinnon, *Toward a Feminist Critique of the State*, p 164-5
112 See CB Macpherson, *The Political Theory of Possessive Individualism: Hobbes to Locke*, Oxford: University Press, 1964
113 Franz Neumann, *Behemoth*, New York: Harper & Row, 1966, p162
114 Franz Neumann, *Behemoth*, p163
115 Catharine Mackinnon, *Only Words*, London: HarperCollins, 1994, p77, pxiv
116 Catharine Mackinnon, *Only Words*, p77-8
117 Carole Pateman, 'The Fraternal Contract' in *The Disorder of Women*, p53
118 *Orientalism: Western Concepts of the Orient*, Harmondsworth: Penguin, 1991
119 *Orientalism: Western Concepts of the Orient*, p190 '"Oriental sex was as standard a commodity as any other available in the mass culture'.
120 *Orientalism: Western Concepts of the Orient*, p3
121 From Immanuel Kant, *Groundwork for a Metaphysics of Morality*, quoted in Avineri, *Hegel's Theory of the Modern State*, Cambridge University Press, 1972, p137. Kant, though, was aware of some of the problems, as implied in his 'Fourth Thesis' of the 'Idea for a Universal History with a Cosmopolitan Intent', where he writes 'I understand antagonism to mean men's unsocial sociability, ie, their tendency to enter into society, combined, however, with a thoroughgoing resistance that constantly threatens to sunder this society', Imanuel Kant, *Perpetual Peace and Other Essays*, Indianapolis: Hackett, 1983, p32
122 'Following Hegel, we find in consciousness itself a fundamental hostility towards every other consciousness; the subject can be posed only in being opposed – he sets himself up as the essential, as opposed to the other, the inessential, the object.' Simone De Beauvoir, *The Second Sex*, pref.
123 Alexandre Kojève, *Introduction to the Reading of Hegel: Lectures on the Phenomenology of Spirit*, Ithaca: Cornell University Press, 1991 p6
124 Alexandre Kojève, *Introduction to the Reading of Hegel*, p3
125 GWF Hegel, *Phenomenology of Spirit*, Oxford: University Press, 1977, p110
126 Alexandre Kojève, *Introduction to the Reading of Hegel*, p8
127 GWF Hegel, *Phenomenology of Spirit*, Oxford: University Press, 1977, p111
128 GWF Hegel, *Phenomenology of Spirit*, p115. The editors of the Miller edition of Hegel's Phenomenology do not capitalise the Other, but in Kojève's Introduction, Queneau does, thereby promoting it from adjective to noun.
129 Simone De Beauvoir, *The Second Sex*, pref
130 Simone De Beauvoir, *The Second Sex*, pref
131 Simone De Beauvoir, *The Second Sex*, pref
132 Jean-Paul Sartre, *Being and Nothingness*, New York: Simon and Schuster, 1966, p328
133 Jean-Paul Sartre, *Being and Nothingness*, p329
134 Jean-Paul Sartre, *Being and Nothingness*, p329
135 Frantz Fanon, *Wretched of the Earth*, Harmondsworth: Penguin, 1971, p30
136 Martin Buber, *I and Thou*, New York: Macmillan, 1987, p6
137 Emmanuel Levinas, *Outside the Subject*, London: Athlone Press, 1993, p124
138 Michel Foucault, *History of Sexuality*, Vol 1, London: Penguin, 1990, p94-5
139 Michel Foucault, *History of Sexuality*, Vol 1, p92
140 Michel Foucault, *History of Sexuality*, Vol 1, p95-6
141 Judith Butler, *Psychic Life of Power: Theories in Subjection*, Stanford: University Press, 1997, p84

142 In Engels' book *Anti-Duhring*, part two, chapters 2, 3 and 4 cover the Force theory
143 Michel Foucault, *History of Sexuality*, Vol 1, p5
144 Engels makes a similar point in a letter to Theodor Cuno: 'Bakunin maintains that it is the state which has created capital, that the capitalist has his capital only by favour of the state', 24 January 1872. Karl Marx gives another account of the priority of direct repression over economic domination in the chapter on 'The Bloody Legislation' in *Capital*, where he argues that early capitalism lacked the spontaneous power to dominate the working class, and was forced to rely upon state repression to augment its power.
145 Michel Foucault, *Politics, Philosophy, Culture: Interviews and Other Writings, 1977-1984*, London: Routledge, 1990
146 Cornelius Castoriadis, 'The Diversionists', originally published in *Le Nouvel Observateur*, 20 June 1977, reproduced in *Political and Social Writings* Volume 3, Minnesota University Press, 1993, p274
147 Bertrand Russell, *Power: A New Social Analysis*, London, 1938, though in fact it was already a 70-year old social analysis in 1938.
148 Quoted in Steven Lukes, *Power: A Radical View*, Macmillan, 1974, p27
149 Cornelius Castoriadis, 'The Diversionists', in *Political and Social Writings* Volume 3, p275
150 Jurgen Habermas, *The New Conservatism*, Cambridge, Polity, 1994, p173
151 Jurgen Habermas, *The philosophical discourse of modernity*, Cambridge: Polity, 1990
152 Jurgen Habermas in Peter Dews (ed), *Autonomy and Solidarity: Interviews with Jurgen Habermas*, London: Verso, 1992, pp 206-7
153 Axel Honneth, *The Critique of Power: Reflective Stages in a Critical Theory*, Cambridge, Mass: MIT Press, 1993, p242
154 Axel Honneth, *The Critique of Power*, p284
155 Martin Heidegger, *Being and Time*, Oxford: Basil Blackwell, 1990, p166
156 Jurgen Habermas, *Autonomy and Solidarity*, p81
157 Jurgen Habermas, *Autonomy and Solidarity*, p188
158 Axel Honneth, *The Critique of Power*, p284
159 Axel Honneth, *The Critique of Power*, p242
160 Jurgen Habermas, *Between Facts and Norms*, Cambridge, 1996, p490
161 Andrew Arato and Jean Cohen, *Civil Society and Political Theory*, Massachusetts: Institute of Technology, 1993
162 Theodore Zeldin, *An Intimate History of Humanity*, London: Minerva, 1995
163 See Anthony Giddens, *Beyond Left and Right: The Future of Radical Politics*. 'Dialogic democratisation is not an extension of liberal democracy or even a complement to it; in so far as it proceeds, however, it creates forms of social interchange which can contribute substantially, perhaps even decisively, to the reconstructing of social solidarity.' Cambridge, Polity, 1990 p112
164 Ulrich Beck, *Risk Society: Towards a New Modernity*, London: Sage, 1994
165 Ulrich Beck, *The Reinvention of Politics: Rethinking Modernity in the Global Social Order*, Cambridge: Polity, 1997, p53
166 Ulrich Beck, *The Reinvention of Politics*, p32
167 Ulrich Beck, *The Reinvention of Politics*, p17
168 Georg Lukacs, *The Process of Democratisation*, Albany: SUNY, 1991
169 Ulrich Beck, *Risk Society*, p49
170 Anthony Giddens, *Beyond Left and Right*, p227
171 Charles Murray and Richard Herrnstein, *The Bell Curve: Intelligence and Class Structure in American Life*, New York: Free Press, 1994, p91
172 See Steven Fraser (ed), *The Bell Curve Wars: Race, Intelligence and the Future of America*, New York: Basic Books, 1995
173 Richard Lynn, *Dysgenics: Genetic Deterioriation in Modern Populations*, Connecticut: Praeger, 1996
174 Anthony Giddens, *Beyond Left and Right*, p220

175 Daniel Dennet, *Consciousness Explained*, 1991; Susan Blackmore, *The Meme Machine*, 1999
176 Quoted in Richard Dawkins, *Unweaving the Rainbow*, London: Penguin, 1998, p307
177 Richard Dawkins, *Unweaving the Rainbow*, London: Penguin, 1998, p308-9
178 Chris Gilligan, unpublished paper, Department of Politics and Contemporary History, University of Salford, 1999. I have benefited from discussions with Chris in the preparation of this section.
179 Erik Erikson, *Childhood and Society*, New York: WW Norton, 1963
180 Erving Goffman, *The Presentation of Self in Everyday Life*, Anchor, 1956
181 See John D'Emilio and Estelle B. Freedman, *Intimate Matters: A History of Sexuality in America*, Chicago University Press, 1998, p324
182 See Stuart Hall and Tony Jefferson, *Resistance through Rituals*, London: Hutchinson, 1976.
183 Juliet Mitchell, *Woman's Estate*, London: Pelican, 1971, p33
184 Martin Heidegger, *An Introduction to Metaphysics*, Yale University Press, 1989
185 Judith Butler, *Gender Trouble: Feminism and the Subversion of Identity*, London: Routledge, 1990, p142
186 Stuart Hall, 'The Question of Cultural Identity', in Hall, Held and McGrew (eds), *Modernity and its Futures*, Cambridge: Polity, 1992, pp276-7
187 Stuart Hall, 'The Question of Cultural Identity', in *Modernity and its Futures*, p277
188 Guy Davenport (ed), *Herakleitos and Diogenes*, San Francisco: Grey Fox Press, 1979, p23
189 Judith Butler, *Gender Trouble: Feminism and the Subversion of Identity*, London: Routledge, 1990, p145
190 Judith Butler, *Gender Trouble*, p147
191 Judith Butler, *Gender Trouble*, p147
192 Judith Butler, *Gender Trouble*, p145
193 See Robin Blackburn, 'Fin De Sciecle Socialism After the Crash', *New Left Review* 185 (1991)
194 Karl Popper, *The Poverty of Historicism*, London: Routledge, 1963, p158
195 FA Hayek, *New Studies in Philosophy, Politics, Economics, and the History of Ideas*, London: Routledge, 1990, p223
196 'I have belatedly come to agree with Josef Schumpeter who 30 years ago argued that there was an irreconcilable conflict between democracy and capitalism', *New Studies*, p107
197 FA Hayek, *Fatal Conceit: The Errors of Socialism*, London: Routledge, 1990, p21. Defenders of Hayek's reputation protest that the book owed more to its editor, WW Bartley III, than the by then elderly economist.
198 FA Hayek, *Fatal Conceit*, p75
199 FA Hayek, *Fatal Conceit*, p63
200 PF Strawson, *Individuals*, p99
201 Richard Rorty, *Philosophy and the Mirror of Nature*, Oxford: Basil Blackwell, 1986
202 Galen Strawson, 'The impossibility of Moral Responsibility', *Philosophical Studies* 75, p7
203 Richard Kearney and Mark Dooley (eds), *Questioning Ethics*, p48

Part Two

1. Alec Callinicos, *Against Postmodernism: A Marxist Critique*, Cambridge University Press, 1989, p168
2. J-F Lyotard, *Libidinal Economy*, London: The Athlone Press, 1993, p100
3. J-F Lyotard, *The Postmodern Condition: A Report on Knowledge*, Manchester: University Press, 1989, p3
4. Alec Callinicos, *Against Postmodernism*, p165
5. for an account, see James Heartfield, 'The Limits of Social Construction Theory', in *Confrontation*, Vol2, No 1, London: Junius, 1996
6. Terry Eagleton, *The Illusions of Postmodernism*, Oxford: Basil Blackwell, 1996, p1
7. Terry Eagleton, *The Illusions of Postmodernism*, p4. In Britain the Liberal Democrat Party is the middle-of-the-road party between Labour and Tory. Voting for it is a sure sign of a sell-out to any leftist.
8. Terry Eagleton, *The Illusions of Postmodernism*, p16
9. In the USA, in 1993 there were just four million days lost through work stoppages 'the lowest tally since 1947'. In Britain 278,000 days were lost in 1994, a figure that has fallen from 29 and a half million in 1979. In Japan in 1986, 252,000 days were lost, the lowest figure and way down on the mid-seventies. In Italy in 1991 20 million days lost was a record low, compared with 39 million in 1986 and 193 million in 1979. In France the figure dropped from 528,000 in 1990, to 497,000 the following year and 359,000 the year after that, and in Canada days lost through strike action fell from 5,700,000 in 1986, to 1,500,000 in 1991 and just 1,200,000 in 1992. Figures taken from Martin Upham (ed), *Trade Unions of the World*, 4th Edition, Cartermill, 1996, and Martin Upham (ed), *Trade Unions of the World*, 3rd Edition, Longman Current Affairs, 1992.
10. See, for example, Peter Morgan, 'Trades Unions and Strikes', *International Socialism*, 69, London 1995
11. A number of writers relegated the mass worker to a past era of industrial production, such as Michel Aglietta (*A Theory of Capitalist Regulation*, London: Verso, 1987) and Alain Lipietz (*Mirages and Miracles: The Crisis of Global Fordism*, London: Verso, 1987). Before he became an adviser at the British Department of Trade and Industry, Charlie Leadbeater wrote about the way that 'changes in the character and distribution of work have undermined the unifying tendencies of production and work under Fordism.' *Marxism Today*, October, 1988
12. Karl Marx and Frederick Engels, *Manifesto of the Communist Party*, Peking: Foreign Languages Press, 1977, p33
13. Jacques Derrida, from *Memoires: For Paul De Man*, quoted in, David Lehman, *Signs of the Times: Deconstruction and the Fall of Paul De Man*, London: Andre Deutsch, 1991, p43
14. He had previously taught in the French Department at the State University of New York, Buffalo in 1970 and 1972, see James Miller, *The Passion of Michel Foucault*, London: Flamingo, 1994, p246
15. See for example Richard Rorty's two volumes of *Philosophical Papers*, Cornel West and John Rajchman's *Post-Analytic Philosophy*
16. 'The taking of the Bastille...made manifest to the entire world a revolution which had begun in France over two years before and had been latent throughout the Western world for the previous twenty', Jacques Godechot, *The Taking of the Bastille, July 14th 1789*, London: Faber & Faber, 1970
17. CLR James, *The Black Jacobins: Toussaint L'Ouverture and the San Domingo Revolution*, London: Alison & Busby, 1980

18   M Vovelle, *The Fall of the French Monarchy*, Cambridge, 1987, p148; George Rudé, *Robespierre: Portrait of a Revolutionary Democrat*, London: Collins, 1975, p102
19   Magali Morsy, *North Africa 1800-1900: A Survey from the Nile Valley to the Atlantic*, New York: Longman, 1984, p78
20   Tarikh Muddat al-Farnsis bi-Misr, quoted in Magali Morsy, *North Africa 1800-1900: A Survey from the Nile Valley to the Atlantic*, New York: Longman, 1984, p79
21   Magali Morsy, *North Africa 1800-1900*, p174 and p286
22   See for example, the discussion of the philologist and orientalist Ernest Renan, in Edward Said, *Orientalism: Western Conceptions of the Orient*, Harmondsworth: Penguin, 1991, esp. pp 130-4. 'The very category of "race" – denoting primarily skin colour was first employed as a means of classifying human bodies by François Bernier, a French physician, in 1684.' Cornel West, 'Race and Social Theory', in Mike Davis *et al* (eds), *The Year Left 2: An American Socialist Yearbook*, London: Verso, 1987
23   Magali Morsy, *North Africa 1800-1900*, p160
24   Charles-Robert Ageron, *Modern Algeria: A History from 1830 to the Present*, London: Hurst and Company, 1990, p39
25   In a letter to the Minister of the Interior, 1877, Magali Morsy, *North Africa 1800-1900*, p286
26   Charles-Robert Ageron, *Modern Algeria*, p39
27   Charles-Robert Ageron, *Modern Algeria*, p53
28   In a letter to the government of Algeria, quoted in J-F Lyotard, *Political Writings*, London: UCL Press, 1993, p173
29   Ian Clegg, *Workers' Self Management in Algeria*, New York: Monthly Review Press, 1971, p32
30   In 1959, J-F Lyotard, *Political Writings*, p248
31   Quoted in Bernard Henri-Lévy, *Adventures on the Freedom Road: French Intellectuals in the Twentieth Century*, London: Harvill Press, 1995, p287
32   Quoted in Bernard Henri-Lévy, *Adventures on the Freedom Road*, p286-7
33   Charles-Robert Ageron, *Modern Algeria*, p114; Ian Clegg, *Workers' Self Management in Algeria*, p37
34   Henri Alleg, *The Question*, London: John Calder, 1958, p47
35   London *Spectator*, 25 June 1994
36   Frantz Fanon, *The Wretched of the Earth*, Harmondsworth: Penguin, 1971, p251
37   Frantz Fanon, *Towards the African Revolution*, London: Writers and Readers, 1980, p78
38   Charles-Robert Ageron, *Modern Algeria*, p108
39   Roland Lew and Jean Pierre Garnier, 'From the Wretched of the Earth to the Defence of the West' in Ralph Miliband *et al* (eds)*Socialist Register*, London: Merlin, 1984, p 311
40   *L'Humanité*, 5 November 1955
41   Paris, 17 March 1957, quoted in Frantz Fanon, *Towards the African Revolution*, p85
42   In Bernard Henri-Lévy, *Adventures on the Freedom Road*, p311. Lyotard makes the correct point that 'solidarity between the proletariat of the old capitalist nations and the liberation movements of the young colonised nations does not appear spontaneously, because European workers do not have an active awareness of the shared goals of the colonial nationalist struggle'. *Political Writings*, p205. But Lyotard's mistake was in thinking that any class-consciousness would appear spontaneously, without people arguing for it.
43   Michael Farrell, *The Battle for Algeria*, Belfast: Peoples Democracy, circa 1972, p15
44   Frantz Fanon, *The Wretched of the Earth*, Harmondsworth: Penguin, 1971, p67
45   Frantz Fanon, *The Wretched of the Earth*, p30
46   Jean-Paul Sartre, Introduction, Frantz Fanon, *The Wretched of the Earth*, p22
47   Jean-Paul Sartre, Introduction, Henri Alleg, *The Question*, London: John Calder, 1958, p13-14
48   Jean-Paul Sartre, Introduction, Henri Alleg, *The Question*, p23
49   Jean-Paul Sartre, Introduction, Henri Alleg, *The Question*, p24
50   In Bernard Henri-Lévy, *Adventures on the Freedom Road*, p313

51 Cornelius Castoriadis, 'The Diversionists', originally published in *Le Nouvel Observateur*, 20 June 1977, reproduced in *Political and Social Writings*, Volume 3, Minnesota University Press, 1993, p274
52 Frantz Fanon 'Algeria unveiled' in *Studies in a Dying Colonialism*, London: Earthscan, 1989, p62
53 Frantz Fanon 'Algeria unveiled' in *Studies in a Dying Colonialism*, 1989, p46
54 Frantz Fanon, *The Wretched of the Earth*, p254, p255
55 J-F Lyotard, *Political Writings*, p278
56 J-F Lyotard, *Political Writings*, p198
57 Roland Lew and Jean Pierre Garnier, 'From the Wretched of the Earth to the Defence of the West', *Socialist Register*, London: Merlin, 1984, p311
58 'The New Battle of France', *Labour Monthly*, July 1958, p305
59 Michael Farrell, *The Battle for Algeria*, Belfast: Peoples Democracy, circa 1972
60 'The New Battle of France', *Labour Monthly*, p304
61 RW Johnson, *The Long March of the French Left*, Macmillan, London, 1981, p52
62 *Spectator*, 25 June 1994. All the imprisoned officers were released later that year.
63 Louis Althusser, 'The facts', in *The Future Lasts a Long Time*, London: Vintage, 1994, p345
64 Louis Althusser, *The Future Lasts a Long Time*, p120
65 KS Karol, 'The Tragedy of the Althussers', *New Left Review*, 124, London, November 1980, p94
66 Louis Althusser, *The Future Lasts a Long Time*, p203
67 Michel Foucault, *Remarks on Marx*, New York: Semiotexte, 1991, p52 (My italics)
68 Louis Althusser, *The Future Lasts a Long Time*, p235
69 Louis Althusser, *The Future Lasts a Long Time*, p250
70 Louis Althusser, *The Future Lasts a Long Time*, p251
71 Louis Althusser, *The Future Lasts a Long Time*, p251
72 Louis Althusser, *The Future Lasts a Long Time*, p252
73 Louis Althusser, *The Future Lasts a Long Time*, p267
74 Louis Althusser, *The Future Lasts a Long Time*, p254
75 Louis Althusser, *The Future Lasts a Long Time*, p241
76 Louis Althusser, *The Future Lasts a Long Time*, p19
77 Louis Althusser, *The Future Lasts a Long Time*, p20
78 Louis Althusser, *The Future Lasts a Long Time*, p21-2
79 Louis Althusser, *The Future Lasts a Long Time*, p8
80 Cornelius Castoriadis, 'The Diversionists', in *Political and Social Writings* Volume 3, p274
81 *Documents: World Congress of the Fourth International*, Intercontinental Press, 14 July 1969, p718
82 *Documents: World Congress of the Fourth International*, p683
83 *Documents: World Congress of the Fourth International*, p687
84 Tom Nairn and A Quattrocchi, *The Beginning of the End*, London, Panther, 1968, p172-3
85 In Stuart Hall and Tony Jefferson (eds), *Resistance Through Rituals: Youth Cultures in Post-War Britain*, London: Hutchinson, 1976
86 Don Milligan, 'British Youth: progressive, reactionary or indifferent', *Marxism Today*, May 1966
87 Quoted in M Kazin, 'A People not a Class', in Mike Davis and Michael Sprinker (eds), *Reshaping the US Left*, London: Verso, 1988
88 Leonard Harris 'Historical Subjects and Interests', in Mike Davis et al (eds), *The Year Left 2: An America Socialist Yearbook* London: Verso, 1987; Cedric Robinson, *Black Marxism: The Making of the Black Radical Tradition*, London: Verso, 1983
89 Leonard Harris 'Historical Subjects and Interests', in *The Year Left 2*, p100
90 *Socialist Register*, London: Merlin, 1990
91 Claus Offe, 'Challenging the Boundaries of Institutional Politics', in C Maier (ed) *Changing the Boundaries of the Political*, Cambridge University Press, 1987, p68

92 In Sean Sayers and Peter Osborne (eds), *Socialism, Feminism and Philosophy: A Radical Philosophy Reader*, London: Routledge, 1991, p205
93 Martin Heidegger, *An Introduction to Metaphysics*, New Haven: Yale University Press, 1987 p46
94 Claus Offe, 'Challenging the Boundaries of Institutional Politics', p70-71
95 Alberto Melucci, 'Social Movements and the Democratization of Everyday Life', in John Keane (ed) *Civil Society and the State: New European Perspectives*, London: Verso, 1988, p245
96 Alberto Melucci, 'Social Movements...', p246-7
97 Alberto Melucci, 'Social Movements...', p247-8
98 Alberto Melucci, 'Social Movements...', p254
99 Claus Offe, 'Challenging the Boundaries of Institutional Politics', in C Maier (ed) *Changing the Boundaries of the Political*, p75
100 Alberto Melucci, 'Social Movements...', p250
101 Alberto Melucci, 'Social Movements...', p249 (Melucci's italics)
102 Claus Offe, 'Challenging the Boundaries of Institutional Politics', p77
103 Claus Offe, 'Challenging the Boundaries of Institutional Politics', p78
104 Russell Jacoby, *The Politics of Subjectivity*, Telos, No 9, Fall 1971 p125
105 Geoffrey Robertson, *Crimes Against Humanity*, pxviii
106 Geoffrey Robertson, *Crimes Against Humanity*, p347
107 See, for example, John D'Emilio and Estelle B Freedman, *Intimate Matters: A History of Sexuality in America*, Chicago University Press, 1988, p311
108 Beatrix Campbell and Judith Jones, *Stolen Voices: An Exposure of the Campaign to Discredit Childhood Testimony*, London: The Women's Press, 1999
109 Eric Hobsbawm, *Age of Extremes: The Short Twentieth Century, 1914-1991*, London: Michael Joseph, 1994, p412
110 See TB and Mary Edsall, *Chain Reaction: The Impact of Race, Rights and Taxes on American Politics*, New York: Norton, 1992, p129
111 Nigel Lawson, *The View from No. 11: Memoirs of a Tory Radical*, London: Corgi, 1993, p13
112 Eric Foner, *The Story of American Freedom*, London: Macmillan, 1998, p304
113 See David Roediger *Wages of Whiteness: Race and the Making of the American Working Class*, New York: Verso, 1991; Theodore W. Allen, *The Invention of the White Race: Racial Oppression and Social Control*, New York: Verso, 1993; Eric Lott, *Blackface Minstrelsy and the American Working Class*, New York: Oxford University Press, 1993; and Alexander Saxton, *The Rise and Fall of the White Republic: Class Politics and Mass Culture in Nineteenth-Century America*, New York: Verso, 1990
114 Margaret Thatcher, *The Downing Street Years*, London: Harper Collins, 1995, p7
115 'When the Thatcher Government first took office in 1979 it inherited an economy beset by all manner of government controls and regulations. We judged these controls and regulations to be among the causes of Britain's economic weakness, and we wished to be rid of them.' Nigel Lawson, *The View from No. 11*, p625
116 George Will, *Suddenly: The American Idea at Home and Abroad 1986-90*, New York: The Free Press, 1992, p159
117 Alan Duncan and Dominic Hobson, *Saturn's Children: How the State Devours Liberty, Prosperity, Virtue*, London: Sinclair Stevenson, 1995, p36
118 Nigel Lawson, *The View from No. 11*, p 301. The former Chancellor blames the rise on 'unofficial claimants groups, who advised their "clients" on how best to exploit the system', not unemployment, which he acknowledges was 'remorselessly rising', p279.
119 'A system of regulation was established under the control of an Office of Telecommunications (OFTEL) with the result that BT had to keep its price increases at a fixed level below the rate of inflation.' Margaret Thatcher, *The Downing Street Years*, p681
120 J Kay and D Thompson, 'Privatisation: A Policy in Search of a Rationalisation', in *Economic Journal*, No 96 March 1986

121 Paddy Hillyard and Janie Percy-Smith, *The Coercive State: The Decline Of Democracy in Britain*, London: Fontana, 1988, p96
122 *EGO Trip*, Democratic Audit/Charter 88
123 Dominic Hobson, *The National Wealth*, London: Harper Collins, 1999, p496
124 Dominic Hobson talks of the 'rise and rise of the quango state' rather in the same terms as Lord Hailsham talked of the 'ratchet-effect' of socialist spending, that only went up, but never down. *The National Wealth*, p496
125 Margaret Thatcher, *The Downing Street Years*, p306
126 Simon Jenkins, *Accountable to None: The Tory Nationalisation of Britain*, London: Hamish Hamilton, 1995, p162
127 Norman Tebbit, *Upwardly Mobile*, London: Futura, 1989, p195
128 Margaret Thatcher, *The Downing Street Years*, p306
129 'We had to fight an enemy without in the Falklands', Margaret Thatcher told a Conservative Party meeting at the start of the year long miners' strike of 1984-5. Now the war had to be taken to 'the enemy within, which is much more difficult to fight and much more dangerous to liberty', in Seumas Milne, *The Enemy Within: The Secret War Against the Miners*, London, Pan, 1995, p26
130 Generally attributed to Margaret Thatcher, though strictly speaking it was Chancellor Geoffrey Howe who coined the phrase in defending the 1981 budget, see Nigel Lawson, *The View from No. 11*, p100. Thatcher, however adopted it, writing 'To coin a phrase, "There Is No Alternative"' in the *Daily Telegraph*, 1 April 1997
131 *Social Trends*, HMSO, 1994
132 In Simon Jenkins, *Against the Grain*, London: John Murray, 1994, p85; David Rose, *In the Name of the Law*, London: Jonathon Cape, 1996, p102
133 See Jock Young, *Oxford Handbook of Criminology*, Oxford University Press, 1994
134 Metropolitan Police Force Appraisal, September 1986, partII
135 'Fear of crime', in Lizanne Dowds and Daphne Ahrendt, *British Social Attitudes*, Twelfth Report 1995/96, Dartmouth Publishing, p33
136 Beatrix Campbell and Judith Jones, *Stolen Voices*, London: The Women's Press, 1999, p120
137 Conor Foley, *Human Rights, Human Wrongs: The Alternative Report to the United Nations Human Rights Committee*, London: Rivers Oram Press, p247. The 1988 Immigration Act removed the last remaining rights to family reunion in the UK, for long-settled Commonwealth citizens.
138 More than 7000 people were detained under the PTA, only a tiny minority of whom was ever charged with any offence. Conor Foley, *Human Rights, Human Wrongs*, p98
139 Paddy Hillyard and Janie Percy-Smith, *The Coercive State*, p260
140 Paddy Hillyard and Janie Percy-Smith, *The Coercive State*, p191
141 Department of Health, *Children and Young People on the Child Protection Register*, 1991, 1994
142 Margaret Thatcher, *The Downing Street Years*, p631
143 US Secretary of State Dean Acheson wrote 'Stalin's offensive against the United States and the West, announced in his speech of 9 February 1946, had begun in Poland in 1945 and would reach its crescendo in Korea and the "hate America" campaign of the early 1950s. This was the start of the Cold War', *Present at the Creation: My Years at the State Department*, New York: WW Norton, 1969, p194
144 Carolyn Eisenberg demonstrates that the decision to divide Germany was not, as generally believed, a Soviet one, but instead imposed by America, at the goading of the British. *Drawing the Line: The American Decision to Divide Germany 1944-1949*, Cambridge University Press, 1996

145 IF Stone argues that MacArthur deliberately provoked the Korean conflict in *The Hidden History of the Korean War 1950-1951*, Boston: Little, Brown & Co, 1988. See also, Walden Bello, *People and Power in the Pacific*, London: Verso, 1992. Today the US army is investigating atrocities committed against Korean civilians in the conflict (*Guardian*, 18 January 2000).
146 In EJ Dionne, *Why Americans Hate Politics*, New York: Touchstone, 1992, p161
147 in EJ Dionne, *Why Americans Hate Politics*, p162-3
148 Robert Goldberg, *Barry Goldwater*, New Haven: Yale University Press, 1995, p226
149 See Fred Halliday, *The Making of the Second Cold War*, London: Verso, 1983
150 26 November 1982, quoted in Fred Halliday, *The Making of the Second Cold War*, p27
151 George Will, *Suddenly*, p108
152 'US forces: Challenges Ahead', *Foreign Affairs*, Winter 1992-3
153 George Walden, *Lucky George*, London: Allen Lane, 1999, p213
154 George Will, *Suddenly*, p95; Margaret Thatcher, *The Downing Street Years*, p769
155 'Quest for a post-Cold War foreign policy', *Foreign Affairs*, Vol 72 No 1, 1993, p17
156 Kevin Phillips, *The Politics of Rich and Poor: Wealth and the American Electorate in the Reagan Aftermath*, New York: Harper, 1991
157 JGA Pocock, *The Machiavellian Moment: Florentine Political Thought and the Authentic Republican Tradition*, Princeton: University Press, 1975
158 WJ Bennet, *To Reclaim a Legacy*, National Endowment for the Humanities, 1984
159 Francis Fukuyama, *The End of History and the Last Man*, London: Hamish Hamilton, 1992; Francis Fukuyama, 'The End of History?', *The National Interest*, Summer 1989
160 Interview with the author, November 1995
161 Vivien Stern, *A Sin Against the Future: Imprisonment in the World*, London, Penguin, 1998, p36
162 See Mike Davis, *City of Quartz: Excavating the Future in Los Angeles*, London: Vintage, 1992
163 Interview, November 1995
164 Reproduced in Georg Lukacs, *Marxism and Human Liberation*, New York, Delta, 1973, p308
165 Anthony Giddens, *Beyond Left and Right: The Future of Radical Politics*, Cambridge: Polity Press, 1994, p78
166 Cited in *Confrontation* Vol II, No 1, London, Junius, 1996, p12
167 John Patten, *Things to Come: The Tories in the Twenty-First Century*, London: Sinclair Stevenson, p1
168 Dick Morris, *Behind the Oval Office*, quoted in the London *Guardian*, 14 January, 1996
169 John Rentoul, *Tony Blair*, London: Warner, 1996, p284
170 Norman Fairclough, *New Labour, New Language?*, London, Routledge, 2000, p24
171 George Stephanopoulos, *All Too Human: A Political Education*, Boston: Little, Brown & Company, 1999, p336
172 Norman Fairclough, *New Labour, New Language?*, p10
173 Norman Fairclough, *New Labour, New Language?*, p157
174 Social Justice Commission, *Social Justice*, London, Vintage, 1996. One hundred and forty years earlier, Karl Marx had poured scorn on those socialists who criticised capitalism for being 'unfair', saying that the very standard of 'fairness' was itself drawn from the market. Denouncing capitalism for being unfair only meant that you wanted it to be more consistent.
175 At the *Guardian/New Statesman* conference, 'What's Left?', June 1994
176 Bill Clinton and Al Gore *Putting People First: How We Can All Change America*, New York: Times Books, 1992, p191
177 Norman Fairclough, *New Labour, New Language?*, p24, about the government white paper by the Department of Trade and Industry, 'Building the knowledge driven economy' (London: HMSO, 1998)
178 Norman Fairclough, *New Labour, New Language?*, p26

179 The song 'The Red Flag' was written in 1889, during a violent dock strike. It was sung at the close of the Labour Party conference.
180 See Dennis O'Hearn, *Inside the Celtic Tiger: The Irish Economy and the Asian Model*, London: Pluto Press, 1998, for an account of the internal pricing regimes that companies use to misrepresent their holdings.
181 'Drivers of Change: Five Key Drivers Will Shape the World over the Next Decades' prepared by No 10's performance and innovation unit for the British Cabinet in November 1999
182 'To secure for the producers by hand or brain the full fruits of their industry, and the most equitable distribution thereof that may be possible, upon the basis of the common ownership of the means of production'. Sidney Webb drafted this clause to the 1918 Constitution, mostly as a sop to stave off the clamour for socialist revolution. Thus the 1922 manifesto finished with a headline 'Against revolution', and claimed Labour's programme is the best bulwark against violent upheaval and class wars.' Tony Cliff, *The Labour Party: A Marxist History*, London: Bookmarks, 1988 p72
183 Labour conference 1963, quoted in Tony Cliff, *The Labour Party*, p280
184 Geoffrey Foote, *The Labour Party's Political Thought: A History*, London: Croom Helm, 1986, p236-7
185 Perry Anderson, *English Questions*, London: Verso, 1992, p338
186 Perry Anderson, *English Questions*, p338
187 The Nairn-Anderson thesis was revived in the 1990s by *Observer* editor Will Hutton, whose bestseller argued that 'British capitalists, politicians and officials have always been driven by the goal of becoming gentlemen, aping the lifestyle of the English aristocrat and aiming to have the same kind of effortless, invisible income'. Will Hutton, *The State We're In*, London: Vintage, 1996, p114
188 Norman Fairclough, *New Labour, New Language?*, p133
189 3 April 2000
190 Philip Gould, *The Unfinished Revolution: How the Modernisers Took Back the Labour Party*, London: Abacus, 1999, p116. In the late 1980s, Clare Short launched a campaign against the British military occupation of Northern Ireland with the slogan 'It's time to go', as though 25,000 troops were simply guests who had outstayed their welcome.
191 Bill Clinton, *Putting People First*, p226
192 George Stephanopoulos, *All too Human: A Political Education*, New York, Little Brown, 1999, p140
193 George Stephanopoulos, *All too Human*, p345
194 Philip Gould, *The Unfinished Revolution*, p92. In fact Kinnock was preparing to retreat from Labour's nuclear disarmament policy.
195 Geoff Mulgan and Helen Wilkinson, *Freedom's Children: Work, Relationships and Politics for 18-24 year olds in Britain Today*, London: Demos, 1995
196 George Will, 'The Miniaturisation of American Politics', in *Suddenly*, p252
197 Robert Reich, *Locked in the Cabinet*, New York: Vintage Books, 1998, p271
198 At the 'What's Next' conference, June 1994
199 Robert Reich, *Locked in the Cabinet*, p152
200 Peter Hennessy, *The Blair Centre: A Question of Command and Control?*, London: Public Management Foundation, p18
201 George Stephanopoulos, *All too Human* p130
202 *Locked in the Cabinet*, p47, 48
203 Martin McElwee, *The Great and the Good? The Rise of the New Class*, London: Centre for Policy Studies, 2000
204 See John Major, *Autobiography*, London: Harper Collins, 1999, p395
205 Bill Clinton and Al Gore, *Putting People First*, p91, p101
206 Philip Gould, *The Unfinished Revolution*, p268, p270
207 George Stephanopoulos, *All too Human*, p122

208 Andrew Sullivan, 'Why Health was too Hot for Hillary', London *Observer*, 18 September, 1994
209 Bob Woodward, *The Agenda: Inside the Clinton White House*, excerpted in the London *Observer*, 19 June 1994
210 Philip Gould, *The Unfinished Revolution*, p181
211 Philip Gould, *The Unfinished Revolution*, p181
212 Philip Gould, *The Unfinished Revolution*, p297
213 John Rentoul, *Tony Blair*, London: Warner, 1996, p289
214 *The World this Weekend*, BBC Radio 4, 10 January 1993
215 John Rentoul, *Tony Blair*, p279
216 Quoted in John Rentoul, *Tony Blair*, p290
217 Philip Gould, *The Unfinished Revolution*, p252
218 Philip Gould, *The Unfinished Revolution*, p203
219 Philip Gould, *The Unfinished Revolution*, p205-6
220 Ridley Memorial Lecture, 22 November 1996. Reproduced in the *Sun*, 7 February, 1997
221 See Paddy Hillyard, *Suspect Community: People's Experiences of the Prevention of Terrorism Acts in Britain*, London: Pluto Press 1993 on the criminalisation of the Irish in Britain, and Keith Tompson, *Under Siege: Racial Violence in Britain Today*, London: Penguin, 1988, esp pp87-9 on criminalising black Britons.
222 Philip Gould, *The Unfinished Revolution*, p254
223 Quoted in James Nolan, *The Therapeutic State: Justifying Government at Century's End*, New York: University Press, 1998, p22
224 James Nolan, *The Therapeutic State*
225 George Stephanopoulos, *All too Human*, p324
226 George Stephanopoulos, *All too Human*, p297
227 See ES Kraemer and J Roberts, *The Politics of Attachment: Towards a Secure Society*, 1996
228 Norman Fairclough, *New Labour, New Language?*, p7
229 Jedediah Purdy, *For Common Things: Irony, Trust and Commitment in America Today*, New York: Alfred Knopf, 1999, p67

Part Three

1. Christopher Lasch, *The Revolt of the Elites and the Betrayal of Democracy*, Norton, p20
2. Mike Davis, *City of Quartz: Excavating the Future in Los Angeles*, London: Vintage, 1992 p244
3. Doug Henwood, *Wall Street: How it Works and for Whom*, New York: Verso, 1997, p288
4. 'In order to protect themselves, the bondholders demanded a "risk premium" on their continued lending.' William Greider, *One World Ready or Not: The Manic Logic of Global Capitalism*, New York: Simon and Schuster, 1997, p299
5. Andrew Hacker, *Money: Who has How Much and Why?*, New York: Scribner, 1997, p11
6. London *Guardian*, 13 April 2000
7. London *Metro*, 12 April 2000
8. James Goldsmith, *The Trap*, Carroll and Graf, 1994
9. Kevin Phillips, *The Politics of Rich and Poor: Wealth and the American Electorate in the Reagan Aftermath*, New York: Harper, 1991, pxviii
10. Richard Brookhiser, *The Way of the Wasp: How It Made America and How It Can Save It...So to Speak*, New York: Macmillan, 1991, p78
11. George Soros, *The Crisis of Global Capitalism: Open Society Endangered*, London: Little, Brown & Company, 1998, p167
12. George Soros, *The Crisis of Global Capitalism*, p111
13. George Soros, *The Crisis of Global Capitalism*, p113
14. George Soros, *The Crisis of Global Capitalism*, p208
15. John Beck, *Morality and Citizenship in Education*, London: Cassell, p93
16. Ron Arnold, Alan Gottlieb, *Trashing the Economy*, Washington: Free Enterprise Press, 1994
17. Sydney Hook, 'The New Failure of Nerve', in *The Quest for Being*, Buffalo: Prometheus, 1991, p73-4
18. *Guardian*, 13 November 2000
19. *Observer*, 9 September 2001
20. *Guardian*, 19 February 1999   David Goodhart
21. *Guardian*, 12 September 2000
22. *Guardian*, 12 September 2000
23. 29 October 2000
24. See Roland Barthes, *Mythologies*, London 1987; *The Eiffel Tower and Other Mythologies*, Toronto, 1984
25. In Lisa Appignesi (ed), *Postmodernism*, ICA Documents 5/6, 1986, p6
26. 'Why don't our distinguished orators come forward as usual to make their speeches, say what they have to say? Because the barbarians are coming today and they're bored by rhetoric and public speaking.' The dénouement of Cavafy's poem, 'Waiting for the Barbarians' is that the barbarians are a figment of the city's imagination. *The Essential Cavafy*, p21, Hopewell, NJ: Ecco, 1995
27. Chris Smith, *Creative Britain*, p3
28. *Observer*, 31 October 1999
29. Heather Macdonald, in Washburn and Thornton, (eds), *Dumbing Down: The Strip Mining of American Culture*, New York: Norton, 1997
30. Melanie Phillips, *All Must Have Prizes*, London: Little Brown, 1996
31. Michael Barber, *The Learning Game*, 1996
32. The concept of sustainability was popularised by the Brundtland Report, produced for the 1987 World Commission on Environment and Development, see Phil MacNaghten and John Urry, *Contested Natures*, London: Sage, 1998, p61
33. Timothy O'Riordan and James Cameron, *Interpreting the Precautionary Principle*, p15-16

34 Quoted in the paper 'The Canadian Environmental Protection Act and the Precautionary Principle', prepared by Dr David VanderZwaag, Director of the Marine and Environmental Law Programme at Dalhousie Law School, circa 1993, for the Canadian House of Commons Standing Committee on Environment and Sustainable development.
35 Dr David VanderZwaag, 'The Canadian Environmental Protection Act and the Precautionary Principle'
36 Dr David VanderZwaag, 'The Canadian Environmental Protection Act and the Precautionary Principle' (My emphasis)
37 John Major, *Autobiography*, London: Harper Collins, 1999, p511
38 Margaret Thatcher, *The Downing Street Years*, London: Harper Collins, 1993, p640-1. It is interesting to note that Sir Crispin persuaded Thatcher to abandon equilibrium theory in ecology where no one could persuade her to abandon it in economics.
39 Crispin Tickell, *Climate Change in World Affairs*, London, 1977
40 Phil MacNaghten and John Urry, *Contested Natures*, London: Sage, 1998, p62-74
41 Istvan Meszaros, *The Necessity of Social Control: Isaac Deutscher Memorial Lecture*, London: Merlin, 1971, p19
42 William Shea. *Galileo's Intellectual Revolution*, p91
43 Brian Wynne et al, *Uncertain World: Genetically Modified Organisms, Food and Public Attitudes in Britain*, Lancaster: Unversity Press, 1997
44 *The Revolt Against Change: Towards a Conserving Radicalism*, London: Vintage, 1993
45 Reprinted in PA Vardin and IL Brody, *Children's Rights: Contemporary Perspectives*
46 The NSPCC asked Mori, the research organisation, to interview 1000 children, aged eight to 15, about their views on family life, discipline, friends and other social issues. The report, *Talking About My Generation*, was published on 10 April 1997.
47 'Children of Crime: Jamie Bulger Update', 14 December 1999, written and produced by Dennis Blakeway for Channel 4
48 Quoted in Sharon Kinsella, *Journal of Japanese Studies*, 24:2, 1998
49 Skov and Moeran (eds), *Women, Media and Consumption in Japan*, p70
50 London *Evening Standard*, 11 April 2000
51 Quoted in Andrew Calcutt, *Arrested Development: Pop culture and the Erosion of Adulthood*, London: Cassell, 1998, p90. Calcutt's *Arrested Development* is the classic on the culture of infantilisation, and I follow it here.
52 Charlotte Raven, 'Middle Youth Ate my Culture', *Modern Review*, London, March 1998
53 Quoted in Andrew Calcutt, *Arrested Development*, p236
54 5 June 1996
55 Robert Reich, *Locked in the Cabinet*, New York: Vintage, 1998 p194-5
56 *Sunday Times*, 28 December 1997. Inclusion of Scotland and Northern Ireland, more traditional parts of the United Kingdom pushes the men back into the majority.
57 *Guardian*, 15 October 1999
58 *LBO*, No 80, November 1997
59 *Daily Telegraph*, 7 October 1999
60 *Daily Telegraph*, 12 November 1997
61 Roger Horrocks, *Masculinity in Crisis*, London: Macmillan, 1996
62 Roger Horrocks, *Masculinity in Crisis*, p182
63 Roger Horrocks, *Masculinity in Crisis*, p95
64 J Taylor Gibbs and JR Merighi , 'Young black males', in T Newburn and EA Stanko (eds), *Just Boys Doing Business? Men, Masculinities and Crime*, Routledge, 1996
65 J Taylor Gibbs and JR Merighi , 'Young black males', p80
66 James L Nolan, *The Therapeutic State: Justifying Government at Century's End*, New York: University Press, 1998, p150
67 *Panorama*, BBC1, 13 April 2000
68 Ben J Wattenberg, *Values Matter Most*, Washington: Regnery, 1995, p167

INDEX

Alleg, Henri 119, 121
Althusser, Louis 20, 37-40, 43, 47, 56, 86, 126, 130-8
Amis, Martin 10
Anderson, Perry 175, 184
Apel, Karl-Otto 28
Arato, Andrew 79
Baudrillard, Jean 10, 11, 25, 103, 108
Beauvoir, Simone de 60, 64, 65
Beck, Ulrich 80, 81
Berlin, Isaiah 9
Bidault, Georges 118, 119
Blackmore, Susan 85
Blair, Tony 44, 176-8, 180, 182, 187, 190, 191, 194, 196-9, 201
Bloom, Allan 171
Bragg, Melvyn 214-5
Buber, Martin 66-7
Buckley, William F 168
Bush, George Snr 170, 175, 210
Butler, Judith 41-3, 90, 92
Callinicos, Alex 102-5, 107
Campbell, Beatrix 152
Castoriadis, Cornelius 30, 73, 74, 124, 137
Cleaver, Eldridge 145
Clinton, Bill 44, 176, 177, 185, 186, 188-94, 200
Clinton, Hillary 194, 199, 200, 225
Cohen, Jean 79
Cooke, Maeve 42
Dawkins, Richard 83-5
Dennett, Daniel 85
Derrida, Jacques 17-21, 26, 27, 104, 108, 126
Descartes, Rene, 27
Eagleton, Terry 104, 105, 107
Engels, Frederick 70-72
Etzioni, Amitai 44-6
Fairclough, Norman 177-9
Fanon, Frantz 117, 120-126
Finkielkraut, Alain 17
Foucault, Michel 20-22, 26, 40, 68-74, 133, 134
Fukuyama, Francis 109, 171, 172
Gaulle, Charles de 127, 128, 129
Giddens, Anthony 81, 175, 177, 181
Gilligan, Chris 88
Goldsmith, Sir James 210, 211
Goldwater, Barry 168, 169
Gould, Phillip 195-6
Green, Thomas Hill 43
Habermas, Jurgen, 75-80
Hall, Stuart 91
Haraway, Donna 35-6
Hayek, Frederick 93-5, 154, 156, 160
Hegel, GWF 9, 24, 25, 26, 60-66, 75, 98, 100
Heidegger, Martin 18, 19, 26, 77, 89
Henwood, Doug 208
Herrnstein, Richard 82
Hobbes, Thomas 7, 9
Hook, Sydney 212-3

Horrocks, Roger 233
John Paul II 15, 16, 100
Kappeler, Susanne 42
Keynes, John Maynard 95
Kojeve, Alexandre 63, 63
Kristeva, Juliet 47
Lacoue-Labarthe, Phillipe 19, 123
Lasch, Christopher 207, 208
Le Corbusier 118, 119
Lenin, Vladimir 100
Levinas, Emmanuel 67
Locke, John 7, 9, 24
Lukacs, Georg 25, 77, 144, 174
Lyotard, Jean-Francois 15, 29, 32, 33, 103, 117, 125, 126, 215
MacIntyre, Alasdair 44
Mackinnon, Catharine 49, 52-4
Macpherson, CB 9, 24, 48
Maistre, Joseph de 43
Manson, Marilyn, 33
Marx, Karl 24-6, 38-40, 75, 76, 130, 131
Massu, Gen 119, 120, 127, 129
Melucci, Alberto 148, 49
Milligan, Don 144
Mitchell, Juliet 89
Mitterand, Francois 120, 185
More, Max 34
Murray, Charles 82
Nairn, Tom 144, 184
Neumann, Franz 51
Nietzsche, Freidrich 26, 27
Nolan, James 234
Offe, Claus 146-50
Parsons, Talcott 74
Pateman, Carole 48, 50-54
Phillips, Kevin 170, 210
Pocock, JGA 171
Popper, Karl 93, 94, 154, 156, 160
Rawls, John 29-31, 44, 45
Reagan, Ronald, 93, 155, 157, 168, 169, 172, 210
Rorty, Richard, 28, 29, 31
Rousseau, Jean-Jacques 7, 9
Russell, Bertrand 74
Said, Edward 57-9
Sandel, Michael 44, 47
Sartre, Jean-Paul, 60, 64-6, 100, 122-5
Seale, Bobby 145
Smith, Adam 100
Sokal, Alan 16
Soros, George 210
Straw, Jack 226, 228
Strawson, Galen 96-8
Strawson, Peter 96-8
Taylor, Charles, 31, 45, 47, 55, 56
Thatcher, Margaret 93, 154-61, 166, 172, 198, 220
Thompson, Robert 197, 225, 228
Venables, Jon 197, 225, 228
Zeldin, Theodore 79
Zizek, Slavoj 12

Made in the USA
Charleston, SC
02 February 2014